International Political Economy Se[...]

Series Editor: **Timothy M. Shaw**, V[...] :ts
Boston, USA and Emeritus Professo[...]

The global political economy is in [...] its
organization and governance. The [...] ɔth
analysis and structure over the las [...] tra-
tion on the global South. Now the South increasingly [...] the
centre of development, also reflected in a growing number of submissions and
publications on indebted Eurozone economies in Southern Europe.

An indispensable resource for scholars and researchers, the series examines
a variety of capitalisms and connections by focusing on emerging economies,
companies and sectors, debates and policies. It informs diverse policy communities as the established trans-Atlantic North declines and 'the rest', especially the
BRICS, rise.

Bringing together some of the very best titles in the International Political
Economy series' history, the IPE Classics showcase these titles and their continued
relevance, all now available in paperback, updated with new material by the
authors and a foreword by series editor Timothy M. Shaw.

Titles include:

Shaun Breslin
CHINA AND THE GLOBAL POLITICAL ECONOMY

Kevin C. Dunn and Timothy M. Shaw
AFRICA'S CHALLENGE TO INTERNATIONAL RELATIONS THEORY

Randall Germain
GLOBALIZATION AND ITS CRITICS
Perspectives from Political Economy

Stephen Gill
GLOBALIZATION, DEMOCRATIZATION AND MULTILATERALISM

John Harriss, Kristian Stokke and Olle Törnquist
POLITICISING DEMOCRACY
The New Local Politics of Democratisation

David Hulme and Michael Edwards
NGOs, STATES AND DONORS
Too Close for Comfort?

Sharon Stichter and Jane L. Parpart
WOMEN, EMPLOYMENT AND THE FAMILY IN THE INTERNATIONAL DIVISION
OF LABOUR

Peter Utting and José Carlos Marques
CORPORATE SOCIAL RESPONSIBILITY AND REGULATORY GOVERNANCE
Towards Inclusive Development?

International Political Economy Series
Series Standing Order ISBN 978–0–333–71708–0 hardcover
Series Standing Order ISBN 978–0–333–71110–1 paperback

You can receive future titles in this series as they are published by placing a standing order. Please contact your bookseller or, in case of difficulty, write to us at the address below with your name and address, the title of the series and one of the ISBNs quoted above.

Customer Services Department, Macmillan Distribution Ltd, Houndmills, Basingstoke, Hampshire RG21 6XS, England

China and the Global Political Economy

Shaun Breslin

Professor, Department of Politics and International Studies,
University of Warwick, UK

palgrave
macmillan

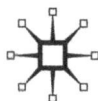

First published 2007
This edition published in paperback 2013 by
PALGRAVE MACMILLAN

Palgrave Macmillan in the UK is an imprint of Macmillan Publishers Limited,
registered in England, company number 785998, of Houndmills, Basingstoke,
Hampshire RG21 6XS.

Palgrave Macmillan in the US is a division of St Martin's Press LLC,
175 Fifth Avenue, New York, NY 10010.

Palgrave Macmillan is the global academic imprint of the above companies
and has companies and representatives throughout the world.

Palgrave® and Macmillan® are registered trademarks in the United States,
the United Kingdom, Europe and other countries

ISBN: 978–1–403–98647–4 hardback
ISBN: 978–1–137–35520–1 paperback

This book is printed on paper suitable for recycling and made from fully
managed and sustained forest sources. Logging, pulping and manufacturing
processes are expected to conform to the environmental regulations of the
country of origin.

A catalogue record for this book is available from the British Library.

A catalog record for this book is available from the Library of Congress.

Contents

Foreword: Learning from the IPE Series Classics Over Three Decades

Timothy M. Shaw

> UNDP 2013 Human Development Report – 'The Rise of the South: Human Progress in a Diverse World' –...will examine the profound shift in global dynamics that is being driven by the fast-rising powers in the developing world – and the implications of this phenomenon for human development...Looking ahead at the critical long-term challenges facing the international community, from inequality to sustainability to global governance...
>
> (www.hdr.org/en/mediacentre/ humandevelopmentreportpresskits/ 2013report/)

I am delighted, honoured and humbled to craft this Foreword for the initial set of Classics to be reissued in paperback from the IPE Series, accompanied by new Prefaces. Both I and my students/colleagues/networks have been greatly informed over a trio of decades as both analytic and existential 'worlds' have changed in myriad ways as indicated in the opening citation from the 2013 UNDP HDR on the rise of the South.

Symbolic of this exponential transformation is this very Series, which has always concentrated on the 'global South'. Thirty years ago, colleagues and editors alike were quite sceptical about the viability of such a limited focus; and indeed initially we only managed to publish a half-dozen titles per annum. By contrast, since the start of the second decade of the 21st century, the IPE Series has been proud to produce over 20 titles a year. As Jan Nederveen Pieterse (2011: 22) has asserted, the established N–S axis is indeed being superseded by an E–S one:

> ...the rise of emerging societies is a major turn in globalization...North-South relations have been dominant for 200 years and now an East-South turn is taking shape. The 2008 economic crisis is part of a global rebalancing process.

This overview juxtaposes a set of parallel/overlapping perspectives to consider whether the several 'worlds' – from North Atlantic/Pacific and onto Eurozone PIIGS versus 'second world' (Khanna 2009) of Brazil, Russia, India, China, South Africa (BRICS) / Columbia, Indonesia, Vietnam, Egypt, Turkey, South Africa (CIVETS) / Mexico, Indonesia, South Korea, Turkey (MIST) / Vietnam, Indonesia, South Africa, Turkey, Argentina (VISTA) – have grown together or apart as global crises and reordering have proceeded (see myriad heterogeneous analyses such as Cooper and Antkiewicz 2008, Cooper and Flemes 2013, Cooper and Subacchi 2010, *Economist* 2012, Gray and Murphy 2013, Lee et al. 2012, Pieterse 2011, USNIC 2012, WEF 2012 and World Bank 2012 as well as O'Neill 2011). In turn, 'contemporary' 'global' issues – wide varieties of ecology, gender, governance, health, norms, technology etc (see part (v) below) – have confronted established analytic assumptions/traditions and actors/policies leading to myriad 'transnational' coalitions and heterogeneous initiatives/processes/regulation schemes as overviewed in Bernstein and Cashore (2008), Dingwerth (2008), Hale and Held (2011) et al. (see part (vii) below). Such extra or semi-state hybrid governance increasingly challenges and supersedes exclusively interstate international organization/law. Clark and Hoque (2012) have assembled a stellar, heterogeneous team to consider any such 'post-American world' (Zakaria 2011): what salient, sustainable features of 'the rest' (Shaw 2012b)?

My overall impression or assumption is that IPE with such a focus on the global South increasingly overshadows – trumps?! – IDS, IR (but cf Bremmer 2012 and Bremmer and Rediker 2012 on resilience/revival of Political Science (PS) as analysis of Emerging Markets (EMs) (www.eurasiagroup.net)), area/business/gender/security studies, and established orthodox social science 'disciplines' such as economics, political science, sociology etc. In turn, IPE may yet increasingly face challenges from analysis broadly construed as 'global studies', especially in the US whose universities never really did 'development'. So I seek to identify areas where such a version of IPE generates similarities to or differences from such approaches, along with 'silences' in each plus divergent ranking of factors among them.

Every title in this set of Classic editions includes a contemporary update on both existential and theoretical developments: from 'Asian' to 'global' crises, from newly industrializing countries (NICs) to BRICs and onto PIIGS and BRICS/CIVETS/MIST/VISTA, Price Waterhouse Cooper's (PWC) E7 (PWC 2013). These sets of Emerging Markets embody slightly different sets of assumptions/directions/implications; PWC expanded the 'Next-11' of Goldman Sachs (i.e. 15 without RSA) to 17 significant EMs by 2050 (Hawksworth and Cookson 2008). Symptomatically, the initial iconic acronym was proposed at the start of the new century by a leading economist working for a global financial corporation – Jim O'Neill (2011) of Goldman Sachs (www2.goldmansachs.com) – who marked and reinforced his initial coup with celebration of its first decade. As he notes, global restructuring has been accelerated by the simultaneous decline not only of the US and UK but also the southern members of the eurozone. Many now predict China to become the largest economy by 2025 and India to catch-up with the US by 2050 (Hawksworth and Cookson 2008: 3). PWC (2013: 6 and 8) suggests that:

> The E7 countries could overtake the G7 as early as 2017 in PPP terms … the E7 countries could potentially be around 75% larger than the G7 countries by the end of 2050 in PPP terms …
>
> By 2050, China, the US and India are likely to be the three largest economies in the world …

But Stuart Brown (2013: 168–170) notes that there are competing prophecies about the cross-over date when China trumps the US, starting with the International Monetary Fund (IMF) advancing it to 2016.

Meanwhile, global architecture is very fluid: the inter-governmental Financial Stability Board (www.financialstabilityboard.org) is matched by think tank networks like the World Economic Forum's (WEF) Risk Response Network (RRN) (www.weforum.org/global-risks-2012) and the Global Risk Institute (www.globalriskinstitute.com); all creations in response to the global crisis towards the end of the first decade. As the G8 morphed into G20 (Cooper and Antkiwicz 2008, Cooper and Subbachi 2010) a variety of analysts attempted to map the emerging world, including Parag Khanna's (2009) second world and Fareed Zakaria's rest: for example: the WEF's Global Redesign Initiative (GRI), which included a small state caucus centred on Qatar, Singapore and Switzerland (Cooper and Momani 2011) (for a readers' guide to GRI see www.umb.edu/cgs/research/global_redesign_initiative), to the Constructive Powers Initiative advanced by Mexico (www.consejomexicano.org/en/constructive-powers), which brought older and newer middle powers together (Jordaan 2003) such as the old Anglo Commonwealth with *inter alia* Indonesia, Japan and South Korea.

And at the end of 2012, from both sides of the pond, the US National Intelligence Council produced 'Global Trends 2030: Alternative Worlds' (GT 2030) (www.gt2030.com), which identified four 'megatrends' like 'diffusion of power' and 'food, water, energy nexus'; a half-dozen 'game-changers'; and four 'potential worlds' from more to less conflict/ inequality, including the possibilities of either China-US collaboration or of a 'nonstate world'. And Chatham House in London reported on 'Resources Futures' (Lee et al. 2012: 2) with a focus on 'the new political economy of resources' and the possibility of natural resource (NR) governance by 'Resource 30' (R30) of major producers/consumers, importers/exporters (www.chathamhouse.org/resourcesfutures): G20 including the BRICs, but not BRICS (i.e. no RSA), plus Chile, Iran, Malaysia, Netherlands, Nigeria, Norway, Singapore, Switzerland, Thailand, UAE and Venezuela.

And in the case of the most marginal continent, Africa, its possible renaissance was anticipated at the turn of the decade by Boston Consulting Group (BCG), Centre for Global Development (CGD), McKinsey et al. (Shaw 2012a), with the *Economist* admitting in January 2011 that it might have to treat Africa as the 'hopeful' rather than 'hopeless' continent. In December 2012, James Francis in the African MSN Report cited Africa's 15 biggest companies: from Sonatrach (Algeria) and Sonangol (Angola) and Sasol (RSA) through MTN, Shoprite, Vodacom and Massmart/Walmart to SAPPI (www.african.howzit.msn.com/africa's-15-biggest-companies/).

The demand or need for 'development' is shifting away from the poorest countries, including 'fragile states' (Brock et al. 2012, www.foreignpolicy.com/failedstates), to poor communities in the second (and first?!) worlds: the other side of the rise of the middle classes in the global South (Sumner and Mallett 2012). Moreover, the supply of development resources is also moving away from the old North towards the BRICS (Chin and Quadir 2012) and other new official donors like South Korea and Turkey plus private foundations like Gates, faith-based organisations (FBOs), remittances from diasporas, Sovereign Wealth Funds (SWFs) and novel sources of finance such as taxes on carbon, climate change, emissions, financial transactions etc (Besada and Kindornay 2013).

(i) Varieties of development

'Development' was a notion related to post-war decolonisation and bipolarity. It was popularised in the 'Third World' in the 1960s, often in relation to 'state socialism', one-party even one-man rule, but superseded by neo-liberalism and the Washington Consensus. Yet the NICs then BRICs pointed to another way by contrast to those in decline like fragile states (Brock et al. 2012); such 'developmentalism' (Kyung-Sup et al. 2012) has now even reached Africa (UNECA

2011 and 2012). But, as indicated in the previous paragraph, while the 'global' middle class grows in the South, so do inequalities along with non-communicable diseases (NCDs) like cancer, heart diseases and diabetes. Given the elusiveness as well as limitations of the Millennium Development Goals (MDGs) (Wilkinson and Hulme 2012), the UN is already debating post-2015 development desiderata (www.un.org/millenniumgoals/beyond2015) including appropriate, innovative forms of governance as encouraged by networks around international non-governmental organizations (INGOs) (www.beyond2015.org) and think tanks (www.post2015.org). As already indicated, Andy Summer and Richard Mallett (2012) suggest that 'development' in the present decade is very different from earlier periods as the number of fragile states declines: given the rise of the global middle class, the poor are now concentrated in the second world. Aid is now about cooperation not finance as a range of flows is attracted to the global south including private capital, foreign direct investment (FDI), philanthropy/FBOs, remittances, let alone money-laundering (Shaxson 2012); Official Development Assistance (ODA) is a shrinking proportion of transnational transfers (Brown 2011 and 2013: 24–28).

(ii) Varieties of capitalisms

The world of capitalisms has never been more diverse: from old trans-Atlantic and -Pacific to new – the global South with its own diversities such as Brazilian, Chinese, Indian and South African 'varieties of capitalisms'. Andrea Goldstein (2007) introduced emerging market MNCs (multinational corporations) in this Series, including a distinctive second index: five pages of company names of emerging market multinational corporations (EMNCs) (see next paragraph). And in the post-neo-liberal era, state-owned enterprises (SOEs), especially national oil companies (NOCs) (Xu 2012), are burgeoning. Both US/UK neo-liberal, continental/Scandinavian corporatist and Japanese/East Asian developmentalist 'paradigms' are having to rethink and reflect changing state-economy/society relations beyond ubiquitous 'partnerships' (Overbeek and van Apeldoorn 2012). Furthermore, if we go beyond the formal and legal, then myriad informal sectors and transnational organized crime (TOC) / money-laundering are ubiquitous (see (vi) below).

For the first time, in the '*Fortune* Global 500' of (July) 2012, MNC head quarters (HQs) were more numerous in Asia than in either Europe or North America. There were 73 Chinese MNCs so ranked (up from 11 a decade ago in 2002) along with 13 in South Korea and eight each in Brazil and India. Each of the BRICS hosted some global brands: Geely, Huawei and Lenovo (China), Hyundai, Kia and Samsung (Korea); Embraer and Vale (Brazil); Infosys, Reliance and Tata (India); Anglo American, De Beers and SABMiller (RSA) etc.

The pair of dominant economies in Sub-Saharan Africa (SSA) is unquestionably Nigeria and South Africa; yet, despite being increasingly connected, they display strikingly different forms of 'African' capitalisms. They both have venerable economic histories, most recently within heterogeneous British imperial networks; and both have gone through profound political as well as economic changes in the new century: from military and minority rule, respectively, both with diasporic and global engagements, including being out of the Commonwealth family for considerable periods each. Whilst distinctive in per capita incomes, they are both highly unequal; for example, Nigeria boasts over 150 private jets owned by its entrepreneurs, pastors, stars, etc.

Nigeria, including its mega-cities like Lagos and Ibadan, is a highly informal political economy with a small formal sector (beer, consumer goods such as soft drinks and soaps, finance, telecommunications etc); by contrast, despite its ubiquitous shanty-towns, South Africa is based on a well-established formal economy centred on mining, manufacturing, farming, finance, services etc. Both have significant diasporas in the global North, especially the UK and US, including Nigeria's in RSA, especially Jo'burg, remitting funds back home. Since majority democratic rule, South African companies and supply-chains, brands and franchises have penetrated the continent, initially into Eastern from Southern Africa, but now increasingly into West Africa and Angola. So MTN's largest market for cell-phone connectivity is now Nigeria; DStv, Shoprite, Stanbic, Woolworth etc. are also present, especially in two of the very few formal shopping malls in Lagos.

South African banks compete in Nigeria with national (established like First and Union and new generation) and regional banks: Access, Eco (in over 30 African countries), Enterprise, Diamond, FCMB, Fidelity, GT (Guaranty Trust), Keystone, Marketplace, UBA (now partially owned by China), Unity, Wema, Zenith etc. And one or two global banks, like Citi and Standard Chartered, are now present in Nigerian cities.

Nigeria's press remains remarkably free and lively despite competition from mobile-phones, social media, TV and websites: *Guardian, Nation, Punch, This Day* etc. Its choice of cell providers includes Airtel, Glo and Etisalat as well as MTN. Its entrepreneurs are developing their own fast food franchises to compete with KFC, Spur etc: Chicken Republic, Mama Cass, Mr Biggs, Rocket Express, Royal Table, Tastee Chicken, Sweet Sensation etc. And it has a huge range of private gas stations in addition to Mobil and Total: Acorn, Bunker, World etc...

Nigeria's variety of African capitalism includes a burgeoning market for second hand EU and US cars and trucks, and a burgeoning born-again religious sector with myriad churches and pastors, some now very large, with endless colourful names such as several Winners' chapels and the (15th in December 2012) Holy Ghost Congress of the Redeemed Christian Church of God at Redemption Camp. Nigerian Pentecostalism has been exported to the diaspora and elsewhere, including the born-again Christian channel on DStv. And characteristic of personal energy, style and networks, Nigeria's Nollywood is now the largest movie industry in the world (*Forbes*, 19 April 2011) in terms of volume – African Magic on DStv. By contrast, South Africa's TV and film production is more limited, formal and international, however stylish. Both countries are sports mad, Nigeria for (men's) soccer: British and EU brands dominate – Arsenal, Barcelona, Chelsea, Manchester United, Real Madrid etc – with Nigerian amongst other players in European clubs.

(iii) Emerging economies/states/societies
The salience of 'emerging markets', especially the BRICs and other political economies in the second world, has led to debates about the similarities and differences among emerging economies/middle classes/multinational companies/states/societies etc, informed by different disciplinary canons; for example, by contrast to Goldstein on EMNCs, Pieterse (2011) privileges sociologically informed emerging societies. In turn, especially in IR, there are burgeoning analyses of emerging powers/regional and otherwise (Flemes 2010, Jordaan 2003, Nel and Nolte 2010, Nel et al. 2012), some of which might inform new regionalist perspectives, especially as these are increasingly impacted by the divergence between BRICS and PIIGS.

(iv) New regionalisms
The proliferation of states post-bipolarity has led to a parallel proliferation of regions, especially if diversities of non-state, informal even illegal regions are so considered. And the eurozone crisis concentrated in the PIIGS has eroded the salience of the EU as model,

leading to a recognition of a variety of 'new' regionalisms (Flemes 2010, Shaw et al. 2011).These include instances of 'African agency' (Lorenz and Rempe 2013) like South African franchises and supply chains reaching to West Africa and the Trilateral FTA (Free Trade Agreement) among Common Market of Eastern and Southern Africa (COMESA), East African Community (EAC) and Southern African Development Community (SADC) (T-FTA) (Hartzenberg et al. 2012) along with older/newer regional conflicts like South China Sea (SCS) and Great Lakes Region (GLR) plus the regional as well as global dimensions of, say, piracy off the coast of Somalia.

(v) Emerging 'global' issues
Over the past quarter-century, the IPE Series has treated a growing number of global issues arising in the global South, as well as those resulting from excessive consumption/pollution in the North such as NCDs like diabetes. In the immediate future, these issues will include environmental and other consequences of climate change and health viruses/zoonoses. They will also extend to myriad computer viruses and cyber-crime (Kshetri 2013). Some suggest that we may be running out of basic commodities like energy (Klare 2012) and water, let alone rare-earth elements (REEs). Finally, after recent global and regional crises, the governance of the global economy is at stake: the financialisation syndrome of Debt Bond Rating Agencies (DBRAs), derivatives, Exchange-Traded Funds (ETFs) / Exchange-Traded Note (ETNs), hedge and pension funds, SWFs etc (Overbeek and Apeldoorn 2012).

(vi) Informal and illegal economies: from fragile to developmental states?
Developing out of the internet, new mobile technologies increasingly facilitate the informal/illegal, as well as otherwise. The 'informal sector' is increasingly recognised in the discipline of anthropology etc. as the illegal in the field of IPE (Friman 2009, Naylor 2005 etc.); these are increasingly informed by telling Small Arms Survey (SAS) annual reports after more than decade with a focus on fragile states (www.smallarmssurvey.org).

Similarly, TOC is increasingly transnational with the proliferation of (young/male) gangs from myriad states (see Knight and Keating (2010), chapter 12). In response, the field of IPE needs to develop analyses and prescriptions from the established informed annual Small Arms Survey and Latin American then Global Commission on Drugs and Drug Policy/Health (www.globalcommission

ondrugs.org); and now at start of new decade onto Ideas Google re the illicit (www.google.com/ideas/focus.html).

Such pressures lead to communities going beyond national and human security towards 'citizen security' as a notion developed in communities of fear in today's Central America and the Caribbean; see UNDP (2012b).

(vii) Varieties of transnational governance

Just as 'governance' is being redefined/rearticulated (Bevir 2011), so the 'transnational' is being rediscovered/rehabilitated (Dingwerth 2008, Hale and Held 2012) following marginalization after its initial articulation at the start of the 1970s by Keohane and Nye (1972): they identified major varieties of transnational relations such as communications, conflict, education, environment, labour, MNCs, religions etc. And Stuart Brown (2011) updated such perspectives with a more economics-centred framework which included civil society, remittances etc.

In turn, I would add contemporary transnational issues such as brands and franchises; conspicuous consumption by emerging middle classes; world sports, such as Federation Internationale de Football Association (FIFA) and International Olympic Committee (IOC); global events from World Fairs to Olympics and world soccer; logistics and supply-chains (legal and formal and otherwise); mobile digital technologies; newly recognized film centres such as Bollywood and Nollywood including diasporas, film festivals, tie-ins etc; new media such as Facebook and Twitter; but such heterogeneous relations/perspectives deserve much more further attention: real IPE in current decade of the 21st century.

(viii) IPE of global development/studies by mid-century?

In conclusion I juxtapose a trio of changes which will probably impact the IPE of the global South in policy and practice and may lead towards the greater privileging as well as theorizing of 'global studies' (O'Bryne and Hensby 2011):

(a) exponential global restructuring in myriad areas, from economics and ecology to diplomacy and security (Besada and Kindornay 2013, Overbeek and Apeldoorn 2012);

(b) changes in the IPE and technologies of publishing including competition from digital and mobile devices; and

(c) shifts in global higher education towards a variety of international interdisciplinary perspectives/methodologies/technologies – from 'ivy' and 'open' universities to Executive Masters in

Business Administration (EMBAs) and Massive Open Online Courses (MOOCs) – so my privileged personal experience of university education on three continents will become the norm, whether virtually or in real time.

In short, to bring my own academic and editorial roles together, I'm delighted to be ending my formal career animating a new interdisciplinary PhD at a public university in the US – University of Massachusetts – (my first time teaching there) on 'Global Governance and Human Security': reinforcing my continuing education, enhanced by the present burgeoning IPE Series, especially its Classics.

Bibliography

Berstein, Steven and Benjamin Cashore (2008) 'The Two-Level Logic of Non-State Market Driven Global Governance' in Volker Rittberger and Martin Nettesheim (eds) *Authority in the Global Political Economy* (London: Palgrave Macmillan), 276–313.

Besada, Hany and Shannon Kindornay (eds) (2013) *The Future of Multilateral Development Cooperation in a Changing Global Order* (London: Palgrave Macmillan for NSI, forthcoming).

Bevir, Mark (2011) *Sage Handbook of Governance* (London: Sage).

Bremmer, Ian (2012) *Every Nation for Itself: Winners and Losers in a G-Zero World* (New York: Penguin)

Bremmer, Ian and Douglas Rediker (eds) (2012) *What's Next: Essays on Geopolitics That Matter* (New York: Portfolio/Penguin).

Brock, Lothar, Hans-Henrik Holm, Georg Sorensen and Michael Stohl (2012) *Fragile States* (Cambridge: Polity).

Brown, Stuart (2013) *The Future of US Global Power: Delusions of Decline* (London: Palgrave Macmillan).

—— (ed.) (2011) *Transnational Transfers and Global Development* (London: Palgrave Macmillan).

Chin, Gregory and Fahim Quadir (eds) (2012) 'Rising States, Rising Donors and the Global Aid Regime' *Cambridge Review of International Affairs* 25(4): 493–649.

Cooper, Andrew F and Agata Antkiewicz (eds) (2008) *Emerging Powers in Global Governance: Lessons from the Heiligendamm Process* (Waterloo: WLU Press for CIGI).

Cooper, Andrew F and Bessma Momani (2011) 'Qatar and Expanded Contours of South-South Diplomacy' *International Spectator* 46(3), September: 113–128.

Cooper, Andrew F and Daniel Flemes (eds) (2013) 'Special Issue: Emerging Powers in Global Governance' *Third World Quarterly* (forthcoming).

Cooper, Andrew F and Timothy M Shaw (eds) (2013) *Diplomacies of Small States: Resilience versus Vulnerability?* second edn (London: Palgrave Macmillan).

Cooper, Andrew F and Paola Subacchi (eds) (2010) 'Global Economic Governance in Transition' *International Affairs* 86(3), May: 607–757.

Cornelissen, Scarlett, Fantu Cheru and Timothy M Shaw (eds) (2012) *Africa and International Relations in the Twenty-first Century: Still Challenging Theory?* (London: Palgrave Macmillan).

Dingwerth, Klaus (2008) 'Private Transnational Governance and the Developing World' *International Studies Quarterly* 52(3): 607–634.

Dunn, Kevin C and Timothy M Shaw (eds) (2001) *Africa's Challenge to International Relations Theory* (London: Palgrave Macmillan).

Economist (2012) *The World in 2013* (London) (www.economist.org/theworldin/2013)

Fanta, Emmanuel, Timothy M Shaw and Vanessa Tang (eds) (2013) *Comparative Regionalism for Development in the Twenty-first Century: Insights from the Global South* (Farnham: Ashgate for NETRIS).

Fioramonti, Lorenzo (eds) (2012) *Regions and Crises: New Challenges for Contemporary Regionalisms* (London: Palgrave Macmillan).

Flemes, Daniel (ed) (2010) *Regional Leadership in the Global System* (Farnham: Ashgate).

Friman, H Richard (ed) (2009) *Crime and the Global Political Economy* (Boulder: LRP. IPE Yearbook #16).

Goldstein, Andrea (2007) *Multinational Companies from Emerging Economies* (London: Palgrave Macmillan).

Gray, Kevin and Craig Murphy (eds) (2013) 'Special Issue: Rising Powers and the Future of Global Governance' *Third World Quarterly* (forthcoming).

Hale, Thomas and David Held (eds) (2012) *Handbook of Transnational Governance* (Cambridge: Polity).

Hanson, Kobena, George Kararach and Timothy M Shaw (eds) (2012) *Rethinking Development Challenges for Public Policy: Insights from Contemporary Africa* (London: Palgrave Macmillan for ACBF).

Hartzenberg, Trudi et al. (2012) *The Trilateral Free Trade Area: Towards a New African Integration Paradigm?* (Stellenbosch: Tralac).

Hawksworth, John and Gordon Cookson (2008) 'The World in 2050: Beyond the BRICs: A Broader Look at Emerging Market Growth' (London: PWC).

Jordaan, Eduard (2003) 'The Concept of Middle Power in IR: Distinguishing between Emerging and Traditional Middle Powers' *Politikon* 30(2), November: 165–181.

—— (2012) 'South Africa, Multilateralism and the Global Politics of Development' *European Journal of Development Research* 24(2), April: 283–299.

Keohane, Robert O and Joseph S Nye (eds) (1972) *Transnational Relations and World Politics* (Cambridge: Harvard University Press).

Khanna, Parag (2009) *The Second World: How Emerging Powers Are Redefining Global Competition in the Twenty-First Century* (New York: Random House).

Klare, Michael T (2012) *The Race for What's Left: The Global Scramble for the World's Last Resources* (New York: Metropolitan).

Kliman, Daniel M and Richard Fontaine (2012) 'Global Swing States: Brazil, India, Indonesia, Turkey and the Future of International Order' (Washington, DC: GMF).

Knight, W. Andy and Tom Keating (2010) *Global Politics* (Toronto: Oxford University Press), chapter 12.

Kshetri, Nir (2013) *Cybercrime and Cybersecurity in the Global South* (London: Palgrave Macmillan, forthcoming).

Kugelman, Michael (2009) *Land Grab? Race for the World's Farmland* (Washington, DC: Brookings).

Kyung-Sup, Chang, Ben Fine and Linda Weiss (eds) (2012) *Developmental Politics in Transition: The Neoliberal Era and beyond* (London: Palgrave Macmillan).

Lee, Bernice et al (2012) 'Resources Futures' (London: Chatham House, December) (www.chathamhouse.org/resourcesfutures).

Lorenz, Ulrike and Martin Rempe (eds) (2013) *Comparing Regionalisms in Africa: Mapping Agency* (Farnham: Ashgate, forthcoming).

Margulis, Matias E et al. (eds) (2013) 'Special Issue: Land Grabbing and Global Governance' *Globalizations* 10(1).

Naylor, R T (2005) *Wages of Crime: Black Markets, Illegal Finance and the Underworld Economy*, second edn (Ithaca: Cornell University Press).

Nel, Philip et al. (eds) (2012) 'Special Issue: Regional Powers and Global Redistribution' *Global Society* 26(3): 279–405.

Nel, Philip and Detlef Nolte (eds) (2010) 'Regional Powers in a Changing Global Order' *Review of International Studies* 36(4), October: 877–974.

O'Bryne, Darren J and Alexander Hensby (2011) *Theorising Global Studies* (London: Palgrave Macmillan).

OECD (2012) 'Economic Outlook, Analysis and Forecasts: Looking to 2060. Long-Term Growth Prospects for the World' (Paris).

O'Neill, Jim (2011) *The Growth Map: Economic Opportunity In the BRICs and Beyond* (New York: Portfolio/Penguin).

Overbeek, Henk and Bastiaan van Apeldoorn (eds) (2012) *Neoliberalism in Crisis* (London: Palgrave Macmillan)

Pieterse, Jan Nederveen (2011) 'Global Rebalancing: Crisis and the East-South Turn' *Development and Change* 42(1): 22–48.

Power, Marcus, Giles Mohan and May Tan-Mullins (2012) *China's Resource Diplomacy in Africa: Powering Development* (London: Palgrave Macmillan).

PWC (2013) 'World in 2050: The BRICs and Beyond: Prospects, Challenges and Opportunities' (London, January).

Ratha, Dilip et al. (2011) *Leveraging Remittances for Africa: Remittances, Skills and Investments* (Washington, DC: World Bank and AfDB).

Reuter, Peter (ed) *Draining Development: Controlling Flows of Illicit Funds from Developing Countries* (Washington, DC: World Bank) (www.openknowledge. worldbank.org).

Shaw, Timothy M (2012a) 'Africa's Quest for Developmental States: "Renaissance" for Whom?' *Third World Quarterly* 33(5): 837–851.

Shaw, Timothy M (2012b) 'The "Rest" and the Global South: Varieties of Actors, Issues and Coalitions.' In Sean Clark and Sabrina Hoque (eds) *Debating a "Post-American World': What Lies Ahead?* (Abingdon: Routledge), chapter 18.

Shaw, Timothy M, Andrew F Cooper and Gregory T Chin (2009) 'Emerging Powers and Africa: Implications for/from Global Governance?' *Politikon* 36(1), April: 27–44.

Shaw, Timothy M, J Andrew Grant and Scarlett Cornelissen (eds) (2011) *Ashgate Research Companion to Regionalisms* (Farnham: Ashgate).

Shaxson, Nicholas (2012) *Treasure Islands: Uncovering the Damage of Offshore Banking and Tax Havens* (New York: Palgrave Macmillan).

SID (2012) 'State of East Africa 2012: Deepening Integration, Intensifying Challenges' (Nairobi for TMEA).

Sinclair, Timothy (2012) *Global Governance* (Cambridge: Polity).

Singh, Priti and Raymond Izaralli (eds) (2012) *The Contemporary Caribbean: Issues and Challenges* (New Delhi: Shipra).

Sumner, Andy and Richard Mallett (2012)*The Future of Foreign Aid* (London: Palgrave Macmillan).

UNDP (2012a)*African Human Development Report: Towards a Food Secure Future* (New York, May)

UNDP (2012b) *Caribbean Human Development Report 2012: Human Development and the Shift to Better Citizen Security* (Port of Spain).

UNDP (2013) *Human Development Report 2013: The Rise of the South: Human Progress in a Diverse World* (New York, March).

UNDP (2014) *Human Development Report 2014: Beyond 2015: Accelerating Human Progress and Defining Goals* (New York, forthcoming).

UNECA (2011) *Economic Report on Africa 2011: Governing Development in Africa: The Role of the State in Economic Transformation* (Addis Ababa).

UNECA (2012) *Economic Report on Africa 2012: Unleashing Africa's Potential as a Pole of Global Growth* (Addis Ababa).

USNIC (2012) 'Global Trends 2030: Alternative Worlds' (Washington, DC: National Intelligence Council, December) (www.dni.gov/nic/globaltrends) (www.gt.com).

Vom Hau, Matthias, James Scott and David Hulme (2012) 'Beyond the BRICs: Alternative Strategies of Influence in the Global Politics of Development' *European Journal of Development Research* 24(2), April: 187–204.

Weiss, Thomas G (2013) *Global Governance* (Cambridge: Polity, forthcoming).

Wilkinson, Rorden and David Hulme (eds) (2012) *The Millennium Development Goals and Beyond: Global Development After 2015* (Abingdon: Routledge).

Wilkinson, Rorden and Thomas G Weiss (eds) (2013) *Global Governance* (Abingdon: Routledge, forthcoming).

World Bank (2012) *Global Economic Prospects June 2012: Managing Growth in a Volatile World* (Washington, DC, June).

World Economic Forum (WEF) (2012) *Global Risks 2012: An Initiative of The RRN* (Davos. Seventh edition)

Xing, Li with Abdulkadir Osman Farah (eds) (2013) *China-Africa Relations in an Era of Great Transformation* (Farnham: Ashgate, forthcoming).

Xu, Yi-chong (ed) (2012) *The Political Economy of State-Owned Enterprises in China and India* (London: Palgrave Macmillan).

Xu, Yi-chong and Gawdat Baghat (eds) (2011) *The Political Economy of Sovereign Wealth Funds* (London: Palgrave Macmillan).

Zakaria, Fareed (2011) *The Post-American World: Release 2.0* (New York: Norton. Updated and expanded edition).

www.africaminingvision.org
www.bcg.com
www.beyond2015.org
www.cgdev.org
www.chathamhouse.org
www.consejomexicano.org/en/constructive-powers
www.dni.gov/nic/globaltrends
www.economist.org/theworldin/2013

www.eiti.org
www.enoughproject.org
www.eurasiagroup.net
www.fareedzakaria.com
www.fatf/gafi.org
www.foreignpolicy.com
www.globalcommissionondrugs,org
www.globalpolicy.org
www.globalreporting.org
www.globalriskinstitute.com
www.globalwitness.org
www.google.com/ideas/focus/html
www.gt2030.com
www.hdr.org
www.isealalliance,org
www.jannederveenpieterse.com
www.kimberleyprocess.com
www.leadinggroup.org
www.mahbubani.net
www.mckinsey.com
www.normangirvan.info
www.openknowledge.worldbank.org
www.paragkhanna.com
www.post2015.org
www.pwc.com
www.reourcesfutures.org
www.smallarmssurvey.org
www.umb.edu/cgs/research/global_redesign_initiative
www.un.org/millenniumgoals/beyond2015
www.unodc.org
www.weforum.org
www.worldbank.org/globaloutlook
www2.goldmansachs.com

Lagos, December 2012 and
Boston, January 2013

Acknowledgements

I started the first draft of this manuscript when I was Visiting Professor at City University of Hong Kong, and I am very grateful for the support provided by City University, and to Kevin Hewison in particular. This work has also benefited from time spent at the Asia Research Centre at Murdoch University and research undertaken in China, and I would like to thank Garry Rodan, Chen Zhimin, Song Xinning, Dai Bingran and Zha Daojiong for their help and financial support, and the Centre for the Study of Globalisation and Regionalisation at Warwick for funding some of them. Special thanks to Bill Abnett and the National Bureau for Asian Research for organising the China-WTO forum which has not only provided an invaluable insight into ideas and opinions of others, but also links to documents and news stories that have been used in preparing this manuscript. Thanks also to Wang Yizhou and Yu Yongding for providing access to the Institute of World Economics and Politics and to Sarah, Patrick and Hannah for putting up with my frequent absences from home over the years.

List of Abbreviations

ACFTA	ASEAN–China Free Trade Area
ADB	Asian Development Bank
AFLCIO	American Federation of Labor and Congress of Industrial Organizations
AMC	Asset Management Company
APT	ASEAN Plus Three
ASEAN	Association of Southeast Asian Nations
BRICS	Brazil, Russia, India, China, South Africa
CASS	Chinese Academy of Social Sciences
CC	Central Committee (of the Chinese Communist Party)
CCP	Chinese Communist Party
CD	China Daily
CECC	Congressional-Executive Commission on China
CFB	Chinese Family Business
CIF	Cost Insurance and Freight
CME	Contract Manufacturing Enterprise
CPPCC	Chinese People's Political Consultative Conference
EPZ	Export Processing Zone
EU	European Union
FAC	UK Parliamentary Foreign Affairs Committee
FDI	Foreign Direct Investment
FIE	Foreign Invested Enterprise
FOB	Free On Board
GATT	General Agreement on Tariffs and Trade
GDP	Gross Domestic Product
GNP	Gross National Product
GSP	Generalised System of Preferences
IPE	International Political Economy
IPR	Intellectual Property Rights
IR	International Relations
ITIC	International Trust and Investment Corporation
JV	Joint Venture
LIPC	Local Investment Platform Company
MFN	Most Favoured Nation
MOFTEC	Ministry of Foreign Trade and Economic Cooperation
NAFTA	North American Free Trade Agreement

NGO	Non Governmental Organisation
NPC	National People's Congress
NPL	Non performing loan
NSB	National Statistics Bureau
OEM	Original Equipment Manufacturing
OECD	Organization for Economic Co-operation and Development
OPEC	Organization for the Petroleum Exporting Countries
PBC	People's Bank of China
PLA	People's Liberation Army
PNTR	Permanent Normal Trade Relations
PPP	Purchasing Power Parity
PRC	People's Republic of China
R&D	Research and Design
RMB	Renminbi
SASAC	State Asset Supervision and Administration Commission
SETC	State Economic and Trade Commission
SEZ	Special Economic Zone
SOE	State Owned Enterprise
TNC	Transnational Corporation
TVEs	Township and Village Enterprises
UN	United Nations
UNCTAD	United Nations Conference on Trade and Development
US	United States
USCBC	United States China Business Council
USGAO	United States General Accounting Office
USTRO	United States Trade Representative Office
WFOE	Wholly Foreign Owned Enterprise
WSCB	Wholly State Owned Commercial Bank
WTO	World Trade Organisation

Note on the Transliteration of Chinese Names

As with most contemporary works, this book uses the hanyu pinyin system of transliterating Chinese into roman script. The only exceptions are where people have chosen to transliterate their own names in different ways – in these cases, their original transliterations are simply repeated here. As there are many references to Chinese authors with the same surname, the Chinese name will be given in full when referenced in the text to help the reader find the correct source in the bibliography where the duplication of surnames might cause confusion.

Introduction: China – Yes, But ...

It seems that Napoleon was right – the world has been shaken by China's awakening. Although China engaged the United Nations (UN) in military conflict in Korea in the 1950s, has been a nuclear power since the 1960s, a permanent member of the United Nations Security Council since 1971 and was a key actor in Cold War politics, China's re-engagement with the global political economy has been a major reason why the world has been shaken into re-evaluating China's importance. To be fair, China's importance has been clear and present in some parts of the world for quite some time – for China's neighbours, long standing fears of potential conflict in Japan, Taiwan and much of Southeast Asia sit alongside actual experiences of military engagement with China in India, Vietnam and the former Soviet Union. What has changed is that the China challenge is now being taken seriously in other parts of the world as well – China is shaking the West, and shaking the United States (US) in particular.

For a relatively loud and influential group of writers primarily, but not only, in the US, China's rise is taken very seriously. It is not just that China will become ever more important and or influential in the international system, but that there is something sinister or dangerous about China's rise. Of course, it's not just about economics alone. Whilst some International Relations (IR) theorists point to the volatility caused when hegemonic stability is challenged by any new rising power, others point to the importance of whether that rising power shares the status quo values and norms (Johnston 2003). It's not being flippant to suggest that China represents a new 'orange peril' to the West, in that it combines the fear of the red communist alternative with the yellow Asian cultural and economic challenge to dominant Western values. What China's leaders do to their own people might be disagreeable to many in the international community, and opposing the policy objectives of Western states can be irritating and problematic. But in the long term, the bigger threat to the global order is seen as lying in the provision of a credible Chinese alternative to the status quo. As Ramo (2004: 3) argues:

> China's new ideas are having a gigantic effect outside of China. China is marking a path for other nations around the world who are trying to figure out not simply how to develop their countries, but also how to fit into the international order in a way that allows them to be truly independent, to protect their way of life and political choices in a world with a single massively powerful centre of gravity.

For some, confrontation and military conflict with the USA as the existing superpower is inevitable (Bernstein and Munro 1998, Timperlake 1999, Gertz 2002, Menges 2005). China's centuries old superiority complex is manifest in an aspiration to return itself to its rightful place of global dominance (Mosher 2000), with China willing to ally with radical Islam to find a means of overcoming the US (Thomas 2001, Babbin and Timperlake 2006). Or at the very least, the growth of an assertive nationalism in China threatens regional stability through military conflict with Taiwan or Japan which might easily escalate into conflict with the US. Why else would China's leaders be spending millions of dollars rapidly modernising and upgrading their armed forces, and continually reminding Taiwan that they will use whatever force is necessary to prevent the creation of a separate Taiwanese state.

Yet even considerations of values/norms/ideas and military capabilities and objectives are at least linked to China's extraordinary economic transformation – it might not just be about economics alone, but economics is usually there somewhere. China's alternative path is partly attractive because of the apparent success of the experience of economic reform. Other developing states might also lean towards the Chinese way not just because China's leaders don't attach democratising and liberalising conditions to bilateral relations, but also because China is coming to provide alternative sources of economic opportunities (with non-democratising strings attached). In terms of military capabilities, economic performance is clearly crucial in providing the resources to upgrade and expand, and also the foreign currency to buy modern equipment from those who are prepared to sell to China. But there is also a less tangible relationship between economic performance and nationalist sentiments and objectives – both on behalf of the government and the Chinese people. On one level, Hughes (2006) argues that nationalism was at the heart of the reform process initiated by Deng Xiaoping – reforming the old system was justified and legitimated by the need to build a strong China that could resist (and even oppose) the existing hegemonic global order.

On another level, the resurgence of nationalism in China is at least partly explained by a new sense of pride in China's economic successes – what Whiting (1995) termed 'affirmative nationalism' – and/or the feeling that key external groups have been trying to prevent China's development and threaten Chinese interests – in Whiting's typology, 'assertive nationalism'.[1] The flip side of this coin is the debates over the extent to which the pursuit of economic gains and the extent of China's economic integration act as a break on popular nationalist ambitions and/or the extent to which the leadership can separate the promotion of nationalism as a source of domestic consolidation and regime legitimation from the promotion of China as a rational predictable and reliable international partner for an international audience.

When the debate is just about economics alone, then there is a relatively strong school of thought that points to China as the engine of growth in the global economy; at least an emerging power well on the way to becoming a global economic superpower that threatens to reconfigure the global political economy around Chinese interests (Weidenbaum and Hughes 1996, Bacani 2003, Overholt 1994, Murray 1998). The prima facie supporting evidence appears to be compelling. The Chinese economy is already the second biggest economy in the world using Purchasing Power Parity (PPP) calculations and is predicted to overtake the US in 2020 or 2041 or 2050 or some time this century. China overtook the US as the single biggest recipient of non-stocks and shares Foreign Direct Investment (FDI) in 2002. China is the fourth largest trader in the world, and has massive foreign currency reserves second only to Japan at the time of writing (and probably even higher by the time of publication). And it is not just size that is important (though it clearly is) but also the incredible speed of change. For example, the fact that China's trade surplus for 2005 was US$102 billion is remarkable – the fact that it tripled during the year even more so. Similarly, it's not just that foreign currency reserves at the start of 2006 were US$819 that generates international interest and much concern, but also that these reserves increased by a third during 2005 (Goodman 2006). And perhaps not surprisingly, this emerging economic superpower is seen by some as the major challenge to the existing global economic order in general, and to US economic interests in particular (Shenkar 2004, Fishman 2005).

Yes, but ...

This extremely brief overview of perceptions of the impact of China's awakening has used sources that depict rather extreme views of China's new global role – not all of them particularly academic in nature – and not mentioned some of the excellent balanced studies of globalisation and China (for example Zweig 2002, Zheng Yongnian 2004). Having established these positions, the next logical step is to knock down and rubbish these interpretations of China. And I am indeed critical of some of the basic assumptions that generate these conclusions. Nevertheless, it would be ridiculous to dismiss the reality of China's amazing economic transformation since 1978 and in particular, since 1992. Even Segal (1999) who answered his own question, 'Does China Matter?' in the negative in reality accepted that China's economic transformation was important and significant – but crucially, not as much as dominant approaches and voices would have us believe. As Yahuda (2004: 1) noted in his assessment of Segal's work:

> The article was intended as a wake-up call for many in Washington and elsewhere. In Segal's view the persistent exaggeration of the significance of China was damaging, as it prevented the development of sustained coherent policies commensurate with the security and commercial interests of the West

I not only share Yahuda's interpretation of Segal's work (see Breslin 2005: 735), but also have considerable sympathy with the aim of tempering such 'persistent exaggeration'.

It is easy to see why China is often posited as an example of successful economic reform and a coming superpower – at the very least economically and perhaps even by any definition of superpower. If you visit Beijing or Shanghai you visit cities that have changed beyond recognition in an amazingly short period of time, and whose populations increasingly live modern urban lifestyles that have much in common with lifestyles of many in the advanced industrial west. Even those who go further afield to other Chinese cities in the interior see clear signs of growth and wealth. And it is not just cosmetic change or an elaborate hoax. The lives of millions of China's urban dwellers really have been changed almost beyond recognition in two decades. Many millions more in the countryside are also much better off than before, with the reduction of people living in poverty in China accounting for most of the overall reduction in global poverty. China's people also have more individual freedom – they have a personal space that was previously denied to them – even though total freedom and political plurality may still be a long way off.

China's engagement with the global economy has also brought many successes, and China is now massively significant for the functioning of the global economy. The way in which parts of the Chinese economy have been inserted into the global economy have already resulted in a reconstruction of the East Asian regional economy, is impacting on the developmental trajectories of developing states across the world, and is altering production processes in (and in the process removing jobs from) even the most advanced economies in the world.

All of this is true – and Chapters 2 and 3 of this book are devoted to exploring how these dramatic changes have come about. But we need to take care not to simply assume that growth equates to development, wealth for all and power – or not yet at least. Yes, China is changing fast, but there are a number of 'buts' that qualify the 'yes'. Yes there has been close to double digit growth for two decades, but despite this, China still remains a relatively poor country in per capita terms coming in at 107th using PPP (US$6,600 per capita) and 128th (US$1,740 per capita) using the atlas method in lists of the world's richest countries in per capita terms. China as a whole may no longer be considered to be 'poor', but is still only ranked as a 'middle income' country at best, and more often as 'lower middle income'. If we take the higher of the per capita income figures using PPP calculations, then China still comes out below Kazakhstan, Namibia, Tonga, Iran, Equatorial Guinea, Thailand, Costa Rica and many others. It is instructive that despite the great successes of China's reform experience, and the fact that it is often favourably compared to the Russian experience, whichever calculation is used, per capita income in Russia is still around 50 per cent more than China's (not least because of the very low base level that China started from).

Yes there has been significant growth in China, but has this growth been accompanied by concomitant levels of development, or have the benefits of growth not been as impressive and immediate as the headline figures suggest. Yes there has been growth, but at what costs? Costs to the environment, and human costs as well. Yes, there have been many millions that have been brought out of poverty, and millions of others that have seen their lives dramatically change for the better. But there are still many millions who remain in poverty and millions whose lives have not improved much at all (or as much as they would like). There are also millions for whom things have got worse. Economic reform in China has entailed a new industrial revolution, but through the transition from socialism, it has also entailed a simultaneous process of de-industrialisation. Yes, economic reform and growth have been an important component in legitimating the continuation of the Chinese Communist Party's (CCP) monopoly of political power, but it has also resulted in class reformulation and social dislocations that might come to threaten that power. Yes it is possible that a new middle class will lead China slowly towards democracy, but it is far from impossible that China might go down an alternative political path. Certainly, those forecasts of China's future(s) that assume a steady and peaceful domestic political situation are making assumptions that China's current leaders amongst others are not prepared to make.

Yes, the way that China has re-engaged with the global political economy has altered the structure of the Chinese economy, and has also impacted on the economies of developing and developed countries alike. But does this mean that China has the economic power that some suggest, or does the locus of economic power, for the time being at least, still reside elsewhere? Has China actually benefited as much as the figures seem to suggest, or is it in fact consumers and companies in the West that gain most from China's 'rise' – even as that rise results in the transfer of jobs from West to East?[2]

Chapter 1 is devoted to exploring different ways of studying China in an era of globalisation, and explains in detail why different assumptions and approaches generate conflicting visions. There is no point in repeating this analysis here, but in essence, this chapter suggests that there are four key issues which in my view create at best only partial understandings.

First, as already noted, there is often an assumption that a linear progression will occur – assumptions that are sometimes based on historical experiences of other societies and which typically discount domestic political turmoil. Second, the concept of 'power' is often left undefined, with an assumption that size and importance is the same as power. Third, too many of these analyses forget or ignore politics. Fourth and very much related (indeed, is it really a separate issue?), these studies tend to take 'China' as the unit of analysis. This might sound strange – not least because this is a book that itself focuses on China. But on one level, we need to consider the differential political consequences of economic reform within China itself. Of course it is important to ask questions about whether x or y – globalisation or joining the World Trade Organisation (WTO) for example – are good for China. But an aggregate answer of 'yes' for China as a whole will almost always miss the fact that what is good for some can be bad for others. So we should ask instead (or at least in addition) who is x or y good for? On another level, many analyses of the political implications of international economic relations assume that these relations are just that – inter (or between) national units. The analysis remains imbedded in conceptions of international, whereas the reality of production is transnational (or globalised). This book builds on these four key areas by providing alternative ways of conceptualising the implication of China's international economic relations in Chapters 4 and 5, and the domestic political implications of economic reform in Chapter 6.

The primary target of this book is those scholars of international relations and/or international political economy who do not have a detailed knowledge of the Chinese case. To this end, it contains some sections of explanatory detail – for example, outlining the process of economic reform and opening in Chapters 2 and 3 respectively. Perhaps most clearly of all, the contents of Chapter 6 – 'Stretching the Social Fabric' – might seem to be so obvious as to be unnecessary for students of Chinese politics. But its inclusion reflects what I continually find to be a rather large gap in general knowledge about domestic dislocations in China amongst academics and some policy makers, which relates back to previous comments about the aggregation of China as a single unit of analysis and the relative neglect of domestic politics in considerations of China's global (economic) role. Jeffrey Sachs might be right that China's experience in poverty reduction is impressive, but his assertion that 'we can see from China's experience that the end of poverty is absolutely palpable and real in the space of a very few years' (Watts 2006) rather overestimates the situation, and skips over the millions or rural Chinese that are still in poverty, the many millions more that are danger of slipping back into poverty, and the increasing numbers of urban poor. Yes, much has been done, but a lot still remains to be done before Chinese poverty can be confined to historical studies.

Although some policy makers are already now thinking of China as rich and powerful, most of the forecasts of Chinese superpower status are still predictions of what will happen in the future. As already noted, I am somewhat critical of the basis of some of these predictions – of their assumptions about where China is now, and about their assumptions of inevitable or at least highly likely future trajectories. Nolan (2003: 252) rightly rebukes those analysts who simply assume that China's developmental trajectory will inevitably (and teleologically) emulate either the early developmental experience of Great Britain or the later developers of East Asia (including the relationship between economic and political change). It is notable that when examples of transition are used to justify evolutionary assumptions, Indonesia is not typically one of the cases referred to, and it is also instructive to remember the hyperbole about the coming 'Pacific Century' prior to the 1997 financial crises. As Zha Daojiong (2005: 780–4) notes, within China itself, the Latin American experience of economic stagnation, domestic social polarisation and international economic dependence is considered to be *a* possible example of China's future (unless the correct policies are adopted now). The analysis will return to conceptions of potential futures in the Conclusion, and to some extent, in Chapter 6 as well. However, the majority of the book focuses on what has happened rather than what will, and to this extent I have to accept that yes China might develop and evolve as some of the predictors of superpower status expect – but then of course, it might not.

In some respects, then, this book provides a 'revisionist' understanding of China's global economic role. For those deeply embedded within the study of China's political economy, this will sound like a grand and probably inflated claim. However this assessment is not mine but the series editor's – which suggests that the visions and interpretations that dominate are not just popular but also non-China specialist intellectual understandings of China fall within the broad typology of analyses that this book does indeed take issue with. So in this respect, the attempt to revise some of the very basic understandings of China's global role and challenge common (mis)conceptions is indeed the starting point of this analysis.

Methodological problems: lies, damn lies, statistics and Chinese statistics (or never trust a statistic that you haven't faked yourself)

In December 2005, the head of the National Bureau of Statistics, Li Deshui, announced that the bureau had revised the 2004 Gross Domestic Product (GDP) figures upwards by almost 17 per cent. This was because the 'Material Product' accounting system developed when the state plan still dominated had failed to correctly measure the extent of economic activity in the services sector – much of which simply went unreported. Using a new accounting system, the bureau had discovered an extra RMB2.13 trillion of activity in the tertiary sector (about a third of the previously reported figure) which meant that it now accounted for 40.7 rather than 31.9 per cent of total GDP (*People's Daily* 2005f). Although this was a high profile case, research on the Chinese economy is always complicated by the possibility of statistical confusion. There are two key issues here – different methods of calculation and the reliability of Chinese statistics.

Methods of calculation

The first problem to be overcome is differing methods of calculating the size of the Chinese economy. Transferring official national income figures collected by the National Bureau of Statistics (Formerly the State Statistical Bureau) into US$ is rather problematic as the value of the Renminbi[3] (RMB) is not set by market forces. Between 1994 and 2005 the value of the RMB was pegged to the dollar. As the pegged rate of RMB8.27 to the dollar undervalued the value of the RMB (by how much was a subject of considerable disagreement), so simple calculations of the size of the Chinese economy that divided the RMB figure by 8.27 similarly undervalued the dollar value of Chinese GDP. Furthermore, when the dollar depreciated as it did in 2003–4, then the dollar denominated size of the Chinese economy artificially changed relative to the dollar based size of other economies with floating exchange rates. The peg was abandoned in 2005 and replaced by a managed floating system. The RMB immediately appreciated by 2.1 per cent and was subsequently allowed to fluctuate to a maximum of 0.3 per cent against the value of a basket of currencies each day.[4] But even after this moderate reform, using simple exchange rate figures remains rather problematic.

PPP calculations provide a means of getting over exchange rate problems by attempting to calculate the cost of a basket of goods in a common currency (international dollars). PPP calculations will be most different from exchange rate methods when that nation's exchange rates are either under or overvalued, and when the nation has considerable economic activity that is not reflected in market prices (ie. subsidised housing). Using PPPs for China generates a figure that is more than four times the exchange rate figure.

These different methods of calculation have important spin-off implications. For example, while most observers shared Huang Jikun and Rozelle's (2003: 115–16) observation that the 'trade-to-GDP ratio increased from 13 per cent in 1980 to 36 per cent in 1997', you can also argue that 'China's trade as a per cent of GDP only grew slightly from 6.6 per cent in 1986 to 7.1 per cent in 1996' (Carter and Li 1999: 4) using a different set of statistics. In trying to understand the importance of (and relationship between) trade and growth, a 40 per cent trade dependency figure generates rather different conclusions than 10 per cent. As we shall see in Chapter 3, different methods of calculating trade statistics and problems in identifying the national origin of trade and investment make interpreting statistics on external economic relations even more problematic.

The reliability of statistics

We also have to be aware that Chinese statistics are not always reliable. It is not pushing a point too far to suggest that China's central leaders themselves do not know the real size of the Chinese economy, or the real distribution of growth and wealth. Despite the recreation of the State Statistical Bureau after its dissolution during the Cultural Revolution, there remain considerable problems in verifying figures. For example, when Premier Zhu Rongji was informed that all but one of Chinese provinces had recorded growth rates of at least 8 per cent in 1998, he is reported to have said that he simply didn't believe them (Kynge 1998). The figures, for Zhu, had to be 'padded' – how could they all have grown at 8 per cent and above when the national growth rate was lower than that? Similarly, in August 2006 the National Development and Reform Commission announced that the aggregate of all provincial GDP figures was US$100 billion more than the national figure. Not only had the problem remained unresolved, the gap between national and aggregate provincial statistics had grown wider.[5]

Reliance on local authorities to collect and collate figures makes a huge amount of sense. China is such a large geographical entity that collecting and collating all statistics centrally is simply unfeasible. Indeed, one of the reasons that the CCP decentralised control to the provinces in the 1950s was the sheer impossibility of planning all economic activity centrally. But giving more authority to local authorities also creates a bargaining chip for those local authorities in their dealings with the central government. It also means that there can be considerable slippage between the collection of information on the ground, and the collation of aggregate national data in central agencies in Beijing:

The village deceives the township, the township deceives the county in deception upon deception as a report moves up the hierarchy.

Officials create figures and figures make official careers (Wu Churen 1998)

Despite the dominance of economic paradigms in contemporary China, elements of old political processes remain. Maoist methods of mobilisation around goal attainment have remained an integral part of the policy process. The central government sets targets for economic growth that local authorities then feel politically obliged to meet. As Young (2000: 4) puts it:

Since officials are rewarded for superior performance and punished for failing to meet targets, it is not surprising that they have a tendency to modify their statistical reports in accordance with central policy objectives.

As just one example, a 1995 survey by the State Statistical Bureau found that the output of Township and Village Enterprises (TVEs) in the previous year had been inflated by RMB1.8 trillion or 40 per cent. Alongside this problem of exaggerated performance, under reporting is also a key problem. Faking deficits or under-reporting profits to avoid paying taxes is, to say the least, not uncommon. Enterprises under-report to local governments, which also underreport to provincial governments to avoid transferring money to the provincial government. Provincial governments then also under-report to the central government to similarly avoid transferring money to the centre. And as we shall see in Chapter 3, a considerable amount of income and trade never gets reported at all because of corruption and smuggling.

The central government tried to redress this situation with the introduction of a new fiscal system in 1994. The system has two main features. First, it distinguishes between fiscal revenues that accrue directly to the central government, revenues that are shared between central and local governments, and local revenues. Second, an independent national tax agency was introduced to collect central and shared taxes to prevent local authorities manipulating figures for their own benefit. While this has reduced the leeway for creative accountancy, and also increased the centre's share of all fiscal revenues, the problem has not disappeared.

Alwyn Young (2000) has undertaken a forensic investigation of the way in which Chinese officials calculate growth. He accepts the Chinese figures as given, and then considers the way in which the accounting system was changed after 1978. By including such elements as passenger transport, finance, insurance and public administration, but not recalculating previous figures accordingly, post 1978 figures were immediately much higher than for the pre-reform era. Furthermore, Young argues that the State Statistical Bureau did not use its own deflation indicators appropriately in generating growth figures. So by adding these two omissions together, it is possible to generate very different conclusions about the levels of growth in the Chinese economy:

> In 1989, a year of economic retrenchment, GDP is now seen to have fallen by 5.2 percent, as opposed to the 4.0 percent positive growth reported in official figures. This provides some insight into the forces which precipitated the political unrest of that year. (Young 2000: 49)

In a similar vein, Khan and Riskin (2001) modified Chinese income surveys and concluded that urban poverty actually increased between 1988 and 1995 – and as we shall see in Chapter 6, statistical problems combine with definitional problems to make reaching reliable figures for poverty (and poverty alleviation) in China particularly problematic (Khan and Risken 2001, Reddy and Minoiu 2005).

For some observers, the 'fuzzy maths' (Rawski 2002a) of China's statistics simply do not add up – 'during the 1997–2001 period, China's energy use, employment and prices all fell. So how could real output have grown by one-third, as Chinese officials claim?' (Rawski 2002b). Rawski points to the scepticism within Beijing about the reliability of figures provided by local authorities, and concluded that total economic growth between 1997 and 2001 was not 34.5 per cent as official figures showed, but 12 per cent at most. In a similar vein, Waldron (2002) noted that:

> Visitors see lots of rural people camped out at urban railroad stations or on sidewalks: Clearly they have nothing to do where they come from, or where they've arrived. Block after block of abandoned construction projects in cities suggest someone's run out of money (as does the recent proposal that money be raised for the Three Gorges Dam by selling stock). Almost daily protests by workers, many violent, are also a clue that all is not well.

We need to take some care with Rawski's and Waldron's observations. The domestic Chinese economy was in recession over the turn of the century, but growth was maintained by exports and by massive pump priming of the economy through a budget deficit. And Carsten Holz (2003a) argues that while there are still problems, statistical reliability is improving, and that reported growth rates are now more or less accurate. Nevertheless, we need to keep the reliability of statistics in mind – particularly because unless they are otherwise cited, the data used in the rest of this book all emanates from the National Statistics Bureau and is therefore subject to some of the questioning outlined above.

Rawski and Waldron are also both scholars who have a strong background in researching the domestic Chinese economy. That their observations sit uncomfortably with not just official Chinese figures, but also popular assumptions about China's inevitable rise to superpower status, highlights the way in which different approaches can generate different and sometimes conflicting conclusions – an issue which will now be discussed in more detail in Chapter 1.

1
Studying China in an Era of Globalisation

Studying China's political economy in the pre reform era was not an easy task. With the plethora of information that is now available from China, it is worth remembering how difficult it was to get data and reliable information out of China for many years after 1949. The sort of information that is available on one visit to the web page of the Institute of World Economics and Politics at the Chinese Academy of Social Sciences (www.iwep.org.cn) would have taken most scholars years to collect. Access to the Tsinghua collection of Chinese academic journals through Eastview (www.eastview.com) – both used in preparing this manuscript – gives more articles on any given subject than you can cope with. Conducting the sort of interviews that are now relatively common with Chinese officials, scholars and business people was impossible. And if Chinese officials or scholars visited the West, it was unlikely that they would engage in free and frank discussion, engage with western ideas and methods, or provide candid observations on the domestic situation in China. As Morgan (2004: 77) notes:

> Twenty-five years ago the China specialist was of necessity a generalist. Since then, mastering the slow dribble of information that can be gleaned from a closed society, has been replaced by the management of a deluge of policies, facts, and figures. Simply keeping pace in one's own small area of expertise has become an onerous task.

We should not fool ourselves that nowadays we know everything that is going on and really understand China – but our chances of making educated guesses that get somewhere close to reality have been vastly improved.

14

In some ways, however, studying the dynamics of change in the Chinese political economy was more simplistic in that it was all but possible to think entirely in domestic terms. To be sure, China was never a purely totalitarian state where central leaders spoke and everybody else just fell in line, and considerable time and effort was spent trying to find the real locus of power, with particular emphasis on elite factionalism, the role of the military, and the power of provincial leaders. And of course, China's leaders always had relations with the superpowers in mind when defining domestic development strategies. But you could all but ignore the global and focus purely on the dynamics of domestic politics.

With China's re-engagement with the global economy in the post-Mao era, and particularly after Deng Xiaoping's southern inspection tour – the *nanxun* – in 1992, such a domestic focus can no longer be efficacious. This is not to say that the domestic context is unimportant – far from it. Domestic considerations must remain crucial for any understanding of the contemporary political economy. It is just that on their own, domestic issues do not let us truly understand the many dynamics at play. Trying to get to grips with the domestic context of reform is hard enough in itself, but the rather daunting reality for students of contemporary China is that it is now essential to also get to grips with the dynamics and workings of the global political economy as well.

Building on Payne's (1998) analysis of the political economy of area studies, the objective of this book is both quite straightforward and rather grand at the same time. It is an attempt to enrich the study of Chinese politics and international relations by deploying the analytical tools of International Political Economy (IPE), to consider the dynamics and implications of China's re-engagement with the global economy. It is also an attempt to enrich the study of IPE by providing a detailed case study to provide a resource for the development of a more comparative basis of theory.

In terms of enriching the study of Chinese IR, in attempting to categorise dominant approaches to considering China's IR in an era of globalisation, we face the risk of caricaturing a vast canon of literature. Nevertheless, and accepting this risk, much of what is written about Chinese IR – particularly from inside China – is methodologically overly-statist and realist. In particular, I suggest that it fails to address the analytical problems of separating the domestic from the international, and separating economics from politics. There are of course exceptions, but by and large, the IR discipline has not widely embraced basic tenets of IPE as a methodological starting point.

In terms of theory building, whilst advancing the efficacy of IPE in general as an analytical tool, many of the theories and approaches that form the basis of IPE have been derived from comparisons of the political economy of advanced industrial Organisation for Economic Co-operation and Development (OECD) states. In particular, there is a dominant conception of a separation between public and private (or state and market) that does not always hold true when we move the focus of attention away from the core heartlands of both the global political economy and the heartlands of mainstream academia. The discipline needs to become more sensitive to case studies from the developing world, with a recognition of the different characters of 'the state' and the nature of capitalism outside the advanced industrialised world.

International political economy and new political economy

There are many different understanding of what the terms 'Political Economy' and IPE are as fields of inquiry. This is partly a disciplinary issue, with most economists who label themselves as 'political economists' using economic models to study 'political' phenomenon – for example, voting power in international institutions. But even within the broad church of political science and international relations, there are wide epistemological and operational differences between different schools of IPE. For example, one of the reasons that 'western IPE' in China is often equated with 'rational choice, game theory, mathematical and statistical methods' (Song Xinning and Chan 2000: 29) is the dominance of such research in major academic journals (Wæver 1998, Marsh and Savigny 2004). At perhaps the other extreme of the spectrum, there also remains a strong neo-realist IPE.

In searching for an analytical framework to explain the nature and significance of China's position in the global political economy, this study is concerned with establishing the relationship between structure and agency without insisting on an ontological separation of the two (Wood 1981). It also aims to avoid the basic pitfall of creating analytical divisions between the international and the domestic, and between economics and politics. It has been particularly influenced by what can be termed the 'New Political Economy' as reflected by the editorial stance of the editors of the journal of the same name in their first edition in 1995. Gamble *et al* (1996: 5–6) reject the adoption of a single theoretical approach, and instead promotes a framework or 'toolkit' which embraces non-exclusionary pluralistic approaches:

The methodology of the new political economy rejects the old dichotomy between agency and structure, and states and markets, which fragmented classical political economy into separate disciplines. It seeks instead to build on those approaches in social sciences which have tried to develop an integrated analysis.

For many scholars, the pathway to a framework for understanding contemporary IPE began with a study of classical political economy. But it is also possible to arrive at a similar position by taking other pathways – by rejecting purely economistic interpretations that ignore power and politics; by rejecting the apolitical and ahistorical tendencies within rational choice theory; and by rejecting the parsimonious explanatory power of statist and realist international relations. For all that divides the numerous critical IPE scholars, this rejectionism is more or less implicitly shared by all. And in this respect, there is resonance for those 'area studies' scholars who are frustrated by the shortcomings of hegemonic discourses in the study of contemporary China. These frustrations relate to the dominance, and failings, of realist approaches to studying Chinese international relations (particularly, but not only, within China itself) and the ongoing battle between 'area studies' and 'discipline' in parts of the US academe.

Studying Chinese IR in China

Although Wang Yiwei (2004) has correctly argued that there is not a single distinctive Chinese International Relations Theory, a number of observers have attempted to draw out the dominant ontologies and epistemologies that re-occur in many of the writings on International Relations within China (Chan 1999, Geeraerts and Men Jing 2001, Song Xinning and Chan 2000, Song Xinning 2001). To varying degrees, they all argue that realism dominates the discipline. As we shall see below, realist approaches are becoming less 'hegemonic' in Chinese international relations thinking, with new approaches, definitions and issues entering the discipline relatively rapidly. Nevertheless, it is still fair to say that there are three key reasons why realist ontologies previously dominated the Chinese international relations discipline – and notwithstanding an increasing pluralism, remain the most commonly used theoretical approach. The first is an over concentration on relations with the United States, and the 'conditioning' element that this places on Chinese IR. It is clearly the case that the US is objectively more important for China than, for example, the European Union, or individual European states for Chinese policy makers and researchers. That being said, it is instructive that in Yong Deng's and Wang Fei-ling's (1999) 'In the Eyes of the Dragon' which outlines Chinese visions of the global order, there is no chapter at all on Europe (including Russia).[1]

Second, 'the overarching constraint [on IR theory in China] is a structural one, being the social setting in which the study of IR in China takes place' (Song Xinning 2001: 71). It is difficult to overstate the importance of policy-relevance in academic research, and the extent to which prevalent political concerns in government shape the concerns of most IR academics. At the very least, the socialising element of appointment and promotion procedures lead scholars toward retaining a strong policy relevance element in all their research. This helps explain both the heavy emphasis on the US in Chinese IR, and the heavy emphasis on statist and realist interpretations, and the overarching interest in state sovereignty.

Third, Song also argues that China's residual ideology impacts on the evolution of Chinese IR. Much of the work in China on IR (until recently at least) was informed by a Cold War framework of power politics. During the Cold War, scholars emphasised the 'strategic triangle' – China's ability to manoeuvre in a political/diplomatic space between Moscow and Washington. With the end of the Cold War, the unipolar world system has removed many of the certainties of the old order and we face the geometric problem of triangles that only have two points. The collapse of the Soviet Union means that the US is now free to impose its hegemony over the international system in general, and China in particular – a hegemony which is deployed to prevent China's development.

This understanding is not simply confined to military conceptions of hegemony. The 'new American hegemony' (Zhou Pailin 2002) includes a wide range of features. On one level, there is the danger of broadly defined 'cultural hegemony' (Liu Weisheng 2002). 'Culture' here refers to the spread of a set of political values and norms – most notably in terms of human rights and democratisation – deployed by the US as a tool of state power to contain China (Wang Jincun 1999). Yang Yunhua (1999) argues that this form of hegemony represents a new type of warfare. This warfare partly has a military dimension, in terms of bringing other countries under the US security umbrella, and providing military capabilities to allies. But importantly, international economic relations are also seen as being part of the US state's hegemonic strategy. Through bilateral pressures such as restricting access to the US market, and through US power in international financial institutions, US power and hegemony can be imposed on the world and developing states in particular without the use of brute military power.

We should note here that this conception of US as the global hegemon is not simply limited to academic and policy circles. Popular perceptions of the US in China can be contradictory. On one level, there is an aspirational element – many young urban Chinese like the trappings of American culture, and the US remains the number one choice if people can emigrate or be educated abroad. But at the same time, there is deep popular hostility to the US which is seen as trying to enforce unfair change on China in an attempt to block China's economic development, and to prevent China from attaining its 'rightful' place as a world power.

This anti-Americanism has been most vocally aired when the US has militarily come into contact with China – once with the bombing of the Chinese embassy in Belgrade, and again when a US spy plane collided with a PLA Air Force plane over Hainan.[2] But this hostility, or at least suspicion, lies not too far below the surface during less turbulent times. There is considerable popular support for nationalist and even xenophobic stances to the extent that the CCP often finds it difficult to keep the lid on the nationalism that the leadership itself often espouses (Hughes 2006). In the mid to late 1990s, this was manifested in the publication of a number of best selling works that portrayed the US as mistakenly attempting to impose its inferior norms and values on China, and calling for China to resist the global hegemon.[3] These sentiments have also been echoed in at least some of the writings of 'New Left'.[4] The importance of the New Left for this study primarily lies in their critique of neoliberalism and their concern with the negative consequences of economic reform. However, in critiquing neoliberalism, these authors do not ignore the fact that neoliberal theory originated outside China, and for some, it is an instrument of US foreign policy designed only to benefit US interests (Fewsmith 2005: 2).[5] For Lu Di (2002), transnational media corporations are part of a cultural invasion enforcing foreign values on China in the same way that the British enforced change on China through the opium wars.[6] And at times of more direct conflict with the US – for example, the aforementioned embassy bombing and spy plane incident – then the US has become a more direct subject of New Left criticisms.

New directions in Chinese IR thinking

It would be wrong to say that all Chinese IR utilises blunt realist methodologies. Zhang Yongjin (2000), for example, has correctly identified an increasing interest in the English School as a methodological tool within Chinese IR. Indeed, there have been important changes in the study of IR in China in the new millennium. IR is still a young academic discipline in China with its origins in the re-establishment of university education in the 1970s in the wake of the Cultural Revolution. Even after the death of Mao and the move towards reform under Deng, academic freedom was still very much constrained by the realities of the political system and the need to reinforce the superiority of the Chinese socialist way. So when the study of Western IR thinking emerged in China, it was simply a descriptive exercise – 'this is what Western IR is' – rather than establishing new approaches and theories for Chinese academics to use in their own research. This situation has changed for four key reasons.

First, Chinese IR emerged from isolation to engagement with IR communities across the world. Almost all Chinese IR researchers have now spent a considerable time working overseas, and many of them have received their doctorates from overseas universities.[7] Whilst there is a considerable diaspora of Chinese scholars who have studied overseas and remained overseas, there is a cohort of scholars who have returned to academic jobs in China bringing with them new ideas and approaches. Conversely, many foreign scholars – and importantly, not just China scholars – have visited China to teach on IR programmes, to help in curriculum development, and to establish joint research projects with Chinese colleagues.

Second, policy has changed, and at least some of the new directions in Chinese international relations writing have followed these policy shifts. For example, China's active participation in or with regional organisations – most notably with the Association of Southeast Asian Nations (ASEAN) and in the Shanghai Cooperation Organisation – has resulted in new research foci on both the theory and process of regional cooperation, and also on the regional cases. In particular, Harris (2001) argues there has been a key change in conceptions of security, with the 1998 White Paper on Defence marking a key turning point by redefining and placing a much greater emphasis on the need for 'economic security'.

Whilst these changes suggest a change in the focus of research rather than a change in theory and approach, it is related to the fourth explanation. The East Asian financial crisis of 1997 brought home the blunt reality that China's economic fortunes were inextricably linked with what happens elsewhere (Fewsmith 1999, Zha Daojiong 1999, Wang Zhengyi 2004). For a set of Chinese thinkers, realist conceptions of IR were found wanting in understanding the impact of globalisation, forcing a rethink of the relationship between political and economic dynamics, and the relationship between the domestic and the international (Fang Li 2000). Perhaps the most cited of authors in this tradition is Wang Yizhou (1995, 1998, 2000, 2003),[8] who argues that studies of globalisation must break down the bamboo fences (*fanli*) between the study of domestic and international politics (Wang Yizhou 2003).

Fourth, the political environment has changed, with academics now allowed much more freedom than before. This freedom is far from complete, and there remain limits to what academics can say and write – advocating the full scale adoption of western political forms and the removal of the CCPs monopoly on power are clearly still taboo. New found freedoms have also sometimes been withdrawn. For example, in the autumn of 2005 academics (and others) were placed under closer official scrutiny and were asked to rethink some of their ideas. The relationship between the Hu Jintao-Wen Jiabao leadership and intellectuals has been a mixed one. On the one hand, they have encouraged academics to share their thinking with policy makers through special seminars and workshops. They have at the very least tolerated an introspective re-evaluation of the basis of Chinese international relations theory/theories (Wang Jun 2004).[9] Whilst these evaluations are careful to defend the basics of Chinese IR thinking, there has been a call for increased distance between theory building and policy – for theorists to move beyond perceptions of the 'national interest' and 'narrow nationalism' (*xia ai de minzhu zhuyi*) that is at the heart of much Chinese international relations scholarship (Shi Bin 2004).

On the other hand, the moderate clampdown of 2005 shows a less liberal side of the leadership. This reversal has formed part of a wider critique over the logic of neoliberalism and the underlying philosophy of reform which has been ongoing in China for some time:

the journals *Dushu* and *Tianya*, along with some other journals, successively published various essays on theories of history and historical capitalism, which, from the angles of theory, history and practice, stringently attacked the market mystifications of neoliberalism. The theories of Karl Polyani and Braudel, as well as those of traditional Marxist political economy, provided important intellectual resources, offering a critical historical horizon informed by political economy and the critique of economism (Wang Hui 2004: 49–50)

These writers are typically grouped together under the umbrella term of 'the New Left' – a label that is rejected by these critical authors who feel that it has been deliberately coined by opponents to suggest unjustly that they want to turn back to the leftism of the Maoist period.[10] As will be discussed in more detail in Chapter 6, many of the concerns of new left scholars about the negative impact of liberalisation on China – inequality, rural poverty, unemployment and corruption – dovetailed with the expressed concerns of the Hu Jintao-Wen Jiabao leadership. Whilst not rejecting liberalisation *per se*, the Hu-Wen leadership were implicitly critical of the idea that growth alone would solve these problems without positive government interference to direct growth. And not simply coincidentally, 'new left' sentiments were subsequently reflected in a renewed emphasis on developmental objectives after 2004.

In terms of ideas and international relations in China, the run up to WTO entry in 2001 provided fertile ground for critics of neoliberalism. Wang Hui (2004: 52) argues that in fact most of the criticisms of WTO entry did not in fact critique the organisation nor the basic tenets of neoliberalism, but were instead about how fast to reform and when it would be in China's best interests to join (and on what terms). However, some key 'public intellectuals' did challenge the entire underlying premise. For Han Deqiang (2000) the key is the relationship between domestic politics and the international economic strategy of central elites. Drawing on insights from classic political economy, Han argues that China needs a new political economy that rejects free market liberalism, and follows the strong state model of 'the national system of political economy' championed by Friederich List, and followed by industrial planners during German and Japanese industrialisation. While domestic issues dominate the agenda of these critical writers (as will be discussed in more detail in Chapter 6), in Han Deqiang at least, we see a conception of political economy that presages not so much the emergence of new ways of thinking of international relations, as a return to the basics of political economy.

A Chinese IPE?

Great power politics continues to dominate Chinese IR both in terms of academic research and policy. But new issues and approaches are increasingly the focus of attention. We have already noted a growing concern with economic security, which has two important sub-streams in energy security and the potential benefits of regional economic cooperation. Conceptions of human security have also gained greater acceptance, notwithstanding the correlation between human security and democratisation for some non-Chinese proponents of the approach. Perhaps most clearly, constructivist approaches have had the biggest impact on changing the nature of Chinese IR thinking. Guo Shuyong (2004) has gone as far as to call for Marxist international relations to be reinvented by incorporating the 'best practice' of American international relations scholarship – realism, neo-institutionalism, and most importantly for Guo, constructivism. I suggest that Fudan University, Renmin University, the Institute of World Economics and Politics, and the Department of International Political Economy at Beijing University in particular have become major sites of theoretical innovation.[11]

But even within these new approaches, there remains a strong focus on the nation state as the unit of analysis in international relations, with the state as the main actor. For Song, developing a Chinese IPE that reflects the importance of economics in international relations and the role of non-state actors is problematic as 'the divides which separate disciplines and institutions are still very deep in China' (Song Xinning 2001: 72). Zhu Wenli (2001) provides an insight into Chinese views of IPE which are particularly instructive here. First, she describes a Chinese IPE which is heavily statist, and largely inspired by non-rational choice US IPE – particularly hegemonic stability theory – for example, Tian Ye (2000). Second, and in a similarly statist vein, whilst accepting that global, rather than just bilateral, issues are now a key area for concern, 'The emergence of global issues is portrayed as the expansion of the diplomatic arena' (Zhu Wenli 2001: 48).

The issues that now face governments may be increasingly transnational in character, but the solution is still often seen as being found in intergovernmental dialogue and processes. Under this approach, economic affairs are often ignored as being a separate sphere of enquiry best left to economists to study, or more often an exercise in the promotion of national interests in a game of mercantilist competition – a subset of politics that can be dealt with by state-to-state diplomatic relations with little attention paid to the role of non-state actors. At the very least, it is fair to say that non-statist critical IPE has yet to make a significant impact on Chinese international relations studies. Little focus is placed on whose interests within individual countries are being served by various political and economic initiatives – the state often remains disaggregated as a unitary actor. Nor is much attention placed on the role of non-state actors – those that Strange (1990) terms the 'international business civilisation' or Cox (1990) would describe as the 'transnational managerial class' – in international relations.

IR, area studies and comparative IPE

China is far from being the only country where the international relations discipline is dominated by a single approach. Realism looms large outside China too, though Wæver's (1998) investigation of publications in the mainstream IR journals showed that rational choice approaches challenge realist ones as the hegemonic theoretical position (and also by authors based in the US). Nor is China the only country where the link between academia and policy making can create methodological myopia. Considerations of the implications of engagement with the global economy by researchers from the international financial institutions unsurprisingly but typically reflect the policy preferences of those organisations. And at least some of the writing on China in the US 'suffers' from the problem of being too closely related to policy issues.

It is still far from uncommon to come across analyses that talk in terms of China as a single unitary entity and actor. Nor is it particularly uncommon to find phrases such as 'the Chinese believe' or 'the Chinese think', implying that over 1.3 billion people have the same beliefs, attitudes and desires. This use of language largely derives from epistemologies that place the emphasis on the national state as the level of analysis, and is built on statist and realist notions of international relations.

It is important to point out that the alternative to these approaches is not a Kenichi Ohmaeesque (1995) argument that the state is irrelevant to the functioning of the international system – that the state is 'dead'. It would be foolish to begin a study of China by ignoring the still hugely significant role of the state in domestic politics and economics, and the importance of 'high' politics at the national state level in China's international relations (both political and economic). We should not throw out the state as a unit of analysis, but disaggregate the state to consider whose interests are represented by state policy at the national level, and also consider the power of sub-state and non-state actors in the global political economy.

On their own, statist and intergovernmental levels of analysis do tell a story, just not the full story. In particular, the focus on bilateral relations at the national level misses key determinants of China's IR, and the way in which external forces partially shape the evolution of China's domestic political economy – particularly, but not only, in light of China's WTO entry. First, mainstream IR literature misses the salience of economic actors – particularly non-state economic actors. Second, national levels of perception miss the uneven geographical and sectoral pattern of China's international economic relations and the political implications of this process. It is true that many in China and outside have long recognised the importance of local authorities in forging China's international economic relations, and there is a considerable literature in this area. But this is not often represented in analyses of China's international relations, and where the local is considered, it is usually in a bilateral framework. Processes of globalisation generate both localised and internationalised networks of relationships that need to be considered alongside the bilateral to gain a full understanding of how best to theorise contemporary Chinese international relations, and to consider how local manifestations of globalisation are linked to wider transnational global capitalist processes.

Area studies and IR

The divergences between dominant IR approaches on one hand, and 'area studies' approaches on the other, are most clear when it comes to assessments of China's future. These different interpretations will be discussed in detail in Chapter 5. Here the intention is to explore the impact of different approaches on conceptions of China, and the perceived defects of 'theory' for some China scholars.

As noted at the start of the introduction, there is a strong and very influential set of literature – much of it specifically policy related – that points to China's impending superpower status, global dominance, and perhaps even inevitable conflict with the US. But while this vision of China seems to dominate popular perceptions, and has considerable purchase in some policy making arenas, there is a strong alternative understanding which sees China not as a global economic powerhouse, but instead in a position of dependency 'in the classical sense used by the Latin American economists in the 1950s' (Nolan 2003: 24), with a political system in crisis having reached the 'limits of developmental autocracy' (Pei 2002, 2006) and on the verge of an internal collapse (Chang 2002) that only a miracle can postpone (Naím 2003). Despite continued economic growth and the increased living standards of many Chinese, there is rural poverty exacerbated by harsh and often corrupt excising of taxes, endemic corruption in general, large and growing levels of urban unemployment, an unprecedented level of ever growing inequality, mass migration from the countryside to the cities, staggering levels of debt within the financial system, and the rapid deterioration of the environment all point to a domestic political economy with massive problems to be overcome. China's social fabric is being severely stretched – a conception that is recognised within China itself – not least by China's top leaders.

These different interpretations of China are explained by the different focuses, epistemologies, and methodologies of observers, academics and policy analysts. They are also explained by the different objectives of researchers. One of Robert Cox's (1981: 128) most oft cited ideas is germane here – 'theory is always for some one, and for some purpose'. So for who, and for what purpose, is the understanding of China as an emerging global power constructed? First of all, we need to accept that the Chinese leadership has placed a heavy emphasis on growth as an indicator of success, and as a means of gaining legitimacy. In the past at least, Chinese authorities have not shied away from triumphing their success in generating growth and doubling, trebling and quadrupling GDP; in the early days of economic reform, the target of raising GDP by a factor of X was an often and loudly proclaimed objective of the Four Modernisations. It is true that this message has been tempered when it comes to the international level. The message from the Chinese leadership to the rest of the world is yes we are important and becoming ever more so – but please don't forget that we are still a relatively poor and developing country so don't place the obligations and expectations of a rich developed state on us. Witness, for example, the attempt to be classified as a developing country during the WTO entry negotiations, and the oft repeated argument that despite China's importance, US actors actually get far more out of US trade with China (which generates China's huge trade surplus) than the Chinese themselves. It is also true that the message for a domestic audience has changed with the transfer of power to the fourth generation of leadership in the guise of Hu Jintao and Wen Jiabao. Nevertheless, the Chinese authorities have at least contributed over the years to a perhaps exaggerated image of Chinese wealth and emerging power.

Images of China are also deliberately constructed to serve specific interests in terms of influencing policy towards China. An overly stark dichotomisation here would point to both those who want to engage and contain China using exactly the same evidence in an uncritical manner to strengthen the arguments for why China should be resisted or engaged. Both sides benefit from depicting China as more powerful, important and either a danger or an opportunity than is really the case. It might also be the case that the focus on China's growth and 'success' is related to the desire to promote the primacy of liberalisation as not so much the best but as the only path to development. Some Vietnamese officials at least seem to have been taught the lesson that Chinese style liberalisation is the obvious way forward for the *doi moi* project.[12]

On reflection, there appears to be a dichotomy between those who study China from the inside out, and those who emphasise international relations, typically conceiving of the nation state as the basic unit of analysis, conceiving of the state as a unitary actor and largely accepting the ontological separation of the domestic from the international. An even bigger degree of separation exists between those who study China and those in policy related institutions and disciplines who study the implications of China in and for other countries, with those who study from the outside largely being the prophets of Chinese power.

Different interpretations are also partly a result of the growth strategy that China's leaders have pursued, particularly since the mid-1990s. With attracting investment to produce exports all but the sole engine of growth, China's international economic profile has obviously increased. But at the same time, the domestic economy hardly grew at all between 1996 and 2002. Double digit growth over two decades has been accompanied by ever increasing unemployment – even as the Chinese economy was growing at 12 per cent in the first quarter of 2004 leading to fears that the economy was overheating, unemployment in China was actually increasing (Yardley 2004).

So while students of the impact of China on other countries and the global economy in general see one picture, specialists on the internal domestic situation see a different one, and are drawn towards the very real social, economic and political problems that exist within China. The external international dimension is not ignored – far from it. It is considered in terms of its impact on the reconfiguration of the domestic political economy, the way in which discourses of international relations and nationalism are used as a tool of domestic legitimacy and social control, and the extent to which domestic political considerations constrain the actions of the Chinese leadership on the international arena. But the conception of a rich and powerful China that can be constructed and have a significant impact on policy makers across the world sits rather uneasily with analyses of serious, though not insurmountable domestic problems.

Area studies and rational choice

Despite the differences, recent debates over the relationship between area studies and discipline – particularly in the US – revolve around the notion that the economics discipline, and the economically inspired approaches of rational choice theory, have become hegemonic in academic discourses. According to Johnson (1997), rational choice theorists are attempting to promote their agenda by discriminating against 'unscientific' area studies.

It is not my intention here to embark on a detailed account of the relationship between politics and economics in IPE – that has been done by others (Higgott 2001, Hay and Marsh 1999). Suffice to say that within the International Financial Institutions, economistic approaches have come to dominate much research, and also to have a disproportionate influence on policy making methodology. But if Johnson and others have a valid claim in resisting the hegemony of a specific theory and discipline, it is important not to fall back into a defence of area studies that denies the relevance and utility of *all* theories and disciplines.

Area studies as an academic programme in the United States in the post War era owed much to the conditions of the Cold War. In perhaps the classic interpretation of the evolution of Area Studies in Cold War USA, Bruce Cumings (1997) notes:

> For a generation after World War II the bipolar conflict between Moscow and Washington and the hegemonic position of the United States in the world economy drew academic boundaries that had the virtue of clarity: 'area studies' and 'international studies', backed with enormous public and private resources, had clear reference to places or to issues and processes that became important to study. The places were usually countries, but not just any countries: Japan got favored placement as a success story of development, and China got obsessive attention as a pathological example of abortive development. The key processes were things like modernization, or what was for many years called 'political development' toward the explicit or implicit goal of liberal democracy.

At the very least, the need to understand what was going on in the 'closed' environments of communist party states inspired the creation of university degrees and scholarships to study language and culture. Building on McGeorge Bundy,[13] Cumings notes the close relationship between many US academics and the US Office of Strategic Studies, and how the US area studies community found much of its funding. In Europe, too, Cold War politics played a part in shaping academic interest, courses and programmes. For example, the special foreign office funding for the School of Oriental and African Studies at the University of London, whilst initially inspired by the needs of serving the British Empire, was at least invigorated by the needs of the foreign policy community to train specialists to understand places like China.

In some respects, then, both the area studies discipline and Chinese international relations need to come to terms with the changing geo-strategic environment within which they function. The Cold War context that Cumings argued drew the lines of demarcation between area studies and international relations has gone. As Zhang Xudong (2001: 4) argues:

> We are experiencing an increasing and intensifying discrepancy between the perceived object called 'China' and the lingering episte-mological models rooted in the Cold War, backed by the even more time-honored machinery of 'knowing the Other' of the long history of the global expansion of capitalism (colonialism, imperialism, etc.). As long as the old regime of knowledge and its reproduction holds sway, the emerging complexity and dynamism of Chinese economy, society, politics, culture, and everyday life will remain concealed, distorted, and oppressed in the global symbolic terrain.

The geo-strategic environment remains important, but so too now is the geo-economic environment based on increased economic interdependence (albeit an asymmetric interdependence) through greater trade and investment flows. This means that the boundaries between the domestic and the international become ever more blurred, requiring an understanding of both the dynamics of the external environment, actors and processes and a detailed country or area studies knowledge.

The debate over the validity and future of area studies versus discipline should not just be conducted within the narrow confines of a revolt against hegemonic approaches in the shape of economics and rational choice theory. As Kasaba (1998) argues, area studies requires a 'revitalizing' impact by combining the study of individual cultures and areas with wider disciplinary understanding – not rational choice 'science', but other disciplines that help us best understand the local-global context of the contemporary world. Kasaba's main interest is in postmodernist approaches – and while this is not my own interest here, I share his basic tenet that the aim is not to replace old discipli-nary barriers between 'area studies' and 'international relations' with new barriers:

> In order not to use this as yet another way of creating divisions, we should start from the premise that the modern era is generating its own comprehensive world view that encompasses all places and groups who are in interaction with each other (Kasaba 1998)

So if we move away from a focus on rational choice, we can find ways in which area and discipline come together to enhance each other. This is done by recognising that there are a set of internation-alised issues most, if not all states, face today – factors that can fall under the broad heading of 'globalisation'. At the same time, we need to recognise diversity, and start from an understanding that the embedded domestic contexts of each individual state will lead to diver-gence and different outcomes in different settings – to recognise the 'historicity of divergent development trajectories'.[14] We need the disci-pline to understand the former, and the area studies to understand the latter.

The basic principles of new political economy outlined earlier in this chapter provides methodological and ontological tools that fit well with the specific knowledge of 'national conditions' of area studies spe-cialists to provide an effective way of studying China in an era of glob-alisation. In addition, the knowledge that area studies specialists have of their case studies can help us develop a more holistic IPE that is truly comparative in nature, and more applicable to the study of deve-lopment and developing nations than is currently often the case. By doing this, we can avoid some of the potential methodological pitfalls of dominant IPE approaches developed primarily from the study of advanced industrialised democracies where a separation of private and public economic spheres is often implicitly taken for granted.

Area studies and comparative IPE

Universalism and comparative capitalisms

The first potential pitfall is one that emerges from trying to make definitive statements that contain universal truths. Trying to find a once and for all answer to, for example, which has power, states or markets, is essentially misguided. The real quest should be to discover differential levels of power in the international political economy – an approach which fits well with conceptions in the Chinese literature regarding the uneven nature of power in a unipolar globalised world. Quite simply, there are clear divergences in different states' abilities to dictate, respond or react to globalising forces. This study, then, shares an understanding with those scholars who perceive globalisation as an uneven process.[15]

IPE should not only allow diversity, but emphasise the fact that there is no single answer; no single set of relationships; no single simple understanding. The researcher should consider, particularly through comparative approaches, how different sets of relationships emerge with different balances of power between actors in different and specific historical, geographical, social and political contexts. This is an approach that does not lead to simplicity, but if the world is complex, then how useful are simple explanations? (Hettne and Söderbaum 2000)

The search for universal truths is helped when the universe is contracted. Tony Payne (1998) has argued that the theories of hegemony were largely constructed around observations of the US experience, moderated by some comparisons with Europe. What we end up with is a concept constructed from a narrow set of cases. More to the point, a concept that because it is so case specific (or a few cases specific) might not have relevance outside that setting. The same argument can be made for many of the approaches within IPE. Once we move outside the setting of the case studies (either explicit or more inferential) that have been used to construct theory, then the applicability of theory becomes more questionable.

One of the major research questions for IPE scholars is to consider the relationship between the state and the market. But much of this literature is based on the experience of advanced industrialised democracies. Such a separation of state and market – or the public and the private – is much less clear in many parts of the world. For example, the concept of neo-patrimonialism has been deployed to explain the blurring of public and private in many contemporary African states[16]. While Weber's conception of traditional patrimonialism saw no distinction between public and private, in the new-patrimonial states, a formal distinction exists based on institutionalised state system underpinned by laws, rules and regulations. But despite the formal legal situation, this separation of public and private is not reflected in the action of political leaders who continue to utilise and dispense public resources as if they owned them themselves. This is in no small part because it is much harder to change practices and cultures than it is to change laws – which has been particularly important in China in relation to local control over the financial system (see Chapter 2). As these political leaders are not only the utilisers of public resources, but also the regulators, there is weak state capacity to enforce control, usually accompanied by weak civil society to act as check and balance on power (Bratton and de Walle 1994, Tangri 1999).

Even in advanced industrial economies, the public-private distinction is not always clear. Van Wolferen (1990), for example, has long argued that analysts from the 'west' fail to understand Japan because they start with false assumptions. A formal separation of 'public' and 'private' exists in that the Japanese government does not own major companies. Nevertheless, Van Wolferen argues that in the eyes of the Japanese people, the government and the company officials themselves, they are 'Japanese companies' that are not considered to belong in a separate 'private' sphere from national public life. For Deans (1997: 17–43), as with the case of neo-patrimonialism in Africa, this is a consequence of embedded historical precedents relating to the way in which market economies were established in Asia. So although Japan has an industrial structure that looks a bit like a western one, the nature of the state and the nature of the state's relationship with the market means that the nature of Japanese capitalism is not the same as the nature of the US state and US capitalism, or European states and European capitalisms. Capitalism in Japan developed in a different way from in the west due to 'pre-industrial legacies, patterns of industrialization, and twentieth-century state structures and policies' (Whitley 1999: 16).

A study of comparative capitalisms, then, is an essential component of recognising diversity, and there are a number of good studies that compare Japanese capitalism with other advanced industrialised economies in Europe and North America (Berger and Dore 1996, Crouch and Streeck 1997). There is a relatively large literature analysing the heavy state involvement in planning and guidance of the market, and overt state control over the financial sector in developing East Asian states.[17] But when what have been termed Capitalist Developmental States (Johnson 1981, 1987, Deans 2000, Leftwich 1995) are studied in a comparative manner, they are typically comparative studies of developmental states, rather than drawing them into wider comparative studies of capitalism.

The blurred relationship between state and market in South East Asia was revisited in the wake of the Asian financial crises, when it became popular in some quarters to refer to the 'crony capitalism' of crisis states. This epithet suggests that South East Asian capitalisms were the wrong sort of capitalism – they departed from the norm of proper and right capitalist practices. And to some extent the conception of Asian capitalisms as different – as something that should be considered when we look at Asia rather than in the mainstream of comparative studies of capitalism – is also evident in academic studies.

In short, I suggest that the study of capitalism focuses (for good reasons) on those cases where capitalism has by and large emerged in advanced industrialised democracies where there is a separation between public and private. Where different systems emerge, where the public-private split is less clear, then they are considered to be per-versions of capitalism or perhaps an entirely different entity altogether. If capitalism is an economic system where the market distributes surplus to the class that owns the means of production, then there are many forms of capitalism where it is difficult to separate the bourgeoisie from the state that regulates the market on their (own) behalf. What is often lacking then is an understanding of varieties of capitalism with different state-market, state-society and public-private relations than is 'normally' the case.

When we do extend the focus of attention to non-core areas of the global political economy, we need to guard against concept stretching. If Van Wolferen is right, and western paradigms are used to try and understand things that look similar in Japan, then the problem becomes magnified when we move on to look at states like China. When China was 'different' – when it was a state planned economy – then it was relatively easy to analyse. We knew that it was different and treated it as such (though sometimes falsely putting it in a box with other 'different' states – assuming that socialist economies were all the same for example). As China has reformed and moved away from socialism, we have perhaps found it increasingly difficult to box it. Dealing with what is still different remains relatively easy. The problem is the problem of the familiar.

The nation state as the unit of analysis

As with much of the economics and IR literature, there is still a ten-dency in IPE to consider the nation state as the unit of analysis. Lasswell's (1936) distributive definition of politics should inform our analysis here – a study of who gets what, when and how – not just within China but also which groups, classes and/or interests within and without China have gained what from China's re-engagement with the global economy. As will be discussed in Chapter 6, economic reform and insertion into the global economy has had a highly differential impact on China. The gap between the urban and the rural populations; between political insiders and normal citizens; between managers and workers; between those in full time jobs and migrant workers; and so on.

In addition, the Chinese case also reveals massive regional differentials – while some parts of China have become embedded within globalised networks of production and are highly integrated into the global economy, other parts of the country are at best, only marginally participating. This is not to say that they are unaffected by globalisation, but to suggest that they are not internationally 'integrated'. This is often explained by making a bipolar division between coastal and interior China. This approach is helpful in establishing the differential nature of the internationalisation of China – but only partially so. There are, for example, many TVEs in the interior which have benefited greatly from internationalisation, and have significantly contributed to the growth of Chinese exports. As such, while geographically based concepts of divergence are clearly important, they do not tell the whole story of the differential impact of globalisation on China.

This recognition of the differential impact within nation states should be crucial for IPE scholars given the emphasis on marrying domestic level and international level analyses, and the importance of the P in IPE. Yet it is not always manifested in theoretical pieces considering the political economy of regional integration.[18] There are a number of good case studies discussing the significance of sub-national and cross-national regional integration in various parts of the world. Nevertheless, work on microregionalism, and the way that globalisation can lead to a disjuncture between the national political and emerging transnational economic spaces remains an understudied phenomenon – something that we attempted to address in *Microregionalism and World Order* (Breslin and Hook 2002). In this respect, the work of area studies specialists (and political geographers) on and in China who emphasise the uneven spatial impact of integration with the global economy are ahead of the game, and have much to offer comparative political economists and IPE theorists in general.

Towards a framework of analysis

The Lasswellian definition of politics as 'Who gets what, when, how?' generates questions of distribution that lies at the heart of the investigation in this book – distribution in terms of power as well as economic rewards, both within China and across national political bound-aries. In order to do this, we need to consider a number of subsidiary questions and approaches, perhaps best encapsulated in a general manner by Bernard and Ravenhill's (1995) assertion that the political economy of East Asia:

> should be understood in terms of the relationship between changes in the global political economy, changes in the political economy of individual states, and changes in the organization of production.

Internationalisation or globalisation?

It would be possible to consider the sort of changes identified by Bernard and Ravenhill under the broad heading of internationalisa-tion. Indeed, in many ways it would be much easier as it avoids the elephant trap of trying to define what globalisation actually is. To say that globalisation is a contested term is something of an under-statement. From Kenichi Ohmae (1995) at one extreme to Hirst and Thompson (1999) at the other, there is a vast literature attempting to understand what globalisation really means (or in the case of Hirst and Thompson, to ask if it is even happening at all). It is a term that has so many different meanings that it has almost become meaningless.

Hurrell (1995: 345) notes that:

> Although rarely tied to any very clearly articulated *theory*, it has become a very powerful *metaphor* for the sense that a number of universal processes are at work generating increased interconnection and interdependence between states and between societies [original emphasis]

In this respect, notions of globalisation as metaphor are useful in recognising the continued importance of states, but also the sign-ificance of societal actors in international relations that are often underplayed when the focus is on internationalisation. Hurrell also draws us to an understanding that, as Susan Strange (1994) forcefully put it in a critique of Stephen Krasner's (1994) understanding of the nature of IPE, we are living in a new era – 'The World *Has* Changed' [original emphasis].

Building on the work of Cox,[19] the new political economy approach suggests that the international economy of the Bretton Woods era characterised by exchange relations between national economies has been replaced by a global economy grounded in production and finance:

> the formative aspect of the new global political economy is seen to be the structural power of internationally mobile capital. States now have to recognise the power not only of other states and international organisations .... but also of international capital, the banks, and foreign exchange markets. (Payne and Gamble 1996: 15)

It is a system where non-state actors play a significant role in shaping financial and commodity flows, but one in which states and state actors do much to facilitate the spread of neoliberal ideas, and the spread of global finance and production. As Underhill (2000: 4) argues, we should not conceive of markets and political authorities as contending and/or separate forces, but rather as part of an 'integrated ensemble of governance'.[20]

Global trade is obviously not new, nor is the fact that production of a single commodity entails activity in more than one country. But in considering China's engagement with the global political economy, we need to be aware of how new and changing patterns of production have shaped this process of engagement. For many, the key to understanding globalisation is a knowledge of 'post-Taylorist 'flexible' (Oman 1999) approaches to the organisation of production within and between firms.

It may be obvious, but it is worth repeating that economic globalisation does not just happen on its own without political decisions. It is true that technological advances have made it easier for production to take place on a global scale. And as will be discussed shortly, it is also true that changing modes of production place a significant element of 'power' in the decisions of non-state economic actors. But financial markets do not liberalise themselves; special economic zones do not create themselves; taxes are not lowered (or removed) on their own; and money can only be freely exchanged across national political borders if governments allow it (well, legally at least). Neither do ports, roads and railways build themselves – as the German Bundestag (2001) report on globalisation forcefully argued. The hard infrastructure that is so necessary for the physical transportation of goods is usually funded by governments rather than by the private sector and 'the growing worldwide integration of economies came not by any law of nature – it has been the result of active and deliberate policies'.

China engaged with the global economy because key decision makers decided that it served specific political interests. As will be argued in more detail in Chapter 2, the key here was changing conceptions of how the CCP could reform the basis of political legitimacy and maintain the party's grip on power. The subsequent way in which this engagement occurred was also a result of numerous government policies. It might be true, for example, that manufacturing capacity has moved across the border from Hong Kong to Shenzhen creating strong economic integration that straddles the border. But it is not a natural 'region state' as Ohmae would term it. Shenzhen's position as a Special Economic Zone (SEZ) was established through political fiat, and supported by other state policies on taxation, distribution, infrastructure construction and so on. This is not to say that the Chinese government has been in total control of the process. On the contrary, and as will be argued in Chapter 3, the investment decisions of non-state actors have been hugely significant, at times forcing a rethink of Chinese policy. But this should not obscure the fact that ideational and policy changes within the Chinese party-state elite came prior to the impact of external non-state actors on Chinese policy – as was once more the case with the decision to join the WTO. In essence, state actors created the space for non-state actors to flourish.

Not only is participation in the global economy dependent on ideational change, it also generates ideational change. Once the process of integration had begun, then if the logic of integration was to be continued, both policy and ideas were increasingly shaped by the need to maintain the growth of inward investment and access to foreign markets (Gill 1995, 2000). Through educational exchanges, the provision of training programmes to allow Chinese officials to become 'WTO compliant', the rise of the internet, and increased access to the outside world, and so on, Chinese academics, government researchers and policy makers are being exposed to new ideas. Business people too are developing new concepts and practices through processes of social and industrial learning. Liberal theorists and neo-Marxian Gramscian's might disagree about whether it is a good thing or not, but they share a belief that increased transnational economic interactions results in ideational change.

Globalisation and China

When considering the implications of these processes for studying China, two of the hypotheses promoted by Jean Grugel and Wil Hout (1998) regarding the implications of globalisation for developing states are apposite here.[21] First, globalisation adds more actors to the policy process and increases the power of 'external' actors over state policy, and second, globalisation engenders the recomposition and renegotiation of relationships between state actors. To the second, we can add Sassen's (1999: 159) argument that effects of economic globalisation often 'materialize in national territories' and that 'the strategic spaces where global processes are embedded are often national; the mechanisms through which new legal forms, necessary for globalization, are implemented are often part of national state institutions' (Sassen 1999: 167).

Following Sassen, then, we need to investigate the impact of globalisation on the institutional balance of power within China's governmental structures. Sassen's main emphasis was on the shifting balance of power between different ministries and agencies within government – the financial agencies may gain power and influence while others may lose. But we also need to consider the distribution of power between national and local state agencies within China. For example, considering the locus of power in China's FDI strategy, Guang Zhang (2000: 49) notes that:

> the central government does not have much power to intervene in individual FDI projects locations. The location is essentially a matter between foreign investors and the governments at the provincial and local levels.

When combined with an understanding of the fragmented nature of post-Taylorist production, this pulls our attention to the relationship between the local and the global. It is entirely correct to focus on the way in which localised relationships between local Chinese officials and Hong Kong and/or Taiwanese businessmen is helping shape China's re-engagement with the global economy, as much good literature on China does. But these local sets of relationships do not exist in isolation. Regional and global modes of production are **primarily** transmitted or linked into China through more localised relationships, and overseas Chinese networks often deliberately exploit cultural links in locating themselves in China. But these localised relationships are themselves predicated on the wider structure of the regional and global economies. The overall structure may be a regional one or even a global one, but the mechanism through which China is integrated can be a local one, or a multitude of different local processes (Smart 2000: 74).

Pulling all this together, the search for political change in China should not be constrained by views that equate political change with democratisation, or those that conceive that economic reform inevitably leads to democratisation (Potter *et al* 1997). Ironically, while such approaches were designed to explain the link between economic and political change, equating political change with political liberalisation can actually contribute to the depoliticisation of analyses of economic change – no liberalisation is equated with no political reform. Abandoning state planning and ownership in favour of market forces and private modes of ownership are clearly not apolitical. But searching for democratisation and liberalisation (at this stage of China's transition from socialism at least) does not allow us to understand the nature of this political change. Rather, we should be assessing the reformulation of political alliances and strategies – alliances within China's political elites, between political elites and new economic elites, between elites and societal groups, and between domestic and transnational actors.

Economic systems and structures do not just emerge on their own but are constructed to serve specific ends. This does not mean that their evolution follows some sort of pre-ordained plan. Often, as is the case with China, the development of the economic system can be dysfunctional in that the system that emerges owes more to the agglomeration of numerous initiatives to interpret and implement economic change to serve particular interests. These may be groups within a nation state, external to that state, or as Sklair (1995) argues, groups that span national political borders. An investigation of China's engagement with the global economy thus allows us to consider the reconceptualisation of interests and the reformulation of alliances as they are emerging.

2
The Transition from Socialism: An Embedded Socialist Compromise?

Despite the assertion in the previous chapter that the divide between the global and the national no longer holds true, this chapter will deal where possible with the domestic context of change, leaving policy towards the global economy and the international context to Chapter 3. It deploys a somewhat blunt tripartite periodisation of the reform period: 1978 to 1984 is characterised as a period of policy reformulation; 1984 to 1994 as abandoning the old system; and the period after 1994 represents the (as yet) incomplete attempt to build a new system of macro economic control based on law and regulation rather than through state planning control.

It is not intended to provide a comprehensive account of domestic reform in China – that would take a book in itself. The first half of the chapter does contain some rather basic information that anybody familiar with the Chinese case will no doubt skip over, and is primarily conceived as providing an understanding of the domestic context for those interested in IPE but who are not familiar with the specifics of the Chinese case. The second half of the chapter returns to the theme of the relationship between the public and the private established in the previous chapter. It shows how different interests influenced the emergence of a public-private relationship by focusing on three factors – the changing bases of CCP legitimacy, formal policy relating to the socialist nature of the Chinese economy and state, and reform of the financial structure. It aims to show that China has moved from a state planned and state owned economy towards state regulation of a hybrid economic system with the existence of a private economic sphere that remains very close to the state system that spawned it. The form of capitalism that has materialised in China is one where state actors, often at the local level, remain central to the functioning of an economic system that has dysfunctionally emerged to suit their interests.

Changing bases of legitimacy

The start of the reform process in China is usually dated from the third plenum of the 11th Central Committee in December 1978. Although Mao had died over two years previously, the continuation of Maoism without Mao – with modifications – under the leadership of Hua Guofeng means that the concept of the 'post-Mao era' often implicitly also starts in December 1978 rather than September 1976. Even though Hua Guofeng retained his chairmanship of the Party until 1981 (and the position of Premier until 1980) the third plenum marked the *de facto* transfer of power to Deng Xiaoping.

To be sure, Deng was not the only leader who favoured a rejection of the extremes of Maoism, and he was never an all powerful leader. His own return to power after a second purge in 1976 owed much to the support of key military leaders, and Deng, like Mao, recognised the key relationship between political power and 'the barrel of a gun'.[1] Nor was he the only key political leader in the post-Mao era – much of his skill as a political leader was in balancing the conflicting demands and interests of different groups of leaders (Bachman 1986, 1988, Dittmer 1990). Nor was he the personal architect of specific reforms in the economic system, and he did not hold the most important formal positions of power for most of the period from 1978 to his death in February 1997. But in terms of dictating the overall direction of China's political economy and in being a key arbiter of who got promoted and who fell from grace, it is entirely understandable that the first two decades of reform are most associated with Deng Xiaoping.

Two key factors should underpin any understanding of post-Mao China. First, no matter what the party has done in loosening its control over the economy, and to a lesser extent society, loosening party control was never conceived as the road to the end of party rule. On the contrary, loosening control was only countenanced as it was perceived to be the best way of ensuring the party's grip on power.[2] In theory, of course, a communist party only exists as a means to an end – to act on behalf of the proletariat to create a classless communist society. But maintaining the party's monopoly on power and the position of its members as societal elites has become an end in itself in China. Mao's alternative strategy for building a revolutionary society might not be palatable, but in many respects he was correct in fearing that the party would transform itself into an authoritarian elite where maintaining the privilege of party members totally overrides any commitment to furthering the revolution.

Second, the party (perhaps more correctly, party members) did not and do not take continued control of political power for granted. The harsh repression of political activists can be seen as a sign of the party's own conception of its fragility, rather than a sign of strength. It is difficult to understand why the CCP responded with such force against the Falungong unless we think in terms of a party that feels that it cannot allow any form of undirected action if it is to hold on to power. It is also interesting to note that after the brutalities of June 4th 1989, the party has subsequently implemented many of those changes that the students were asking short of multi-party liberal democracy.

In 1978, Deng and other reform minded leaders were well aware that the party had haemorrhaged popular support as a result of the Cultural Revolution. The masses had lost their trust in the party, their belief in communism and subsequently had a crisis of faith over where China might go in the future (Zhao Suisheng 2000). A new basis of polity was required that rejected mass campaigns and political programmes based on ideological indoctrination as a source of legitimation. Looking back at the Mao era in 1981, the 'Resolution on Party History' called the Great Leap Forward a 'serious mistake' and declared that the Cultural Revolution was 'responsible for the most severe setback and the heaviest losses suffered by the party, the state and the people since the founding of the People's Republic' (CCP CC 1981).[3] In Zheng Shiping's (2003: 54) words, the party changed from being a 'revolutionary party' based on class struggle and mass mobilisation to a 'ruling party' based on stability and order.

Initially, simply not being the old party and not being the Gang of Four and not pursuing leftist policies was enough to provide a considerable degree of support. The post-1978 leadership attempted to rebuild legitimacy by repudiating the old party under Mao, where a single individual could direct policy.[4] Under the banner of 'Socialist Democracy' the new benign modernising party based on collective leadership and inner party democracy in decision making would deliver the Chinese people a new period of economic prosperity (Goodman 1985). The Socialist Democracy campaign included the introduction of competitive elections at the county levels of administration (Womack 1982). Village and township elections were also introduced in the 1990s (Li Lianjiang 2002, O'Brien 2001, Shi Tianjian

1999) in an attempt to build a legal rational basis of legitimacy. And after their assumption of the top positions in the leadership in 2003, Hu Jintao and Wen Jiabao attempted to present the CCP as a more listening party with a more open democratic system in yet another attempt to reinvent the bases of party power and secure a degree of legal rational legitimacy. But while the party continually stresses the importance of building democracy (but not liberal democracy) as one of its key tasks, three much more important pillars of party legitimacy have emerged to maintain party rule and the privileged societal position of party members.

The first is ideology. It is certainly true that with the de-radicalisation of the revolution and a rejection of the Maoist past, the nature of this ideology has changed. As we will see later in this chapter, attempts were made to justify economic reform in terms of ultimately establishing a fully communist society at some distant point in the future. But for all practical reasons, ideological legitimacy no longer has anything to do with rallying popular support for revolutionary agendas. But even under Mao, Chinese Marxism was always as much about China as it was about Marxism, and as many commentators have noted, nationalism remains an important element of the CCPs approach to maintaining legitimacy.

At the risk of oversimplification, the party establishes the national interest, and then does what it can to defend that national interest in the face of what is depicted as a hostile west committed to preventing China's development. As noted in the previous chapter, this nationalist approach finds fertile soil in popular hostility towards perceived enemies – most often Japan followed by the United States. At times this is manifest in overt xenophobia and/or racism (particularly towards the Japanese) to the extent that the problem for the Chinese leadership is not so much harnessing nationalism as a means of legitimation, but keeping a lid on the extreme expressions of such nationalism – particularly if and when it is directed at China's most important economic partners (Hughes 2006).

The second is legitimacy through performance, with performance largely defined in terms of economic success. T.H. Rigby (1982) referred to communist party states as pursuing 'goal rational' legitimacy. To put it very simply, the party set goals, mobilised the entire population to attain those goals, and ensured that the propaganda organs made sure that everybody knew when these goals had been realised (or more typically, exceeded ahead of time). There have been times when the process of economic reform resembles a Maoist campaign of mobilising the people to achieve the goals of market liberalisation. For example, in the initial post-78 period the population was assured that the pursuit of personal wealth was politically acceptable and compatible with socialism, and the party would do what it could to help people to develop personal wealth. To get rich was 'glorious' and the people were exhorted to emulate the success of those who had (always by hard work alone) increased their income to live in '10,000 Yuan' households. However, in general, performance-based legitimacy in contemporary China does not entail the active mobilisation of the population. On the contrary, it encourages a passive acceptance that the party will deliver economic growth for the people on their behalf.

Crucially for this study, the emphasis on economic performance as a key basis placed a primacy on rapid capital accumulation, and increasingly, the best way of ensuring this rapid capital accumulation and economic growth was seen as the adoption of modified capitalist methods and insertion into the global economy. Whilst the logic of capital accumulation was initially tempered by the logic of maintaining a commitment to building socialism, the balance of commitments soon shifted. Maintaining and increasing growth rates became all important irrespective of how this was achieved, and if socialism had to be redefined to fit this reality, then so be it.

The third basis of legitimacy is stability. The party presents continued CCP rule as the only way of providing the political stability and personal safety that disappeared in other communist party states. Crucially, the stability provided by party rule is seen as being a prerequisite for economic growth and prosperity. The CCP tolerates no challenge to its monopoly on political power, but calculates that the vast majority of the people will accept this so long as their economic wellbeing is improving, or at least not declining. What has emerged is an unwritten social contract between the party and the people whereby the people do not compete with the party for political power as long as the party looks after their economic fortunes.

These bases of legitimacy can lead in contradictory directions. For example, as Hughes (1997) has noted, the economic logic of participating in the global economy to generate growth has at times sat uncomfortably with nationalist sentiments, necessitating careful justifications of how China controls the terms of its participation resisting the unfair practices of dominant powers (often shorthand for the US). More fundamentally, while the acceptance of market forces and integration into the global capitalist system was perceived as the best way of generating quick economic growth, market competition – both domestic and international – was perceived as potentially damaging for those employed in the state sector, and also for many rural workers.

It is difficult to overestimate the importance that the Chinese leadership ascribes to maintaining employment. Particularly in urban centres, maintaining employment is seen as the pre-requisite for the maintenance of social stability, and perhaps even the CCPs continued grip on power. While growing unemployment is worrying for any regime, we should bear in mind that despite the introduction of a form of social welfare (see Chapter 6), it only has a limited coverage in urban areas. China developed a system of workplace socialism after 1949, through which the *danwei* in urban centres and the collective in the countryside provided health, education and welfare. With decollectivisation and the desocialisation of the economy, many of the certainties that they provided have disappeared, and have yet to be fully replaced by a comprehensive national welfare system. Before the accession of China into the WTO, at least, the task of reform then was to open up new opportunities for economic growth whilst providing a palliative for those who stood to lose from the desocialisation of the economy – 'reform without losers' (Lau, Qian and Roland 2000).

Thus, policy, until 1994 at least, entailed a careful balance between the economic task promoting market economic reforms that would increase growth and wealth, whilst simultaneously undertaking the political task of protecting those who might suffer from the introduction of those same market reforms. Policy thus represented a compromise between the embedded residual socialist system, and the ever increasing importance of market liberalisation. The extent of domestic interventionism was too extreme to fit with Ruggie's (1982) conception of an 'embedded liberal compromise'. As we shall see in Chapter 3, this compromise was not accepted as being legitimate by much of the international community. However, the concept of an embedded domestic system coming to terms with these norms (and gradually reforming closer to them) does inform our understanding here. As such, we can think of the way in which China managed the relationship between conflicting interests as an 'embedded socialist' compromise. As we shall see in the next chapter, the same characterisation also holds true when considering the relationship between domestic protectionism and the process of gradually conforming to international neo-liberal economic norms.

The transition from socialism

Establishing reform

The reforms that began in 1978 generated a plethora of consequences – they set in motion the process of liberalisation of agriculture, and although the impact on the urban sector was somewhat delayed, provided the basis for the use of 'the law of value' in industry. This is not to say that those who set the reforms in process in 1978 had a plan or blueprint for change. On the contrary, White (1984) and Hamrin (1990) both argue that the lack of any coherent plan explains why the reform process evolved in the way that it did in the 1980s. Individual reforms would generate consequences that were often dealt with on an individual and ad hoc basis, often generating unexpected and dysfunctional consequences that had to be dealt with in an unplanned responsive manner (Naughton 1995: 224). This incremental approach to reform has been widely described as a process of 'crossing the river by reaching for the stones'. While this gives the correct impression of a leadership searching for the right policy after they have seen how previous reforms have worked out, we should not assume that reformers knew where they were eventually going to end up – where the other bank of the river was. Despite a general acceptance of the rejection of the Maoist path – particularly by 1982 – there was no uniform acceptance of the wisdom of moving beyond a return to the correct policies of 1956. Some opposed further reform on ideological grounds. Quite simply, they perceived that creating a more market based system and embracing capitalist practices was not something that a communist party should be doing. Others were opposed to specific individual policy changes that they perceived as being misguided or undermining their positions of bureaucratic power, or both.

Writing during an early stage of the reform process, Solinger (1982: 68) argued that even amongst those leaders who accepted the basic logic of reform, there were five key areas of conflict over how reform should be carried out. First, the extent to which market regulation should be allowed to replace administrative control and state planning of the economy. Second, whether power should remain in the hands of the central leadership, or whether it should be decentralised to provincial leaders. Third, whether a fast or slow rate of growth was most conducive to stability. Fourth, whether heavy industry should be given a privilege position in the economy and protected accordingly. And finally, the extent to which foreign trade should be encouraged.

From state planning and ownership to state regulation

The Third Plenum of 1978 was the first of a number of official changes to the basics of CCP polity reflecting important ideational shifts. Although the CCP formally remained committed to class struggle after the Third Plenum, this political priority of CCP rule was relegated to a secondary place behind the goal of economic modernisation. To be sure, Deng Xiaoping and others had previously argued that economic development should be the party's main task in the short term – and public statements relating to the colour of cats and raising output came back to haunt Deng during the Cultural Revolution. But by moving the basis of party rule from a politically to an economically mobilised model (Wang Huning 1988a), the Third Plenum created a benchmark for polity that laid the foundations for the more radical changes that were to come.

The 1981 'Resolution on Party History' condemned Mao's 'grave left errors' – the idea that a great leap to communism could be achieved either before or alongside the creation of a modern industrialised economy through the promotion of socialist ideology and willed human change. Rather, the transition to communism would have to wait until after the economic revolution had been completed under the guidance of a benign communist party that would ensure that the Chinese people did not become oppressed or alienated during the process. In the 'Decision on the Reform of the Economic Structure' in 1984, the Chinese economy was accordingly characterised as a planned 'socialist commodity economy' *shehuizhuyi shangpin jingji* – an economy where the state still played the key leading role in guiding the drive towards industrialisation and economic modernisation.

At this stage, the promotion of private ownership and the formal acceptance of capitalist methods remained politically difficult, but in practice, the emergence of non-state controlled but not really private enterprises had already played a significant role in generating economic growth. This took two forms. First, the drive to encourage foreign investment led to a change in policy towards forms of foreign ownership. In order to encourage more inward investment, the Wholly Foreign Owned Enterprise (WFOE) Law of April 1986 freed foreign investors from the need to set up joint ventures with domestic Chinese companies. To be sure what they could was still heavily controlled by the state. Article Three of the 1986 law gave the State Council the right to restrict or ban WFOE from specific industries and 'The establishment of wholly foreign-owned enterprises must be beneficial to the development of China's national economy. The state encourages to establish such enterprises as shall export all or most of their products or adopt advanced technology'. Although at this stage they were still relatively small in number, WFOEs were accepted as legitimate privately owned organisations and 'no interference shall be allowed in the operation and management activities of a wholly foreign-owned enterprise' (Article 11).

Second, private economic activity outside of state control had emerged in the countryside through the decollectivisation of agriculture. Freed from total control over what they could produce and how much they received for their produce, rural households developed sideline activities. Third, the search for greater efficiency in farming forced many off the land, but the government was keen to prevent a massive influx of migrants into the cities, and encouraged them to leave the land but not the countryside. Many of the surplus workers were absorbed by the creation of TVEs which proved to be one of the main engines of economic growth. Johnson (1999: 5) suggests that the move to non-agricultural jobs in the countryside secured employment for up to 100 million people between 1984 and 1997 when the TVE sector began to retract.

We should note here that there are a number of definitional problems in identifying the role and importance of the state sector in China. State Owned Enterprise (SOEs) in China are nominally 'owned by all the people – *quanmin suoyou*', rather than the state as such – the state exercises control on behalf of the masses. But in practice, the enterprises are not just controlled by government agencies at both the national and local level but owned by them as well (though ultimately theoretically responsible to the State Council) and are typically referred to as state owned (*guoyou qiye*). But through equitisation, the concept of strict and formal state ownership has become diluted as non-state actors can take shares in the firms where the state is still the biggest share-holder. As a result, Chinese information sources now usually refer to 'state owned and state controlled (*guoyou guokong*) enterprises' in official statements.[5] However, it is not always clear if a simple reference to 'state owned' refers only to those enterprises that are still formally state owned, or both state owned and state controlled enterprises.

This complication, however, is only very minor when compared to the issue of how to classify collectively owned enterprises. In particular, TVEs are not strictly state-owned under Chinese definitions. But nor are they strictly speaking privately owned:

> TVEs in most areas of this country are best defined as 'the local government sector of the Chinese economy' or 'the collective sector'

which is a constituent part of public ownership.' (Guo Sujian 1998: 46)

In their summary of the literature on TVEs, Jin and Qian point to three key features that distinguish them from truly private enterprises; they have special and preferred access to credit,[6] benefit from trading relations with SOEs, and receive political protection from local governments not afforded to individual or private enterprises.[7] So TVEs are strictly speaking 'non-state' but also not 'private'. And this classification can created massive methodological problems in considering the nature of the Chinese economy depending on whether TVEs as a sector are considered to be part of the state sector, or part of the private sector (Chang Chun and Wang Yijiang 1994, Weitzman and Xu 1994). But no matter how they are formally classified, I suggest that they would be categorised as being part of a state sector in most of the rest of the world – or as Guo Sujian (2003) puts it, part of the 'public' rather than the 'private' sector.

The *de facto* reality of quasi-private – or at least, non-state – ownership preceded formal *de jure* legal changes. A form of private ownership was first implicitly accepted through the acceptance of 'individual ownership' – *getihu* – as a legitimate form of ownership in 1981. Individually owned enterprises could originally employ no more than five people (raised to seven in 1988) and initially at least, these employees were restricted to family members. Any enterprise employing more than the stipulated number was considered to be a form of 'private ownership' (*siying*). Liu Yingqiu (2002) suggests that the number of employees was chosen from Marx's example that it would take eight employees before an employer could extract sufficient surplus to receive an income twice the size of the employees', and have the same amount available for investment.

However, Liu goes on to argue, the example was a wholly hypothetical one and the calculations were based on a specific set of circumstances that had nothing to do with the Chinese context. So rather than attempt to find a theoretical justification for this division between individual and private ownership, we should instead focus on the reality that some in the leadership felt that they needed to do something to formally recognise the emergence of these quasi-private enterprises, but were not prepared to call them 'private' and to legitimate them for fear of arousing opposition from more conservative leaders. Indeed, even the designation and legitimation of 'individual ownership' resulted in complaints that the socialist basis of the economy was being abandoned.

The problem for conservative opponents was that the non-state sector was increasingly highly successful in economic terms – it sucked in surplus employment and was typically much more efficient than the state sector. In Wenzhou in Zhejiang Province, rapid economic growth resulted from the local government's promotion of the non-state sector. The 'Wenzhou Model' provided the justification that reformist leaders such as Zhao Ziyang were looking for to promote the benefits of allowing the non-state sector to grow, and did much to validate the decision to legitimate individual ownership (Liu 1992, Parris 1993).

This legitimation was taken a step further in 1987 at the Thirteenth Party Congress when Zhao Ziyang provided a theoretical framework that explained the dominance of economic development as the party's primary goal. In what was effectively an ex post facto justification for what had gone before, Zhao explained that as the Chinese economy was still hugely underdeveloped when compared to:

> industrialised capitalist nations .... China must go through *an extremely long* primary stage so that it can achieve the industrialization and the commercialization, socialization and modernization of production that other countries have secured through capitalistic means [emphasis added]

Expanding the productive forces was the key priority, and if non-state enterprises could help in this task, then they should be 'encouraged to expand'. In effect, the non-state actors were ultimately helping to build socialism – a concept that Kwan (2002) believes is more akin to justifying primitive capitalism rather than socialism. This theoretical justification for allowing the non-state sector to grow was supported by legal reforms introduced in 1988. In April, the state constitution was amended to recognise the legitimate existence of the private sector, followed in June by the delightfully entitled 'Tentative Stipulations on Private Enterprises' which established private enterprises as a formal business category.

Not surprisingly (and ultimately wisely) there was no great enthusiasm to take advantage of the legal ability to register enterprises as privately owned. As inflation grew in the late 1980s, Premier Li Peng restored elements of state control, pricing and planning at the third plenum of the 13th Central Committee (CC) in September 1988. The retrenchment campaign was not as successful as Li would have hoped, largely because many local leaders resisted central policy and maintained their own quasi-independent development strategies. And as a result of the previous retreat from socialism, the central government's ability to enforce retrenchment was much diminished. Nevertheless, the number of private and individually owned enterprises 'declined significantly' between 1989 and 1991 through a combination of specific reforms – for example, demands for payment of back taxes – and the conservative political wind of post-Tiananmen that saw increased attacks on the private sector and market economics in general (Liu Yingqiu 2002: 3).

The turning point back to reform came with Deng Xiaoping's inspection tour of southern China in 1992 (the *nanxun*). Despite holding no formal position of power at the time, Deng made his last significant intervention in the direction of reform – an intervention that on hindsight marked the defeat of conservatism and marked a key watershed. Acting in an ad hoc manner, Deng praised the emergence of proto-capitalist practices in open areas and called for a new policy of rapid economic reform and further opening. Deng did not formally reject socialism or embrace capitalism, but rather dodged the issue of definitions:

> The fundamental difference between socialism and capitalism does not lie in the question of whether the planning mechanism or the market mechanism plays a larger role. [The] planned economy does not equal socialism, because planning also exists in capitalism; neither does [the] market economy equal capitalism, because the market also exists in socialism. Both planning and market are just economic means.[8]

With the increasing importance of the non-state sector and concomitant decline in the significance of state planning made the concept of a planned socialist commodity economy increasingly out of step with reality. Thus, in October 1993, the Chinese economy was redefined as being a 'socialist market economy' – 'socialist' because public ownership remained conceived as the dominant form;

> The state-owned economy, i.e. the socialist economy with ownership by the people as a whole, is the leading force in the national economy. The state will ensure the consolidation and development to the state-owned economy. (Article 7)

But 'market economy' as the law of value rather than state planning should be utilised. As a result, the rights of all sorts of enterprises to purchase, produce and sell what they wanted was increased (though not wholly liberalised – liberalisation is relative) and the number of products where the state set the price and planned production was further decreased. Within five years, over 80 per cent of all prices were determined by market forces rather than set by the state (*People's Daily* 2000).

Protection, reform and the perceived national interest

Despite the vacillations in policy towards the non-state sector, and the incremental and largely reactive nature of legal changes, there was a consistent basis to reform up to 1994. Whatever the policy towards new economic practices and new forms of ownership, existing enterprises and potentially vulnerable sectors of the population were protected from potentially damaging market competition. In 1994, a key sea-change occurred. Rather than viewing the national interest as being served by protecting key sectors from the market, the national interest was now viewed as being best served by forcing market competition, and creating a more efficient market economy.

Between 1978 and 1993, SOEs share of urban employment fell from 75 per cent to around 60 per cent (although migration and urbanisation meant that this was a smaller share of a bigger pie). Over the same period, its share of industrial output dropped from 78 per cent to 43 per cent (Cao, Qian and Weingast 1999: 103). By 1994, key leaders, notably Zhu Rongji,[9] considered that keeping the SOEs out of market competition had to be reconsidered. Rather than reform the existing structure to make it work better (*gaige*), the system itself had to be fundamentally alerted (*gaizhi*) (Yang Yao 2004). Under the policy of 'grasping the big and letting go of the small' (*zhuada fangxiao*),[10] small SOEs were allowed to be transferred to private ownership – officially referred to as 'shareholding transformation' (*gufenhua* rather than 'privatisation' (*siyouhua*). These SOEs were typically transferred into the hands of previous factory managers, or relatives of local party-state officials (Chen An 2003), with one report suggesting that 80 per cent of firms at the county level and lower had been privatised by as early as at the end of 1998 (Zhao Xiao 1999: 26). Overall, around 60,000 SOEs were privatised in the decade from 1996 to 2005.

Larger SOEs remained within the state sector, but mergers and consolidation were encouraged to create large conglomerates (*qiye jituan*) that would form the backbone of the residual state owned economy and become national champions in the global economy – a policy that might not have formally emulated the Japanese experience, but which was inspired by the success of the zaibatsu and South Korean chaebols (Nolan 2003: 19). According to Li Rongrong, the Director of the State-owned Assets Supervision and Administration Commission (SASAC), the ultimate aim is

> to accelerate the growth and expansion of 80 to 100 major companies or corporate groups that are technologically advanced, reasonably organized, flexibly managed, possessing independent intellectual property and strong international competitiveness, thus speeding up the reorganization and adjustment of centrally-owned enterprises, pushing state capital towards critical areas of important enterprises involved in relevant state security and state economic lifeline activities and to pull SOEs towards those major companies that are internationally competitive. (Chinanews 2005a)

Efficiency was also 'encouraged' through removing protection and forcing competition, and through the shedding of excess workers. From 1995 to China's WTO entry at the end of 2001, there was a 40 per cent reduction in the number of workers in the state sector (46 million), and a 60 per cent reduction in workers in collectively owned urban enterprises (18.6 million), with a further 34 million state sector workers registered as laid off (Giles, Park and Fang 2003: 1).

The spatial dimension is important here because of the uneven regional distribution of industry. The state owned sector is heavily and disproportionately concentrated in the interior and north-east provinces which specialised in extraction and heavy industry sectors in the old planning days. Profit making joint-venture and foreign owned enterprises, and the most efficient TVEs are conversely heavily and disproportionately concentrated on the coast of China from Zhuhai in the south to the Bohai Rim and the Liaodong Peninsula in the north (Ito 2002). As such, the impact of allowing loss making industries to sink or swim in the face of market disciplines has a geographically uneven impact.

The change in policy reflected a new emphasis on promoting economic efficiency. Maintaining the SOEs irrespective of their performances resulted in the waste of large amounts of cheap industrial inputs which could have been utilised much more efficiently in the non-state sector.

In 1998 approximately a third made profits, a third made losses, and the remaining third broke even. This is not what you would call the outcome of successful reforms. An indication of the low productivity of the SOEs is that in 1997 they had 65 percent of the total employment in industry, had 57 percent of the value of assets, produced just 46 per cent of the value added in industry and made only 25 percent of the industrial profits. It is hard to imagine a more dismal record. (Johnson 1999: 14)

Zhou Shulian, argued that the lack of reform in the state sector was the single most important obstacle to the creation of a more efficient and competitive Chinese economy: 'With the majority of state enterprises staying out of market competition, it is difficult to redistribute resources for better efficiency'.[11] On one level, the 'top slicing' of scarce raw materialsw and energy supplies denied more efficient producers access to those resources. On another, the quality and reliability of supplies from the state sector was often so low that in 1997 the World Bank estimated that 17 per cent of China's GDP consisted of 'unsaleable' goods manufactured by SOEs.[12]

Protection, reform and the financial system

Perhaps more important, keeping the SOEs afloat was costing billions in subsidies and loans contributing to the near bankruptcy of the Chinese financial system. As non-productive loans in support of political stability increased in the 1980s, then the returns on assets of China's specialised banks dropped dramatically from around 1.4 per cent in 1986 to virtually nil by 1997 (Lardy 1998: 100). And while the capital of state banks increased by 1.88 times between 1987 and 1996, the balance of loans provided by state banks increased by 5.25 times.

In 1996, prior to the Company Law which put into operation real SOE reform, official sources[13] said that around half of all SOEs officially made a loss (though interviews in China at the time suggested a real figure nearer two thirds), the amount that the sector as a whole lost had increased by 46 per cent year on year, and unpaid loans to various levels of government by SOEs accounted for around 10 per cent of Chinese GNP – and this does not even start to take into consideration the huge loans through the banking system that had very little chance of ever being paid back. While the ratio of debts to the equity of SOEs was a mere 23 per cent at the start of the reform process, this grew to 440 per cent by 1998 (Bonin and Huang 2001: 8–9). The policy of *zhuada fangxiao* subsequently reduced the figures by 'letting go' small SOEs – around three quarters of which were losing money in 1997

(Zhao Xiao 1999: 15). Nevertheless, although the number of SOEs fell dramatically, O'Quinn (2005: 4) reports that over a third were still running at a loss in 2004, and those SOEs that were still unprofitable appeared to be losing more money each year.[14] As a result, the SASAC set 2008 as the deadline by which residual loss making enterprises must either be in profit or face closure (Chinanews 2005b) – though whether political concerns over social stability trump market based economic efficiency rational remains to be seen.

Thinking back to the changing bases of legitimacy outlined at the beginning of this chapter, then we can see that financial reform entailed something of a trade-off between two conflicting considerations. On one side, the desire to generate rapid economic growth; on the other the concern with ensuring stability and ensuring that important sectors did not lose too much during the transition from socialism. Initially, this compromise was maintained by utilising the planning system. By the end of the 1980s, official Chinese figures showed that subsidies constituted almost a quarter of total central government expenditure. And while subsidies and budget deficits continue to be a key tool for ameliorating perceived detrimental impacts of reform, the use of the financial system to provide loans to favoured enterprises became increasingly important.

The dysfunctional manner in which the financial system changed was also largely a result of the way in which the old was eliminated and the new created. As early as 1987, Zhou Shaohua (1987) complained that although 'central government's comprehensive management system has been dismantled .... new economic pillars have not yet been erected'. Over a decade later and five years after the start of financial reform, Gao Zhanjun and Liu Fei (1999: 55) argued in a very similar vein that:

China is now in an important historical period during which an old financial system is shifting to a new one and the two are hitting each other ....New financial institutions and business lines are constantly emerging, whereas the old financial system has not been broken up completely, nor has a brand new financial system taken shape

Technical changes can be introduced moving towards a more market oriented system. But changing the preferences and actions of state officials is an entirely different matter. Effectively, when the People's Republic of China (PRC) moved from a plan based to bank based source of credit, many officials continued to act as if the banks' money was the state's money. It was to be utilised by state officials based on their considerations of what was politically necessary, rather than controlled by bank officials based on considerations of what was economically prudent and profitable.

In many respects, we should throw away our understandings of what financial systems are and how they should work when we are considering the Chinese financial structure. For example, Wang, Liu and Liu (1999: 6) argue that bank debts in China are not the same as bank debts in the West. The loans have been based on political considerations and often ordered by government officials rather than on financial prudence and commercial objectives. Western governments provide social safety nets through the fiscal system. In China, basic standards of living and access to health education and welfare is often assured by extending loans to keep loss making enterprises operating. What is more, the state can and does step in to bail out the banks if they themselves face financial ruin, and as Jia Kang (2003: 16) points out, even ultimately shoulder the burden of the foreign debts of Chinese enterprises

> some enterprises raise money through foreign debt, which are directly or indirectly guaranteed by local governments. When those enterprises have debt crises, the local government has to take the responsibility. If there is still difficulty for the local government to cover this debt, the responsibility will be finally shouldered by the central government.

As such, bank loans – both domestic and to a lesser extent foreign – should be conceived as 'para-fiscal investment', and bank debt can be conceived as quasi-government debt.

Furthermore, the financial system in China has largely worked. It perhaps hasn't worked in terms of allocating scarce capital efficiently – nor has it worked as some of China's leaders wanted it to. But it works in terms of serving the purposes that many in China – particularly party-state elites at the local level – want it to serve. It maintains employment, allows local companies to flourish to generate local taxes and incomes, and of course, it works in terms of providing some people with individual wealth. Using the financial system to replicate elements of the old planning system provided a crucial means of reforming whilst not creating too many losers. Nevertheless, the extent of debts that will never be repaid in the financial system has long been considered by both external observers and the Chinese leadership to be unsustainable in the long term, and has been one of the single biggest challenges for the leadership to deal with in overcoming perceived detrimental side-effects of reform.

Building a new financial system: still muddling, not yet through

The first major attempt to build a new financial system (rather than modify and tinker with the old one) came with a set of financial reforms in 1994. Ultimately, though, these reforms failed to address the key issue of policy directed lending, and thus failed to provide an effective solution to the growing level of bad debts. The reforms saw the four policy banks replaced as policy based lenders by three policy banks. The State Development Bank of China took responsibility for long term projects: notably infrastructure, and the development of strategic industries. The Agricultural Development Bank took responsibility for procurement of agricultural produce and agricultural development projects, and the Import-Export Bank was established primarily to provide credit to promote exports. Theoretically at least, the 1994 reform introduced effectively commercial banks for the first time, and also fostered the development of competition between banks at both central and local levels.

The banking reforms highlight two key features of China's reform process. First, when new systems are introduced, they often do not replace the old systems, but are grafted on top of (or alongside) the existing system. Thus, when the new policy based banks were introduced, the four old specialised banks continued to operate, and retained responsibility for all their previous debts. Second, despite repeated commitments to the independence of the banks (not least in the Central Bank Law and Commercial Bank Law, 1995), political interference remains a hallmark of lending decisions. Even the theoretical independence of the People's Bank of China (PBC) is somewhat limited. Quite apart from the authority of Zhu Rongji over the bank whilst vice premier in the mid-1990s, the PBC remains a government department under the State Council, and the State Council is mandated to approve major policy initiatives (Xie Ping 1999: 5). The autonomy of specialised commercial banks was also limited. As Chen Yixin (2000) put it (before WTO entry):

> With directed lending operations (especially those financing the working capital of SOEs) still ongoing, the specialized banks can hardly be said to be commercial in any real sense.

Indeed, Victor Shih (2004) argues that the reforms weren't really intended to reduce state control over the banks in the first place. Rather that being driven by ideational preference, Zhu was simply playing power politics, acting to consolidate financial power in central state agencies where he or his supporters held sway.

The 1994 reforms then essentially achieved little. They did nothing to deal with the existing bad debts of the now commercial banks, nor did they put an end to the extension of more bad debts in pursuit of political objectives. In a rather damning assessment of whether the 1994 reforms achieved their ends, Sayuri Shirai (2002: 51) concluded that they had failed on all of their criteria:

> First, the banking sector has remained dominated by the four WSCBs [Wholly State Owned Commercial Banks] in the reform period since 1994. Competition has emerged, but only at the lower end. Second, the impact of the financial reforms has not had a noticeable impact so far on the performance of WSCBs. Their profitability and cost-efficiency (measured by the ratio of operating cost to operating income) have remained poor and more or less constant throughout the reform period, and earnings-efficiency (measured by total income as a percentage of assets) has steadily deteriorated. Third, and more worrying, is that the performance of the other commercial banks (i.e., profitability and cost efficiency) has deteriorated in recent years.

Indeed, because the fiscal reforms of 1994 generated an overall budget deficit for local governments taken as a whole, many local authorities turned to the banks to service the deficit increasing financial instability (Jia Kang 2002: 5–6).

As the debt continued to grow, the government issued an unprecedented RMB270 billion special treasury bonds on 18 August 1998 to replenish the capital of the four major state owned banks. The bonds allowed RMB120 billion of bad loans to be written off, and were intended to keep capital adequacy at above eight per cent for five to eight years. But this was not the end of the story. In 2003, the government took US$45 billion out of its foreign currency reserves to recapitalise the Bank of China and the China Construction Bank. The intention here was to prepare the two banks for floatation on at least domestic stock markets, and ideally in Hong Kong and New York as well. Private and international capital, then, is seen as a key means of creating liquidity, as it also is in 'debt to equity' initiatives. These simply convert some of the debt of selected SOEs and financial institutions into equity which are then sold on to private and institutional investors. In the first instance, the equity is held and managed by four Asset Management Companies (AMCs) established to help clear the debts of the four big commercial banks. Thus, Huarong handles the bad debt of Industrial & Commercial Bank of China, Xinda those of the China Construction Bank, Great Wall those of the Agricultural Bank of China, and Dongfang (Orient) those of the Bank of China.

One of the problems with the scheme, according to the Bank of International Settlements, is that the initial capitalisation of RMB10 billion each is too little for them to survive in the long run.[15] Furthermore, it is only really applicable for essentially healthy companies – those who took out loans before 1995 and whose deficits are 'mainly' a result of the burden of interest payments. Thus, it is an attractive option for those that are basically sound, but does nothing for the hopeless cases. In fact the scheme is so attractive that it has given rise to intense lobbying from government organisations that want to help revenue generating firms in their own sector. And as Zeng Paiyan argues, if the same political pressure that frequently led to the creation of bad debt in the first place is placed on the AMCs, then 'the whole process will increase and not reduce financial risks and expenditures for the state'.[16] Bonin and Huang (2001: 20) came to similar conclusions, but with an emphasis on the structural relationship between the AMCs, the banks and the state. In particular, because there is a single AMC for each of the state banks, 'such an arrangement could lead to the expectation that a parent bank can continue to dump bad loans with its AMC offspring'. Chi Lo argues that the programme has not worked properly because the AMCs and the SOE managers simply have different motives and incentives:

> The AMCs want to use debt-equity swaps to address the bad debt problems by identifying bad SOEs for restructuring. But many state firm managers still see these as just another way to save the crumbling SOEs. The banks have no incentive to recover bad loans because they see the AMCs as public bailout agencies to absorb their losses. This situation has improved recently, but the bailout mindset still overwhelms the pulse of market discipline.[17]

But even if the last non performing loan has been lent and all new loans will be repaid, there is still the problem of existing debt to be dealt with. There are so many different figures for the extent of bad loans within the Chinese financial system that you can almost pick whichever figure you want (Bhattasali 2002: 5). At times, the figure has suddenly radically reduced as the authorities have turned US$170 billion of debt into equity held by AMCs (see above) or recapitalised the banks. In 2006, Chi Lo calculated that all told, 'China has spent US$260 billion on cleaning up its banking system. The amount is about twice as much as Korea spent on restructuring its banks after the 1997–98 Asian crisis'.[18] We also have to consider that at least as much again of bad debt is thought to be held by local institutions (Brown 2004), though in honesty nobody really seems to know the true figure.[19] Searching for a definitive figure Dornbusch and Giavazzi (1999: 44) gave a range from as low as 20 per cent of all loans based on official Chinese figures to a high of 70 per cent. Standard and Poor's came out at 40 per cent of all loans and roughly 55 per cent of GDP, while Roubini and Sester provided a range of between 45 and 56 per cent of GDP (O'Quinn 2005: 8). The highest estimates of US$1.6 trillion worth of non performing loans (NPLs) in the four big banks in 2003 would equate to something like 60 per cent of China's GDP (Ferguson 2003). Rather than search for a definitive figure, perhaps it is easiest simply to accept that Harding's (1997: 3) assertion back in 1997 that 'China's banking system is insolvent: its bad debts exceed its capital' remains true. It is notable that at least one major international company has assumed that there will be a banking crisis in China at some point in the future in building its scenario planning for China's economic future.

Interviews in China and Hong Kong suggest that commercial decisions are becoming ever more important in informing lending decisions, and that things are changing quickly. Through increased regulation by the China Banking Regulatory Commission, interest rate management, commercialisation of the banking sector, and a growing role for foreign capital (if still relatively small in overall percentage terms), the Chinese financial system is changing quickly. Nevertheless, local governments in particular still seem to exercise considerable power over the allocation of capital. Putting new systems in place has proved to be easier than getting people to act differently, and the distribution of economic power within the Chinese state and state actors' conceptions of what best serves their interests – often what serves the local interest – mean that new regulatory reforms have not always produced expected outcomes.

Decentralised authoritarianism

If the financial system is crucial to understanding the state-private relationship, the key to understanding the financial system is an analysis
of the fragmented structure of economic power in contemporary
China. There is now a relatively large literature on the relationship
between central and local authorities in China. Chung's (1995) 'mid
term appraisal' of centre local relations in 1995 showed work on
centre-local relations already constituted a sizeable and growing sub-
field within Chinese studies. Not surprisingly, this canon of work has
undergone substantial growth in the subsequent years, including the
establishment of the journal 'Provincial China' in recognition of the
diverse nature of politics and society beneath the national level.
Although Lynn T. White (1998, 1999) rebuked the mainstream 'cen-
tralist' literature on China in his study of Shanghai, the idea that the
study of China's political economy must look at what happens at the
sub-state level is now all but firmly accepted by scholars of contemporary China, even if some non-China specialists still seem somewhat
surprised to discover that it is not a monolithic political structure with
all power emanating from Beijing.

In recognising that central control is limited by local autonomy, we
should not assume that all localities have the same levels of power; or
that they use power in the same way to produce the same (or similar)
outcomes. David Goodman has long been a proponent of this key
understanding of the nature of the centre-local relationship. In his
assessment of Guizhou and Sichuan, Goodman (1986) pointed both to
the local autonomy granted to (and taken by) provincial leaders well
before the post-Mao reforms, and also the differences in both the desire
and ability of local leaders to exert independence from central control.
In essence, he argued that there was a danger in making the false
assumption that there was a single group called 'province' and thus, a
single centre-province relationship.

Cheung, Chung and Lin (1997) explain differential provincial power
by taking a leader-centric approach, considering the specific role of
individual provincial leaders in developing local strategies for reform.
But while leadership is clearly important, it does not exist in economic,
social or political isolation from other factors. Goodman (1997) developed his earlier ideas regarding the diffused and differential nature of
centre-local relations by focusing on different processes and dynamics
of economic and social change within a number of provinces,[20] with a
particular emphasis on class formation and reformulation. It is these

internal dynamics that guarantee different case specific sets of centre-province relations. Hendrischke and Feng (1999) also emphasised the way in which local political and cultural identities influence individual policy based process and outcomes. In her comparison of reform in Shanghai and Guangdong, Linda Li (1998) takes issue with much of the centre-province literature by arguing that Guangdong was simply allowed more autonomy than Shanghai by the central government due to the different roles they play in the national economy. But even though Li might question how it came about, her analysis is nevertheless built on an understanding of differing levels of autonomy, and asymmetric centre-province relations.

In considering the nature of the Chinese state, it is not only important to acknowledge the role of the local state (Oi 1995) alongside the national state, but also to acknowledge that state power exists at different levels of the 'local' from the still relatively centralised provincial level right down to towns and villages. Township and village level governments have also been crucial in establishing new enterprises, and also being the basic level of revenue collection across the country, often deploying innovative and proactive means of generating income (Bernstein and Lu 2003). With a blurring of functions at the local level, governments are often left to regulate both themselves and the local economies – local economies that they might not directly own, but with which they have a hand in glove relationship.

Chung (1999a, 1999b) has gone further than most in developing a sub-provincial framework of analysis, assessing the successes (and failures) of a number of large cities' development strategies. The Pearl River Delta has also become a fruitful laboratory for considerations of sub-provincial development strategies, particularly in relation to local government interaction with the global economy (Khanna 1995, Yeung 2001, Sasuga 2004). Jane Duckett (1998) takes an even lower level of analysis. Her focus is on the competition between different bureaux within a single provincial level municipal authority (Tianjin) to develop economic strategies that are frequently in competition with each other. There are three inter-related elements to this relationship between local state control over China's emerging and evolving post-plan financial system – the fiscal system, extra-budgetary revenues, and local control over financial institutions.

The fiscal system

In dismantling the planned financial system in the 1980s, the central leadership deliberately and consciously created a link between local collection and control of finances as they wanted to unleash local initiative and enthusiasm for reform. This is not to say, however, that they anticipated all of the outcomes of decentralising economic authority. While individual policy changes to the banking system, the fiscal system and in terms of ownership might have had their own internal logic, they were not planned in conjunction with each other. The planned consequence of reform in one area was frequently undermined by reform in another related area (Wong 1992) – hence the idea that the development that decentralisation helped generate was 'dysfunctional'. So while it was a deliberate policy to give up some of the central government's share of national revenues, the leadership was soon surprised by the extent of its losses (Wong 1991).

After a period of experimentation beginning in Jiangsu Province in 1976, a new system of centre-local revenue sharing was introduced in 1980, allowing provincial authorities to retain a proportion of locally collected revenue for locally defined projects. Crucially, these initial reforms aimed at decentralising financial autonomy deliberately treated China's provinces in an unequal manner. For example, the three municipal provinces of Beijing, Shanghai and Tianjin were under much tighter central control, and expected to return a greater proportion of revenue to the centre than Guangdong and Fujian (Donnithorne 1981, Tong 1989). While Shanghai returned around 70 per cent of its income to the central authorities, Guangdong Province remitted only 15 per cent (Wang Huning 1988b). As such, the first stage of financial reforms not only resulted in an increase in local revenues vis-à-vis central funds, but also resulted in inter-provincial tension (Breslin 1996a) and intense political lobbying to be given the same treatment as the apparently favoured 'Gold Coast' (Hamrin 1990: 83).[21]

As the reforms implemented by Zhu Rongji after 1994 were intended to claw back control over national finances from local authorities to the centre, they have been referred to as a process of 'recentralisation' (Lam 1999) or 'selective recentralisation' (Zheng Yongnian 1999). While they were intended to increase the power of the central authorities, we should be careful not to associate these processes with previous attempts to recentralise the economy in the 1980s. The intention was not to return to the draw backs from the market as was the case with the last serious attempt at recentralisation in 1988–9. The then Premier Li Peng did try and restore planning control through the reintroduction of price controls, and by strengthening central planners' control over investment capital. While Li Peng saw the solution to financial instability in returning to the plan, failings of which had led to the decision to introduce economic reform in the first place, Zhu Rongji's solution was to create new mechanisms of macro-economic control over the Chinese economy. Zhu's attempts to 'recentralise' the economy in the 1990s were the first step in a more fundamental attempt to make a clear break with the old state-planned political economy and to create a new regulatory state.

The reforms of the fiscal system in 1994 were intended to redress the balance of fiscal power between centre and provinces by creating three categories – central taxes, local taxes and shared taxes. Importantly, the central government established its own national tax service to collect both central taxes, and also those taxes that are subsequently shared with the local governments (Zheng Yongnian 1999: 1168–9). Under the old system, the central authorities entrusted local authorities with the task of collecting and reporting fiscal revenues. The creation of the new national tax service was a sign that the centre no longer trusted the localities. At the very least, it represents another attempt to formalise an institutional relationship between centre and province that acknowledges the pivotal role of local authorities and local interests within this structure.[22]

The immediate result of the fiscal reforms was to increase both the total amount of tax revenue, and also the proportion accruing to the central authorities rising from around 30 per cent to around 50 per cent of all fiscal revenues. The dramatic increase in the total revenue base can only be explained by either previous lax tax collection, or the deliberate underreporting of local fiscal revenues to avoid making remittances to the central authorities. It is notable that the tax revenue continued to increase in the 1990s despite the low levels of domestic economic growth later in the decade. This was partly due to increased customs duties resulting from a surge in imports. But it was also partly due to campaigns against corruption and smuggling (particularly in Guangdong Province).

Extra-budgetary revenue

On the face of it, then, the fiscal reforms were successful in that they increased the total volume of fiscal resources. More important, they partially redressed what the central leadership perceived to be a structural imbalance in the division of finances between centre and locality. However, tax revenues are only part of government income in China. Fan Gang (1999) suggests that revenues collected outside the tax system probably exceed fiscal revenues, while Gao Peiyong (1999: 41 and 45) suggests that fiscal revenues are as little as 40 per cent of all government revenue at all governmental levels. The rest is what Gao terms 'extra system' revenue, defined as those 'revenues whose regulations are formulated independently by various departments and localities and which are collected and disposed of by them as well'.

Complaints about impositions of ad hoc fees by local authorities rank high in the list of problems faced by foreign companies operating within China. But while foreign companies might feel that they are being treated unfairly, they are effectively being treated in the same way as many Chinese companies. Anyone or anything that makes a profit is likely to face new fee charges, which to a large extent are beyond the scope of the central government to control (Wong 1997). In fact the biggest burdens of the fee culture have fallen not on foreigners, but on the already burdened Chinese peasantry. Partly out of the desire to create a more manageable financial structure, and partly out of concern over the growing rural discontent and social instability, the central government is attempting to transfer all fees to taxes – a process that at the time of writing was still incomplete. The government also abolished the Agricultural Tax from 1 January 2006 in an attempt to reduce the financial burdens on peasants and partially offset the large and growing income differentials between rural and urban China (an issue we shall return to in detail in Chapter 6). But as Yep argues, these technical changes miss the fundamental cause of the *need* to impose fees which is 'the systematic discrimination against peasants and the consequent deficit in financing rural governance' (Yep 2004: 43). The existing financial structure in China means that if local rural interests are to be served, then local governments have little choice but to use 'flexible' means of raising revenue such as raising fees:

> Despite their large size, [central government] transfers have nonetheless proved inadequate to provide sufficient financial support to the provision of essential services such as rural education and rural public health' (Fedelino and Singh 2004: 39)

Thus, while a financial system where fees play such an important role might appear to be wholly irrational, it is an entirely sensible policy for local authorities to follow given the constraints of the system that they operate within.

The importance of the growth of fees as a source of local revenue (and the relatively slow process of turning them into taxes) is just one example of how the Chinese financial system has proved difficult for the central authorities to control. An example of how the financial systems are moulded to serve specific interests. Another example – perhaps more important for an understanding of financial reform – is the way in which banking reforms altered the relationship between central and local authorities. In 1984 the PBC was designated as the Central Bank, and four large specialist banks were introduced, each channelling capital for different sectors of the economy. Thus, the Industrial and Commercial Bank was responsible for channelling finances into SOEs; The Construction Bank of China was responsible for new investment projects; The Agricultural Bank of China was responsible for agricultural procurement, and rural investment (including rural industry); and the Bank of China took control of foreign exchange business.

This was followed in 1985 by a key transition from the plan, in that China switched from a grant based to loan based investment system. In order to facilitate the transition from central grants to bank loans, the power of specialised banks in the localities was increased in 1985. The move to bank loans sponsored a huge boom in investment in capital construction by local governments. While investment in state planned projects recorded a 1.6 per cent year-on-year increase in 1985, investment in unplanned projects by local governments was increasing by 87 per cent. Crucially, while state planning agencies and financial authorities controlled the provision of 76.6 per cent of internal national investment capital at the start of the reform process, this proportion fell to 33.2 per cent in 1986 as a result of the new banking reforms (Zhu Li 1987).

Here we need to focus on the notion of dual control of local level organisation in China. Administrative organisation is built on twin and simultaneous functional and geographic channels. Thus, a provincial branch of a bank was vertically responsible to the bank's central offices, and ultimately to the Ministry of Finance. But at the same time, it was also responsible to the provincial finance bureau and the provincial government. The latter had the advantage of hands on contact with the branch, since it was in direct day-to-day contact with bank officials. Furthermore, it possessed considerable power in terms of allocating goods, services and personnel to the banks. As we will see, changes in the 1990s formally altered this structure of power, centralising regulatory functions in the financial sector, and creating a new Finance Work Committee to ensure the correct implementation of central policy at the local level (Heilmann 2005); but in practice, the reality of hands on day-to-day contacts combined with the persistence of old patterns of interaction mean that local authorities still can and do exert considerable political influence over local financial agencies. Thus, while not formally an agency of local government, local branches of banks still sometimes act as if they are part of the local government structure.

While fiscal reform went some way to restoring the central authorities' ability to control the national economy, it was, in itself, not enough. As we have seen, both the levying of fees, and control of local branches of central financial institutions shifted the balance away from the centre to the provinces. Furthermore, there is financial 'chaos and mismanagement' resulting from the expansion of local financial institutions (Gao Zhanjun and Liu Fei 1999: 53). Many local governments established International Trust and Investment Corporations (ITICs) that borrowed money on international markets to provide funds for local investment projects. In 1998, the Guangdong ITIC collapsed with US$4 million worth of outstanding debts owed to foreign investors as a result of imprudent investment. The central government refused to support the Guangdong ITIC, and also refused to honour its international debts. As a result, foreign investors lost confidence in working with ITICs, and many local authorities moved to merge and stabilise their local companies over the following 12 months – but even at the end of this period of retraction, there were still over 200 ITICs controlled by local authorities at various levels.

ITICs emerged to provide a degree of financial autonomy for local governments – to sidestep, and even undermine, official government policy through innovative new ways of raising finances. As has often been the case, the establishment of an effective regulatory mechanism for ITICs only took place after they had already proliferated, and after severe problems emerged that needed redressing. In this case, it was not until 2001 that the PBC issued detailed regulations governing ITICs actions, rights and responsibilities, requiring them for the first time to be registered and approved, and banning them from issuing bonds overseas. It took another four yeas 'after years of crackdown' that the China Banking Regulatory Commission announced that the remaining 59 ITICs were now essentially economically viable (*People's Daily* 2005a). Again, as has often been the case, the creation of new central regulation were at the very least complicated, if not obstructed, by local governments keen to protect their own financial interests and autonomy.

In addition, to the ITICs, there are literally thousands of small scale locally controlled rural and urban credit cooperatives – in the region of 2000 urban and around 50,000 rural credit cooperatives – that effectively exist outside the reach of the central macro-economic control and central financial regulatory institutions. Local governments not only dictate the direction of investment, but also act as the local branch of national regulation, which can be ignored if it runs counter to local interests, and also control the local judicial system (Xie Ping 1999: 13).

It was this concern with local control over local financial institutions that led the PBC to undertake a major structural reform in August 1998. The central bank abolished its 49 provincial branches and replaced them with nine multi-provincial regional offices. Yet six years later when the central government attempted to slow growth over fears of inflation and a shortage of raw materials and energy, it was still not able to control the national flow of credit due to local control over local financial resources (Cheng 2004).

Local financial autonomy: engine of economic growth or economic irrationality?

A strong case can be made for arguing that the devolution of financial autonomy proved to be highly successful in generating economic growth[23] (Oi 1999). But there is also a strong case for arguing that it has resulted in negative or at least problematic outcomes as well. The lack of macro-control resulted in a highly inefficient use of scarce investment capital, and allowed local authorities to pursue development strategies irrespective of national goals and strategies (Tsai 2004).[24] Such strategies can take place without knowledge of what is happening in other localities – what is termed 'blind investment' (*mangmu de touzi*) or copying other localities' successful ventures. In order to maintain production in local factories they set up trade barriers preventing 'imports' from other parts of China. This not only maintains employment in enterprises that might not be able to exist in a competitive market, but also provides finances for future local projects through local revenue collection (Li Jie, Qiu and Sun 2003). After the 1994 tax returns resulted in the central government keeping all of the consumption tax and three-quarters of the new value added tax, fiscal revenue from local enterprise income tax became even more important as a source of revenue for many local authorities (Tsui and Wang 2004: 80).[25] While local authorities as a whole had an overall surplus in 1993, local government expenditures outstripped revenues in 1994 and the deficit has been increasing ever since with business tax providing the largest amount of local government finances – 30 per cent of the total in the country as a whole (Jia Kang 2002: 7–8).

While Wedeman (2003) perceives this as a 'positive' force for the transition towards capitalism, engendering competition between rent seekers, others are less convinced:

> Regional protectionism – by protecting the backward, inflating trade costs, blocking the equitable allocation of resources, and hindering the formation of large-scale economies – is becoming the main cause for the weakening international competitiveness of Chinese enterprises (Hou Yu 2004: 24)

The power of local authorities to collect and impose fees and local influence (if not control) of local banks contributes to the characterisation of many local governments as acting like old feudal economies (*zhuhou jingji*) (Shen Liren and Dai Yuanchen 1990). The notion of a dukedom economy is not just that the local government is in control of finances etc, but also controls the judicial system as well; 'Since courts and judiciary departments are subject to local Governments, justice cannot be brought along in many fields' (Xie Ping 1999).[26] Warning of the dangers of assuming that China constitutes a single market, the British Chamber of Commerce in China argues that 'it is important to appreciate that the country is far more like the European Community of the 1970's than the United States of America today' (FAC 2000 Appendix 15). Such local protectionism includes:

> import bans, discriminatory product and health certification standards, tariffs and dumping charges, confiscations of profits earned on marketing foreign–provincial goods, as well as subsidies to local commercial units for buying locally produced products aimed at curtailing competition with home-province products and sustaining employment and the survival of uncompetitive local enterprises (Poncet 2005: 411)

Chou (2006) also points to local governments control over issuing licences to operate as a key means of not only generating significant local finances, but also of controlling who can do business within any locality.

In addition to contributing to the rather large holes in the financial system, duplication of production has resulted in over capacity in many areas. As local governments protect their local producers, this has created strains on raw material and energy supplies. For example, in 2004, despite large increases in the production of steel, China was still forced to import steel, forcing international prices up in the process, due to the poor quality of the steel produced by many locally controlled factories. Local protectionism has also contributed to the lack of a fully functioning internal market within China. But while there is a wide acceptance of the importance of local protectionism, there is little convergence over whether the phenomenon is increasing or decreasing as market mechanisms have become more important. Although Naughton (2003) has argued that inter-provincial trade has increased, Tsai (2004) suggests that his data set is problematic as Naughton compared 1987 with 1992 – a limited period and one in which a central policy of retrenchment under Li Peng was still shaping the economic environment. Surveys conducted by Fan Gang as part of the index of marketisation of China's provinces suggest that at best, considerable barriers to internal trade remain and have not been notably reduced by the growth of the market, whilst Huang (2003), Young (2000) and Poncet (2005) point to an increasingly less integrated national market in the 1990s. Sasuga's (2004) analysis of Fujian and Guangdong found that both provinces were more integrated with external economies than they were with each other. Notably, even those authors who suggest increasing inter-provincial trade accept that local control and local protectionism remains an important feature of China's political economy (even if it is less important than before).

Contemporary China: what kind of state, what kind of capitalism?

The formal relationship between party, state and economy has been established by structural changes to the organisational principles and structures of the Chinese state, and ideational change reflected in reforms to the party and state constitution. In terms of structures, government restructuring after 1998 were designed to make a final move from government control over the economy to macroeconomic supervision and regulation. The key pillars in this supervision and regulation were initially the Ministry of Finance, the PBC and the State Planning Commission (renamed the State Development Planning Commission in 2000).

In 2003, the China Banking Regulatory Committee took control of banking regulation and supervision from the PBC. In name at least, 'planning' disappeared altogether, as the Planning Commission was merged with the Structural Reform Office of the State Council to create The National Development and Reform Commission. In addition from

April 2003 SASAC took over responsibility for the state's interests in SOEs as shareholder rather than as direct manager/owner/planner. Crucially, the need to put in place a new regulatory framework resulting from China's WTO commitments (see Chapter 3) led to the merger of the Ministry of Foreign Trade and Economic Cooperation (MOFTEC) with the State Economic and Trade Commission (SETC) to create a new Ministry of Commerce. For the first time, the relationship between the international and the domestic was officially accepted. In combination, these reforms established a governmental structure designed to regulate the economy rather than control it through the plan[27] – albeit relatively strong regulatory control.

In ideational terms, the key turning point came in a speech by the then Party leader, Jiang Zemin on the 80th anniversary of the creation of the CCP in 2001. Jiang's proposal to allow private entrepreneurs to join the communist party raised concern and bitter protests from many party members (Dickson 2002, 2003). Despite the protests, the party constitution was amended at the 16th Party Congress in November 2002 to add Jiang's theory of the 'Three Represents' (*sange daibiao*) to Marxism-Leninism-Mao Zedong Thought-Deng Xiaoping Theory as the Party's guiding principle. As a result, the CCP now formally represents not just the Chinese proletariat, but also China's advanced productive forces, China's advanced culture, and 'the fundamental interests of the overwhelming majority of the Chinese people'. As a consequence, the CCP is no longer just the vanguard of the proletariat, but of 'Chinese People and the Chinese nation', and membership is open to 'any advanced element' including private entrepreneurs. The following year, the PRC constitution was also amended to not only include the 'three represents' but also to commit the state to guarantee the right to have and inherit private property.

In truth, few people in China are really concerned about how the party theoretically justifies its oversight of economic reform as long as that economic reform is bringing tangible economic results. It is not so much what the party says as what it delivers that conditions popular attitude to its continued grip on power. However the Three Represents is significant as it marks the official recognition that the fundamental basis of CCP rule, and thus the fundamental basis of the Chinese political regime, has changed.

Occupying space(s)

In creating an understanding of the contemporary Chinese state, it is perhaps helpful to think in terms of different types of space. Political space remains occupied by the CCP. To be sure, the party has become more flexible and listening – for example, to think tanks, intellectuals, and to the delegates of the National People's Congress (NPC). It might be becoming a more internally democratised party, and has an evolving class basis that makes it a very different party than before. But whatever the party is and whatever it represents, the party resists any substantial challenge to its domination of this political space by any possible means. However, alongside this monopoly of political space, we need to consider the fragmentation of authoritarian power in the national space. Any analysis that ignores the role and power of local authorities at different levels will simply fail to understand the real dynamics of economic, social and political change in China. If China is becoming a regulatory state, it is a voluntary regulatory state, with local authorities still able to decide whether to adhere to central regulation or not.

Since the end of the Maoist period, the party has allowed its control of social space to diminish. On one level, there is now a private space, with the de-politicisation of the private life of individuals. To be sure, there are limits – the One Child Policy perhaps being the single most important exception. There are also societal limits based on conceptions of morality that many in the west would regard as conservative. But by and large the party does not dictate what individuals can do in their private lives as long as it does not cross the line into political action. This may not seem like a particularly remarkable degree of freedom unless one considers the intense politicisation of private individual action that characterised the pre-reform political system.

On another level, the party has allowed social groups to emerge and play a role in the social space. However, these social groups do not necessarily play the same role as civil society in other states. It is perhaps misleading to try and seek examples of civil society that we would recognise as such in the West, though some have tried. Rather, we have what Howell (1998: 72) calls a policy of incorporation. While there are agents of civil society that are now more independent from the state than before, they are largely independent because the state wants them to be. Zhang Ye (2003: 4) argues that 'there is no independent sector'. The state uses these nascent groups and agencies to deliver on its behalf, rather than allowing them real independence.

For example, business associations in China are mandated to represent both their membership and the government. In this respect, they perhaps serve the role of transmission belts between party and society that the Leninist mass organisations of the pre-reform era failed to perform. If it is civil society, it is party dominated civil society that reflects only a relative relaxation of control over society that, for the time being, the party is still able to reverse if and when it sees fit. And of course, the party state has removed itself from the provision of health, education and welfare in the countryside – an issue that will be dealt with in more detail in Chapter 6.

In terms of economic space, the relationship between state and economy is, to say the least, blurred. Strong elements of state control remain in place. The unashamedly pro-neoliberal Heritage Foundation ranked China as 127th out of 157 countries in a league table of economic freedom in 2003. Based on individual criteria, with 5 representing the lowest levels of freedom, China scored a 5 for trade policy; 4 for government intervention, restrictions on foreign investment, government regulations, control over banking and finance, and property rights infringement; 3.5 for black market activity; and 3 for control over wages and prices. And this was *after* the liberalisation policies that had been put in place after WTO entry.[28]

As Wank (1998: 2–3) argues, in reality it is all but impossible to distinguish between the public and the private, and formal legal property rights and definitions are less important than the 'social environment' in determining market activities. By this, Wank means that having a good relationship with local party state officials is much more important for doing business than the formal ownership classification of that enterprise. Chan and Zhu (2003) also discovered that formal ownership registration often bore little resemblance to who was actually running factories in their study of export oriented enterprises. Commercial rationality in China is less about searching out market opportunities than searching for strong ties with local officialdom that in turn will guarantee those market opportunities (Wank 1998). Whilst accepting that personalised networks of relationships in business are not unique to China, and that the need for these relationships are a result of the nature of the Chinese market than any cultural norms, establishing what the Chinese call *guanxi* relationships are an essential form of social capital in China (Gold, Guthrie and Wank 2002: 7).

Transparency (and the lack of it)

Another source of power in the emerging Chinese market is a lack of transparency which means that only insiders – those who have the social capital or *guanxi* – have true market knowledge. And this market knowledge provides them with significant economic power. The US Trade Representative Office (USTRO) has accused the Chinese authorities of deliberately retaining an opaque system in order to defend Chinese national interests – the lack of transparency in decision making, and the use of data collection and dissemination is a deliberate tactic aimed at privileging domestic Chinese companies and discriminating against foreign companies.

There is some truth in this assertion – but the lack of transparency is sometimes a consequence of the nature of institutional reform rather than design. For example, in 1998, the central authorities introduced a new system aimed at providing effective regulation of the increasingly complex financial system. In keeping with the transition from central planning to supervision and regulation, a new tripartite system was introduced in 1998 that gave different areas of responsibility in to the Central Bank, the China Securities Regulatory Commission, and the China Insurance Regulatory Commission.

Despite the best intentions of the reforms to increase transparency and accountability, the reforms, initially at least, just led to confusion and bureaucratic battles. It appears that the three authorities tended not to coordinate their activities, and were given ample leeway to interpret central regulations in sometimes contradictory manners because the regulations were often ambiguous and conflicted with other central edicts. It was not too little regulation that was the problem, but too much. So it was not necessarily the case that the central government was deliberately ignoring transparency to serve the national interest (though this was clearly true in some cases), but that the lack of transparency was an unintended consequence of reform.

Crucially, the lack of transparency has been exploited by party-state actors to capture the benefits of the introduction of the market and use political power to attain economic benefit (and economic power). The development of stock markets in Shenzhen and Shanghai provides an excellent example of this process. Stock markets were introduced in China as a means of raising capital for Chinese enterprises. But in practice – in the early years of their functioning at least – they proved more efficient at taking money out of the hands of private investors and into the hands of networks of insiders clustered around the local party-state machinery.

Stockbrokers in Shenzhen emerged from within the state system, and operated in companies owned by the local government. Furthermore, there was no prohibition on them dealing on the markets as personal actors. This created a situation where the local government was in a position of privileged information within the emerging structure.

Through its relationship with local banks and other financial institutions, it had privileged knowledge of investment decisions and was often the initiator of these decisions in the first place. Through its control and/or influence over local enterprises, it also had privileged knowledge of management decisions. And through its control over stock-brokers, it had influence and privileged access to the stock-market.

A network of insiders, then, dominated the decision making process – a network of people who were organisationally linked through a governmental structure, and also linked through personal contacts and connections. Their insider knowledge of future key economic decisions gives them considerable advantage over 'private' investors. And as insider dealing was not illegal, they utilised this insider knowledge to 'buy low and sell high' using a computer programme developed by an academic mathematician to decide the optimal point at which to sell. When asked where this leaves private investors, the reply was 'vulnerable'.

The extent of this use of information for local gain prompted the reorganisation and strengthening of supervisory and regulatory mechanisms in 1998, and a new securities law on 1 July 1999. In the same year, the Central Working Committee on Finance established small groups in (theoretically at least) all financial institutions to guarantee that central (and indeed, party) policy was implemented throughout the country (Heilmann 2005). And as Green (2003) has documented, the financial regulatory structure in China is now much more effective than in the late-1990s – though still far from perfect. But the lack of transparency still means that market knowledge is a key source of economic power within China, and a key means through which political elites use their position of political power to capture the benefits of the market and create economic bases of power.

Bureaucrat capitalists

By the summer of 2005, the Minister of the National Development and Reform Commission, Ma Kai, announced that the task of replacing state planning with a 'socialist market economy' was now completed. Market forces now determined the price of 96 per cent of retail commodities, 97 per cent of agro and sideline products and 87 per cent of capital goods; over half of the residual 3,000 state owned or controlled large enterprises had been transformed in stock-sharing enterprises; and the private sector accounted for a third of GDP, and four-fifths of all new jobs (*People's Daily* 2005b). Using a broader definition, Fan Gang (2000) had previously calculated that by the end of the 1990s, the non-state sector (as opposed to just the private sector) accounted for 63 per cent of GDP, 80 per cent of GDP growth, and 'more than 100 per cent' of new jobs (Fan Gang 2000).[29] Nevertheless, the state–economy relationship remains extremely strong in contemporary China. Much of what is considered non-state remains heavily connected to officialdom through various mechanisms. As Duckett (1998: 162) argues:

> State institutions .... have retained control over many resources and still exert considerable influence over policy formulation and implementation. They can use that influence to direct the economic transition process in ways favourable to themselves

For example, Chou (2006) argues that the regulatory structure gives local authorities in particular the ability to control who gets licences to operate and who doesn't – and also allows the local governments to revoke these licences for not just economic reasons.

Much of the non-state sector in contemporary China has its origins in the party-state sector that spawned it. Dickson (2003) focuses on the emergence of new entrepreneurial elites from the ranks of the political elites, concentrating on the children of party state officials, and those entrepreneurs who have left formal political office to become economic elites – the process of *xiahai*. Guo Baogang (2003: 16) suggests that a third of all private enterprises in 2003 were owned by party members. Particularly at the local level, power holders are switching the prestige, influence and wealth that came from forming part of the political structure for the wealth that comes from being a factory manager, or a member of the board. To be more accurate, they are not so much swapping one source of power for another, but using their political positions to increase their economic potential and bargaining power.

Walder (2002) argues that a wave of privatisation that began in 1988 gave a new impetus to this process. But rather than own or run the enterprises themselves, officials more often retained control by proxy. On one level, they established new enterprises run by their relatives, or transferred ownership of publicly owned assets to private enterprises owned by 'cadre kin'. They then allocated state contracts to these enterprises and provided protection through local state power. On another level, when public enterprises were privatised, the existing managers of the enterprises, with whom local officials had a close working relationship, were typically the first people to be considered as potential new owners. This form of privatisation did not entail government officials directly taking control of public enterprises and assets, but a form of 'insider privatization' (Walder 2002: 13, Li and Rozelle 2003) whereby officials directed the privatisation process towards close contacts or relatives, and ensured that the success of these enterprises remained contingent on the new owners' relationship with the local government (see also Cai Yongshun 2002).[30]

Ding (2000a) has referred to the resulting relationship between political and economic elites as 'nomenklatura capitalism' and considers this process of privatisation as comprising 'illegal asset stripping' (Ding 2000b). According to Zou Dapei, the main forms of achieving such asset stripping are not including liabilities to banks or responsibilities to workers in the sell-off; not allowing competitive bidding, thus ensuring that a very low bid wins; ensuring losses in the period before privatisation to depress the sale price, and to discourage competitive bids; pricing the firm based on its industrial assets when its land was worth much more; discounts for cash payments; and through outright corruption by faking deficits and other forms of fraud:

> Zuo cited a study by finance ministry researcher Zhou Fangsheng who pointed out that a state firm with 300 million yuan (US$36 million) in total assets could end up valued as having net assets of only 20 million if its nominal and implicit liabilities (to banks and workers respectively) were 'forgiven'. This would mean it could be sold to its managers, after 'discount', for as little as 10 million yuan! (Cheng 2005)

Furthermore, after privatisation, the new managers utilise their hand-in-glove relationship with the state to ensure that they have the best possible chance of making a profit. For example, existing state owned companies would remain in existence, but perform a role of providing cheap supplies to a new privately owned company; or alternatively, state firms and organisations would purchase from the newly private enterprise at above market prices; or employees would remain on the books and be paid by state owned enterprises, whilst actually working for affiliated private companies (usually officially classified as being collectively owned for legal purposes). Whatever the specific tactic employed, losses would be located in the state sector, and profits in the private. And if the worst comes to the worse, many new entrepreneurs sourced the loan to buy the enterprise through the original (or an ancillary) state firm meaning that the state rather than the individual was left with the financial burden if the new enterprise failed to make a profit.

But the coalescence of political and new economic elites is not just a one way process. Private entrepreneurs in China find it difficult to make headway unless they have a good relationship with the party-state elites. Even those who have no formal contacts with the party-state are essentially dependent on strong support from local authorities in order to survive. Successful 'private' local enterprises usually succeed thanks to the protection and aid afforded to them by local state elites. In an economy where land, raw materials, transport and finance capital are still in relatively short supply, occupying a gatekeeper role (or knowing somebody who does) has an important economic premium. As such, a form of business-local state alliance is an essential prerequisite for successful economic activity. Krug (1997) argues that this is particularly important when 'private exchange exceeds the jurisdictional boundary'. As local barriers to trade abound in China, anybody that wants to transport goods across local administrative boundaries has to gain the cooperation of the local administrative authorities.

Thus, there is, and long has been, a tendency for emerging private enterprises to form an alliance with local governments. This has often resulted in what are effectively private companies being officially classified as collectively owned 'in order to obtain the security and privileges that those governments extend to collective firms' (ADB 2003: 63) – 'red hat' enterprises. This can include extending ownership to the local government, local party-state leaders taking a seat on the company board in a private capacity, or simply paying a fee relative to output or turnover to the local authorities. In addition to hard factors, such as easier access to capital, being classified as collectively owned ameliorated what Liu Yingqiu (2002: 4) refers to as 'ideological harassment'.

Furthermore, Krug's (1997) and Goodman's (2004b) research has shown that new entrepreneurial elites are trying to stabilise their positions by joining the party. And crucially, even before the formal decision to allow 'advanced productive forces' into the party, some local organisations were more than happy to accept these entrepreneurs into the party. They deemed the economic growth that new enterprises provided for local development and the provision of revenues for the local government as beneficial. Party membership and the benefits it provided for the private entrepreneurs were also often provided as a prid pro quo for more tangible private economic rewards for party state officials in the form of a seat on the company's board, or other means of remuneration.

This hand in glove relationship has led a number of observers to describe China as a corporatist economy.[31] There is some value in this concept, particularly if we modify the idea and think in terms of local corporatism where local governments develop 'institutional ties with civic and professional groups to bring them into the state' (Dickson 2003: 4). But the classic idea of corporatism with governments interacting through peak organisations with representatives from economic and social groups perhaps involves a conception of a greater degree of independence from the state (or party, or party-state) than is really the case in China. Yep (2000) also argues that peak organisations such as business organisations lack the necessary coherence and homogeneity to represent their sectors as a whole, and provide the effective means of state-society dialogue foreseen by corporatist models.

However we want to term it, one of the features of the Chinese reform process is the transformation of relationships between existing state actors, and the changing basis of their power. There is a symbiotic relationship (at the very least) between state elites and new economic elites. They have effectively co-opted each other into an alliance that, for the time being, mutually reinforces each other's power and influence, not to mention personal fortunes. What we see, then, is a process of reformulation of class alliances within China. As Hong Zhaohui (2004: 33) notes, what he terms the 'New Private Entrepreneurs' represent:

> a unique socio-economic entity, has the highest percentage of party members compared with all other social groups/classes, even higher than the Chinese working class, which is supposed to play a leading role within the CCP

Furthermore, Hong argues that this political alliance has gone beyond simply party membership, with party-entrepreneurs increasingly seeking representation on the NPC or Chinese Peoples Political Consultative Conference (CPPPC); 'Statistics show that 17.4 per cent of the private entrepreneurs are the members of the NPC and 35.1 per cent are the members of the CPPCC at various levels' (Hong Zhaohui 2004: 34). In numerical terms, this means that '5,400 entrepreneurs belonged to people's congresses at the county level or higher, and over 8,500 belonged to political consultative conferences at the county level or above' (He Li 2003: 90).

(Quasi) Capitalism with Chinese Characteristics

> It is currently accepted that socialism with Chinese characteristics means the abandonment of 'state socialism' for 'people's socialism', and that 'people's socialism' is analytically hard to differentiate from 'people's capitalism'. (Woo 1999: 8)

This chapter has traced the transition from a state planned and state owned economy towards state regulation of a hybrid economic system with the existence of a private economic sphere that remains very close to the state system that spawned it. The form of economic system that has materialised in China is one where state actors, often at the local level, remain central to the functioning of an economic system that has dysfunctionally emerged to suit their interests.

Bowles and Dong (1994: 62) argued that 'attempting to classify China's industrial system at this point in its evolution is a hazardous (some might say futile) exercise'. I have some sympathy with this view, but they were writing at a very early stage in the transition from social- ism, and notwithstanding the hazardous nature of the endeavour, it is time to raise the question of whether the Chinese economy is a capital- ist one. It is certainly nothing like the sort of capitalism that we see in the advanced developed democracies of the West.

But why should we search for convergence towards a single model of capitalism? If we conceive of capitalism as a mode of production where private ownership of the means of production prevails and in which surplus value is appropriated by the bourgeoisie in the market, then China does appear to have something equating to a primitive capitalist system. The most problematic part of the definition is 'private owner- ship'. As Guo Sujian (1998) has forcefully argued, the role of the state in controlling TVEs (if not formally owning them) means that the public sector still dominates ownership of the means of production. But it is an economic system where the state creates the space for the private sector to be increasingly important, and regulates the market to ensure that the new bourgeoisie can appropriate surplus value thanks to the bourgeoisie's close relationship with the party state – capitalism with Chinese characteristics.

So for the time being, the Chinese economic system works as it serves the interests of key elites – both economic and political. This does not mean that it is necessarily 'efficient' as the problems of the financial system indicate. Nor does it mean that it is necessarily 'fair' – but while there have been losers of reform (either absolute or rela- tive), the interests of those groups that count most in the power structure are served by the system that they have (often dysfunction- ally) generated. It works because it serves the political and economic interests of those who have had the most control over its evolution. Whether the interests of all of those elites will remain the same, and thus be served by the maintenance of the status quo, is entirely another question.

The system that has emerged has not only created the opportunity for external actors to become involved in the Chinese economy, but has also been reinforced by interaction with external economic actors. So despite the emphasis on the domestic context in this chapter, the distinction between the domestic and international is an increasingly artificial one that has been used here for ease of analysis. Thus, if we are thinking in terms of different types of space, and who or what occupies this space, it is important to turn away from national conceptions and towards an understanding of economic spaces that are either transnational and/or global in nature – the task for Chapter 3.

3
Re-engagement with the Global Economy

Twice in the space of a century and a half, China emerged from relative isolation and autarky to engagement with the international system. On the first occasion, this engagement was a consequence of imperialism and the forced opening of China by military power. Re-engagement of the post Mao era had a shared feature with the first case – the international system was not of China's making, Chinese elites did not accept the norms of the system, and many in China perceived external actors as hostile forces opposed to China's national interests and determined to prevent Chinese development.

Of course, there are many differences between the two eras. Key amongst them is that whilst the post-Mao leadership were, and in some ways remain, suspicious of the dominant norms in the international system, and reluctant to accept and embrace all of these norms, re-engagement with the global economy was a matter of deliberate choice by Chinese elites. But choosing to participate in the global economy is not the same thing as being able to control the way that such participation occurs. As noted in Chapter 2, the original logic for participating in the global economy created new logics, interests, and power relationships that influenced the way that China's re-engagement has evolved.

So this Chapter traces the way in which the relationship with the global economy evolved from a position of relative isolation to the liberalising logic that accompanied WTO entry. The basic argument is a simple one; in overseeing this transition from relative isolation to engagement, the Chinese leadership pursued a very simple and logical strategy – trade and investment was encouraged where it was deemed beneficial, and resisted where it was perceived to threaten domestic Chinese producers. The key question, then, is why the leadership decided to move to a new basis of polity by joining the WTO? Or more correctly, why join the WTO by accepting membership criteria which the Chinese side had previously rejected and were far more stringent than those previously negotiated by new developing country members?

The way in which prospective members of the WTO have to negotiate the specific terms of their entry with existing members is important here. So too is the shifting understanding of at least some Chinese leaders of the benefits of WTO membership – the importance of having a say in how the organisation evolves in the future and the importance of ensuring access to key foreign markets. Furthermore, WTO entry is a manifestation of a key shift in perceptions of the relationship between embedded domestic interests and the global economy. Whilst the original strategy of re-engagement was originally designed to protect domestic producers from market competition, the final agreement is a manifestation of the transition from *gaige* to *gaizhi* outlined in the previous chapter (Yang Yao 2004). And in part at last, WTO compliance reforms have been used as a tool to enforce reform on sceptical and resistant domestic actors.

Given the artificial divide between the domestic context discussed in Chapter 2, and the international context in this chapter, much of what needs to be said relating to basic principles has already been said. The changing bases of legitimacy, the fragmentation of power and the differential importance of local authorities, and the reformulation of interests and power relations are just as important for studying the process of re-engagement as they are for studying the domestic context.

Opening China

There is a tendency to describe China in the Maoist period as a 'closed economy'. This popular perception rather exaggerates the level of isolation, and is primarily a product of equating the capitalist world with the international economy (Harding 1987: 131). As Zhang Yongjin (1998: 26–31) has demonstrated, while China did look to self-reliance where possible in economic development, foreign trade also played a role 'as a balancing sector' of the Chinese economy. Nevertheless, despite the fact that trade increased after 1949, it is fair to say that China was not a significant player in the global economy during the Maoist era. After China's break from the Soviet Union and the gradual and moderate programme of re-engagement with the West in the 1970s, trade did increase, but trade volumes remained relatively low. Total Chinese trade was a meagre US$4.8 billion in 1971, and even after an almost five-fold expansion in trade, still only totalled US$20.6 billion in 1978 (Howell 1993). But as with the domestic context discussed in the previous chapter, 1978 marked a watershed in Chinese economic policy.[1] The initial moderate reforms initiated in 1978 gave only a strictly limited role for international economic interaction, and China's re-integration into the global economy was initially a slow and gradual affair. Indeed, in many respects, China's re-engagement with the global economy only really took off in earnest in the early 1990s. But whilst rather modest compared with later changes, the adoption of a more open policy towards the global economy in 1978 marked a fundamental ideological shift that was a pre-requisite for all that was to follow. We can divide the opening of China into four stages – all of which provide stark delineations between the 'before' and the 'after', but roughly correspond to important sea changes in policy.

Phase one: unlocking the door, 1978–86

The first phase, from 1978 to 1986 marked the gradual opening of parts of China to the global economy. Following the decision to place economic modernisation above class struggle in the list of party objectives, interaction with the global economy was conceived as being beneficial to this modernisation drive. But given that the party leadership had railed against the evils of the capitalist global economy for much of the preceding 30 years, insertion into the capitalist global economy had to be handled with care. Thus, following the Third Plenum, China opened just four SEZs with the (limited) freedom to conduct international economic relations.[2] In July 1979, the National People's Congress passed a supporting law which provided a legal basis for the existence of joint ventures and foreign investment. These SEZs were conceived as 'windows on the world' for China – allowing international economic contacts to grow, but limiting them to specific areas to allay fears from political conservatives that such contacts would lead to 'bourgeois spiritual pollution' (Bachman 1988).

China's SEZs were very similar both in intention and policy to the Export Processing Zones (EPZs) that had previously been established in other regional states. Following the example of the Kandla export-processing zone in India, Taiwan opened its first EPZ at Gaoxiong in 1966 to attract inward investment to produce exports. A similar strategy was pursued in South Korea, which opened its own EPZ at Masan, and by Malaysia which established EPZs in and around Penang. As

Jackson and Mosco (1999) note, the EPZs in Malaysia were intended to dis-embed the globalised sectors of the Malaysian economy from the domestic economy as a whole. We should of course be aware of the very different contexts of the Chinese and other experiments in creating processing zones. Cold War politics ensured that anti-communist regimes in East Asia gained preferential access to the benefits of the global economy, primarily through preferential trading relations with the United States. This entailed both a toleration of the maintenance of barriers to imports to protect emerging industries in the region, and a privileged access to the US market for regional exporters. Thus, regional states were permitted to benefit from export led strategies and relatively unhindered access to lucrative foreign markets without being subject to all the reciprocal impact of the global economy on domestic producers (Cumings 1987: 68). The developmental successes of East Asia cannot all be put down to the relationship with the US and Cold War politics. But it is undeniable that this relationship certainly helped.

In the Chinese case, the argument for moving away from this geographically limited integration came not on ideological grounds, but because of the success of the SEZs in attracting investment and facilitating rapid capital accumulation. This success resulted in considerable lobbying from other local authorities to be allowed the same access to the global economy. In 1984, the government decided to open five more cities to trade, but as a result of lobbying from local leaders, a total of 14 cities were instead 'opened up' (Hamrin 1990: 83), all of them along China's coast. Whilst the rest of the country gradually opened up to international economic contacts (in geographic terms at least) a striking feature of China's re-engagement with the global economy is a continued uneven geographic distribution, with the vast majority of investment and trade still concentrated on the coastal regions.

Phase two: from permitting to facilitating, 1986–92

Fung, Iizaka and Tong (2002: 4) argue that while the period up to 1986 entailed the government developing policies that permitted international economic contact, in 1986, a new period of facilitating such contacts began with the passing of what have now come to be known as the 'twenty-two regulations'. In combination, these regulations created a more beneficial environment for foreign investors including lower fees for labour and rent, tax rebates for exporters, and made it possible for foreign companies to convert limited profits earned in RMB into foreign exchange and repatriate profits. It also extended the joint venture contracts beyond the original 50-year limit, and created a legal basis for wholly foreign owned enterprises, rather than the previous insistence on foreign companies working in joint venture with a Chinese partner. This move considerably increased the attraction of investing in China – not to produce in China, but to produce exports to be sold on other markets. While Foreign Invested Enterprises (FIEs) only accounted for two per cent of exports and six per cent of imports before 1986, the figure increased to 48 per cent and 52 per cent respectively by 2000 (Braunstein and Epstein 2002: 23). Since then, export based investment has not only dominated investment into China, but has also been a major motor of Chinese export growth.

Phase three: accelerating opening, 1992–9

As with domestic reform, the third key change came in the *nanxun* of 1992. And in many respects, it was only now that China began to emerge as a global trading power. From 1993, exports increased by 60 per cent in two years (53 per cent in real terms), and doubled in the space of five years.[3] In the process, a US$12.2 billion trade deficit was transformed into a US$5.4 billion surplus the following year, the start of a period of continual trade surpluses that have done much to politicise China's international economic relations – particularly, but not only, with the United States. It is no coincidence that 1993 also marked the emergence of China as a major recipient of FDI, with the figure for that year exceeding the entire preceding 14 years of reform put together. Attracting this FDI was conceived as a major – perhaps *the* major – means of providing the new jobs required to allow domestic reform to proceed without too great an impact on urban employment.

A dualistic economy

In theory at least, the benefits of engagement should have been offset by the impact of international competition on vulnerable and inefficient domestic sectors:

> if we pursue more open policies to encourage global competition, the less competitive national industry would be in competition with powerful international capital owners which could lead to problems in the future.....In this world, it is not possible to satisfy both sides (Jin Bei 1997)

To understand how the two sides were satisfied, we need to follow Naughton (2000) and divide the focus of analyses into two distinct and largely separate spheres.[4]

Where foreign actors did not compete with domestic actors, then they were encouraged to come to China. This almost always entailed encouraging FDI to produce exports for external markets. The extent of incentives offered to investors will be discussed in more detail below, but what is important here is the extent to which China constructed a liberal *internationalised* export regime. Investment was made simple, as was bringing in components to be used in export industries – as China joined the WTO entry, some 60 per cent of all imports came into China tariff free.

But this liberal export regime sat alongside a relatively closed and protected *domestic* trading regime. This regime was partly designed to protect domestic producers from competition in order to maintain production, profitability and jobs. Thus, it protected inefficient loss making SOEs from international competition, and also ensured relatively stable incomes for agricultural producers. But it was also partly designed to provide price advantage to domestic exporters. For example, Zweig (2002: 160) has shown how small scale TVEs swapped access to China's domestic markets in return for international capital and access to international markets'. Such TVEs accounted for around half of all Chinese exports in 1996 when the significance began to tail off, and alongside FIEs, were a key source of Chinese export growth in this early period.

From 1995, this dualistic approach has a formal manifestation in the form of 'The Catalogue Guiding Foreign Investment in Industry' jointly produced by the State Development and Planning Commission, the SETC and the MOFTEC. The Catalogue stipulated into which sectors investment was prohibited, permitted but restricted with conditions specified on an industry by industry basis, or encouraged (later revisions to the catalogue will be discussed later). Although encouraged sectors include those where there are no significant domestic actors and where there is an urgent need for capital,[5] the vast majority are where investment produces exports. Even if a sector is officially restricted, any investment that promises to export 100 per cent of its produce is promoted to the encouraged sector.[6]

External pressure to reform

As we saw in Chapter 2, national and local authorities have used the financial system to support exporters and to protect domestic enterprises from international competition. They have eased access to investment capital by providing loans through the creation of specialist banks, and provided a number of tax exemptions and other incentives for exporters. In addition, the government has also used import plans, licenses and quotas and retained some of the highest import tariffs in the world to protect key domestic sectors (though notably these were steadily reduced even prior to WTO entry). In 1995, USTRO drew up the 'November Roadmap' outlining the areas in which the US government thought China was 'unfairly' protecting domestic producers. Although this list provides a snapshot of issues at a specific point in time, it nevertheless provides a rough overview of those issues that emerge time and time again in discussions with foreign companies trying to compete in the Chinese market.

In addition to 'normal' trade issues such as tariffs, trading rights, and access to 'closed' sectors of the Chinese economy, USTRO pressed for a number of other reforms. For example, incomplete currency convertibility resulted in restricted access to foreign currency and also meant that converting and repatriating profits was difficult if not impossible; the lack of transparency in China's policy making (and in particular, the monopoly of the state news-agency, Xinhua, in the dissemination of economic information) placed outsiders at a disadvantage; intellectual and property right infringement was costing millions to copyright owners; and the differential application of fiscal system where local companies typically negotiated tax free deals with the local government, effectively provided a hidden fiscal tariff for foreign companies.

Furthermore, US trade officials claimed that the lack of full price reform in China also acted as a hidden state subsidy for those Chinese producers in the state sector, or private enterprises that retained close and warm links with the state administration. They paid cheap state set prices, while external actors were forced to pay the higher market rate (Barshefsky 1999). And as we have seen in Chapter 2, Chinese enterprises were also supported through massive subsidies, which often took the form of 'loans' from government or the banking system that will never be repaid.

The manipulation of currency rates was also a key area of concern. The RMB was not fully convertible on international markets, and exchange rates remain under central government management and control today. However, in the early 1990s, a market rate of sorts appeared as the government relaxed regulations on currency exchanges. To facilitate increased international economic contacts, a number of 'swap shops' were established where individuals could trade RMB for foreign currency. Although the official exchange rate at the time was RMB5.7 to the dollar, the swap shop rate was influenced by supply and demand, and was closer to RMB9 to the dollar. In 1994, the government 'unified' the two rate, which essentially entailed moving to the swap shop rate. The new official exchange rate of RMB8.7 to the dollar apparently representing a 50 per cent devaluation. But in reality, the headline figure of a 50 per cent devaluation misses the point that most companies were already using the market rate for the majority of their foreign currency trading. As such, the headline 50 per cent devaluation was probably nearer 20–30 per cent for most exporters – and Fernald, Edison, and Loungani (1998: 2–3) put the figure at a mere seven per cent.

Maintaining a currency peg also allowed the Chinese authorities to decrease interest rates to boost growth without suffering any impact on exchange rates. But while we can argue over the real extent of this devaluation, and its impact on other regional states, producing for export in China after 1994 became increasingly attractive. And with the RMB pegged to the dollar, the maintenance of a stable exchange rate as the dollar devalued in 2003–4 renewed complaints about currency controls acting as an unfair government protection of the Chinese economy.

In its own terms, the policy was a great success – domestic producers were protected from competition, domestic exporters were helped to gain a competitive foothold, and investment to produce exports increased. The relative lack of liberalisation – particularly financial liberalisation – also had the added, if unplanned for, benefit of ensuring that China escaped the Asian crises relatively unscathed (Yu Yongding 1999: 15). Perhaps even more than the first generation of late developing states in East Asia, China's re-engagement with the global economy appeared to be a great example of how to reap the benefits of the global market-place whilst maintaining strong defences against the dangers of globalisation.

Phase four: joining the WTO 1999

As Lardy (2000) notes, protectionist measures had incrementally eased in the years preceding China's WTO entry. For example, average tariff rates of 50 per cent in the early 1980s had been reduced to 17 per cent by 1998. Nevertheless, it still came as something of a surprise to many (not least many within China itself) when the government moved to end years of at times rather bitter negotiations by signing an agreement with the US government in November 1999 with the aim of facilitating China's entry into the WTO (finally achieved at Doha in 2001).

The first initiative to join what was then the General Agreement on Tariffs and Trade (GATT) came in July 1986, and according to Fewsmith (2001b) was a source of political friction throughout the 15 and a half years of negotiations. Deng Liqun has been the main voice of Marxist (if not Maoist) opposition to not only WTO entry, but liberalisation in general. A former Minister of Propaganda, Deng Liqun was considered by some outsiders to be a candidate for Party leadership in 1982 when he remained a close ally of Deng Xiaoping. Deng Liqun subsequently distanced himself from Deng Xiaoping over ideological issues, and maintained continued criticism of the political conse-quences of economic reform via his position as head of the 'leading group to oppose bourgeois liberalisation.' After Deng Xiaoping's death, Deng Liqun became ever more vocal in his criticisms of the direction of reform, and in particular, Jiang Zemin's moves towards allowing private entrepreneurs to join the party. For Deng Liqun, WTO entry was another step on the road towards the creation of a new capitalist ruling class in China which exploits the Chinese workers and farmers (Masaharu Hishida 2002).

Others were less concerned about class, and focused instead on the relationship between the economic benefits of increased economic integration on one hand, and the concomitant potential political prob-lems of being subject to the vagaries of global capitalist economy dom-inated by China's (potential) enemies on the other (Hughes 1997). Major actors (which almost always meant the US) could use economic levers to not only pressure China to undertake domestic economic reform, but also to threaten economic repercussions if China did not comply with US political and security interests. Thus, divisions emerged within the leadership between those emphasising the logic of economic transformation, and those who argued that traditionally conceived national security issues should take predominance.

The wisdom of WTO membership was also debated in the wider population. Han Deqiang (2000) captured a popular mood by claiming that not only would WTO membership endanger Chinese jobs and incomes, but would also subject China to the vagaries of a global economy dominated by US hegemony. Other 'new left' writers joined the criticism – but according to Wang Hui (2004) the vast majority of works that appeared at first sight to be an attack on neoliberalism and/or US hegemony and/or the WTO were in reality much more prag-matic and practical. What they were really opposing was the timing and/or specific conditions of membership, and the impact that this might have on societal groups and social stability. Further liberalisation might be good in the long term, but what about the impact of rapid change on rural incomes, on employment in uncompetitive SOEs, and the fragile (to say the least) financial system?[7]

China's changing negotiating stance

For much of the period from 1986, the Chinese position reflected the sceptical or pragmatic view and was built around gaining entry on terms that allowed China greater and more stable access to external markets than it would reciprocally grant to others.[8] Initial claims that China was simply retaking the China seat vacated by the Republic of China in 1950, and therefore didn't need to do anything in terms of further liberalisation were slowly but firmly rebuffed. Unlike the UN, GATT was open to membership from a legal entity that has autonomy over external commercial relations and not states. There was thus no 'China seat' as such, and if the PRC wanted in, then it had to negotiate agreement with existing members (and indeed Taiwan also joined the WTO in 2001 as the separate Customs Territory of Taiwan, Penghu, Kinmen and Matsu). If this was a slightly strange basis to start the nego-tiations on, in some ways the next definitional conflict was even stranger. Chinese negotiators made much of the importance of being allowed in as a 'developing country' as this would allow them to main-tain some protection for key domestic sectors, to partially subsidise exporters, and to have a longer period of post-entry adjustment than that afforded to developed countries. It is true that previous 'developing country' new members had not all been forced to fully liberalise imme-diately (Trebilcock and Howe 1999), but this preferential treatment declined significantly after GATT became the WTO in 1995.[9]

More important, special treatment for developing countries is not mandatory and the definition and legal basis of WTO membership is astonishingly vague (Jackson, 1989: 279). 'Least Developed Countries' are classified according to United Nations Conference on Trade and Development (UNCTAD) definitions, but there are no definitions of what constitutes a developed or developing country in the WTO rules at all. A country can decide to classify itself as a developing country, but this can be challenged by any other member. Moreover, in provid-ing preferential treatment to other members through the Generalised System of Preferences (GSP), it is up to the developed country to decide which countries qualify. So even if China calls itself a developing country, it is up to the UK and the US and other countries to decide whether to accept this and add China to their GSP list (Jackson 1989: 278).

More important still, this only applies once a country has joined, and the definitions and legal basis of membership provide even greater levels of ambiguity. There are no set processes at all, with the specifics of each individual attempt to join the WTO worked out on a case by case basis. The WTO will establish a special working party to undertake negotiations in consultation with interested member country parties (as established by Article XII of the WTO Marrakech agreement). But this working party does not act on behalf of the members with power to make an agreement. Any existing member can demand a bilateral negotiation with the prospective member and can block entry until or unless they are happy (or can agree to membership on the condition that it doesn't treat the new member as a member at all).[10] As such, Chinese negotiators' insistence that China be treated as a developing country were wholly pointless. The terms of Chinese entry would be determined by the individual negotiations with existing members, what they wanted from China and what they were prepared to offer up, irrespective of how China classified itself.[11]

Just to add even more confusion, all these bilateral negotiations took place individually without full consultation amongst existing members. For example, there was considerable conflict in negotiating Chinese entry between the European Union (EU) and US negotiators – the latter claiming that an agreement that they had reached with China was subsequently undone by a later agreement negotiated between the EU and China.[12] So ironically, membership of a key multilateral organisation where decisions are usually reached through multilateral consensus is achieved through multiple, overlapping and at times conflicting sets of hard nosed bilateral bargaining.

Quite simply, China was considered too big and too potentially important to be allowed in on its own terms even if it had already liberalised as much as other developing countries, and perhaps more so than Japan and South Korea had done when they were allowed in (*Economist* 1995). And trying to negotiate entry conditions that allowed considerable residual protection was not likely to succeed while China was running massive trade surpluses with the EU and the USA, and while many in the US in particular were warning about the future rise of China to challenge the existing global order. Charlene Barshefsky was in part correct when she argued that China would only be allowed in on terms that were 'commercially meaningful' to the US and that debates over what 'developing' and 'developed' meant were in fact meaningless.[13] But there was more to it than just economics – domestic politics in the US and elsewhere certainly also played their part.

So it is rather easy to understand why the existing members tried to push the Chinese side into accepting rather far reaching conditions on membership (which will be outlined in more detail below). What is perhaps harder to understand is why the Chinese side agreed given that they had previously held out for entry on their own terms, and given that the Chinese economy was not exactly in a crisis at the time that could only be solved by WTO membership. The first explanation is the desire to have a say in shaping any future changes to the global trading system. To influence the organisation, you have to become a member, and to become a member, you have to accept its existing rules and norms (in the short run at least). Second, and very much related, there was some concern at the time that the WTO might set new agendas in the Doha round that would require even greater liberalisation from new members, so best to get in now before it gets even harder. However, the most important explanations are found in the need to secure access to export markets – and particularly the US market – and the changing understanding of the impact of competition on domestic sectors.

The politics of Sino-US trade relations

The first explanation lies in the importance of exports as a means of generating growth, and in particular, the uncertainties relating to the annual vote in the US congress over whether to extend Most Favoured Nation (MFN) status to China. In the words of Long Yongtu after the negotiations had been completed:

> the question concerning MFN status had long been the crucial factor for difficulties in China–US negotiation, US Congress' involvement in it had made the negotiation more politicized.... I want to point out that entry into the WTO would make future trade disputes between us and other countries and regions not easily be politicized (*People's Daily* 2001c)

The Jackson-Vanik amendment to the 1974 US trade act (officially Title IV of the Trade Act) was introduced to provide an economic means of punishing authoritarian states. In inception, the amendment was designed to block normal access to the US market for those states that were considered to unfairly prevent emigration. 'To assure the continued dedication of the United States to fundamental human rights' normal trade relations could be denied to any 'nonmarket economy' that 'engages in practices prohibiting or severely restricting free emigration of its citizens'.

The Jackson–Vanik amendment was designed to discriminate against the Soviet Union and the Communist Party States of Eastern Europe for preventing the emigration of Jews, and was not intended to deal with China. If a President wants to waive the discrimination on a Jackson-Vanik listed state like China, then they have to inform congress 30 days before the expiry of the annual waiver (June 3rd) of the decision and show that allowing MFN will 'substantially promote the objectives of this section' *and* that 'he has received assurances that the emigration practices of that country will henceforth lead substantially to the achievement of the objectives of this section'. Congress has the right to block the extension of MFN, but the Presidential power to veto any no vote means that a two-thirds majority was necessary in both houses to override the President.

In the Chinese case, the letter of the law was replaced with its spirit only. The decision to extend the waiver was argued on the lines that notwithstanding China's poor human rights record, 'constructive engagement' through the extension of economic relations was the best way of ultimately improving this Human Rights situation. Perhaps successive Presidents really did believe that engaging China in commercial terms would lead to political and social change in China, but not everybody was convinced. The annual Presidential proposal to renew MFN always resulted in a welter of complaints about China's human rights record, one child policy, treatment of Tibet, policy towards Taiwan, unfair trade practices, trade surplus, labour abuses, arms sales, military technology transfer, environmental degradation and so on.

But notwithstanding the voices calling for trade sanctions on China from the groups mentioned above, there were also strong voices calling for the separation of human rights from commercial relationships – particularly during the Clinton Presidency. Here, we should note that if the waiver and MFN were not extended, then US companies would not be eligible for export credit and investment guarantees from the US government. For major corporations like Boeing, Chrysler, and General Motors, these guarantees were essential for their growing relationship with China.

Roden (2000) also points to the divisions that existed within the administration itself. On one side were those who wished to maintain a strong political basis for relations with China and a maintenance of Human Rights as the underlying discourse – typically the National Security Council and the State Department. On the other were those agencies that primarily had economic relations with China – Treasury, Commerce and the National Economic Council. Is it any coincidence that it is the same people that make so much of the potential of the Chinese market? Ron Brown whilst commerce secretary placed great emphasis on China as an emerging market that would provide rich pickings for US companies – indeed the US Department of Commerce targeted China as one of the ten 'Big Emerging Markets' that would increasingly dominate US economic relations (Roden 2000: 82).[14] Given that EU states in particular were perceived as being less interested in Human Rights in China than developing commercial contacts, if the US took a moral stance, then US companies would simply lose out to their European competitors.

Perhaps not surprisingly then, every President renewed the waiver and MFN – even though each new president was always critical of the incumbent President's China policy during the election campaign. With hindsight, we can see that the withdrawal of MFN was never really on the cards. But at the time, there were no such guarantees for the Chinese authorities. The importance of exports as an engine of economic growth meant that guaranteeing access to the US market in particular, and those of the developed world in general, was essential for job creation. And the best way of achieving this was through WTO entry – a means of depoliticising market access issues, and of taking some of the bilateral out of trade relations with the US by providing access to multilateral dispute resolution mechanisms.

But to truly understand the importance of export markets for Chinese development, it is essential to consider the relationship between export growth and 'domestic' growth. China's desire to join the WTO peaked twice – once in 1989 and again at the end of the 1990s. At both times, the domestic Chinese economy was in deflation, leaving export growth as essentially the only means of generating growth, and in turn minimising the impact of deflation on unemployment. In 1989, this was fired by a real fear that the EU and North Atlantic Free Trade Agreement (NAFTA) might become economic fortresses that developing countries outside the global trading organisation would be unable to penetrate. In the late 1990s, continued export growth was seen as providing the breathing space required to tackle domestic inflation, and to close down the high proportion of loss-making state owned enterprises. As one of China's most influential trade official, Wu Yi, puts it in 1998 (when the spillover of the Asian financial crises threatened briefly to reduce FDI and export growth):

If we cannot keep exports and investment growing, our macroeconomic growth target will be at risk .... It's not exports for exports'

sake, we have to help achieve an 8 per cent growth rate in GDP ....
It's a political issue to boost exports .... proper export growth is critical in helping the nation reform State-owned enterprises, create
jobs and promote social stability (Wang Yong 1998).

Abandoning the embedded socialist compromise

Wu Yi's comments bring us to the key issue of the changing understanding of the benefit of protecting domestic producers and the transition from *gaige* to *gaizhi* outlined in the previous Chapter. By the late
1990s, key Chinese leaders had come to believe that the system needed
to be changed, not simply tinkered with at the margins and reformed.
The residual elements of the old system that were still largely protected
from international competition were no longer perceived as the sacred
cows of the Chinese economy, but instead were seen as obstacles preventing the full transition to a new economic paradigm. Key amongst
these leaders were Premier Zhu Rongji (who would clearly not have
been able to push the agenda without the support of Jiang Zemin), and
China's chief WTO negotiator, Long Yongtu.

But despite the support of China's top leaders, WTO entry was not
supported by all. There was considerable resistance to further liberalisation both within the central bureaucratic agencies and in particular,
from local authorities in areas where agriculture and/or the residual
state sector continued to dominate economic activity. According to
Fewsmith (2001: 574b), 'frustrated by bureaucratic obstruction to fundamental reform, Zhu was willing to avail himself of foreign competitive pressures to force restructuring'. In the first instance, this entailed
apparently offering considerable concessions in a bid to gain US
support for China's entry during an official visit to Washington in
March 1999. If the Chinese participants at a conference taking place in
Beijing at the time were anything to go by, this was not a popular
move. Subsequent discussions in Beijing also suggest that many within
the Chinese policy elites thought that these concessions went too far –
and if anything, there was even greater anger that this had all been
done with minimal consultation.

When these concessions were rejected in the US, Zhu's position as
Premier and liberaliser in chief came under scrutiny. He was not helped
by the fact that the anti-inflation strategy pursued after 1994 did not
result in the expected soft landing, but instead turned into deflation.
To say that Zhu was saved by his another turn to the US authorities in
November 1999 is to go too far, but had US officials not accepted this
second attempt to push through with an agreement, his domestic posi-

tion would have been weaker, and the prospects of WTO entry more distant (Groombridge and Barfield 1999). To some extent at least, the desire to bolster reformers and to encourage China's engagement with multilateral organisations appeared to inform US policy makers as well. Clearly, the deal would have to be on the 'commercially beneficial' terms that Barshefsky set as the bottom line, but if this helped lock China into a liberalisation path and reduce the possibility of any future reversal, then all the better.

The terms of the agreement

There is a wide acceptance that the terms of China's accession protocol entailed significant concessions far exceeding the obligations of previous 'developing country' members. For example, China agreed to subsidies for agricultural production at 8.5 per cent of the value of farm output rather than the 'normal' 10 per cent enjoyed by developing countries (but more than the 5 per cent for developed countries). In addition, China agreed to adhere to Article 6.2 of the WTOs Agriculture Agreement, which, according to the US Department of Agriculture Foreign Agricultural Service, means, 'China agreed to forego the developing country exemption'.[15] Even observers from the World Bank office in Beijing who were highly supportive of China's entry argue that the concessions exceeded even developing countries obligations (Kawai and Bhattasali 2001: 2). In particular, Lardy (2002) argues that other countries can maintain restrictions on Chinese imports for 15 years after Chinese entry – much longer than 'transitional safeguard measures' usually allow.[16]

WTO membership did bring some very early tangible results. For example, trade increased, as did foreign investment (though of course we cannot know what the trade and investment figures would have been if China had not joined in 2001) and both have continued to grow with exports outstripping imports. In urban China in particular, one of the most visible early impacts was the large increase in private car ownership as import tariffs were cut and obtaining loans to buy cars became simpler with the approval of car financing ventures by General Motors, Volkswagen and Toyota. The more apocalyptical forecast of a collapse in rural incomes has failed to materialise, though grain prices did drop back and were still below the 1996 level a decade later.

Nevertheless, it is still far too early to come to any firm conclusions over the long term impact of WTO membership on China – not least because the process of ensuring WTO compliance is still ongoing (hence the lack of an end date for phase four in the heading for this section). Becoming WTO compliant entails a significant transformation of the Chinese administrative legal system. As we saw in Chapter 2, the merging of (MOFTEC) with the (SETC) into the Ministry of Commerce was largely a result of WTO entry. The Chinese authorities have also put in place a number of legal changes to ensure WTO compliance. Perhaps the most relevant for the issues under discussion in this chapter were the changes in relation to ownership of foreign enterprises, customs regulations, and the new Foreign Trade Law which came into effect in July 2004. The Foreign Trade Law was the result of two years of negotiations between interested parties across a range of different administrative units in national level bureaucracies. The new law had three major changes from the previous Trade Law adopted in 1994. First, individuals rather than just companies were permitted to engage in foreign trade. Second, legally registered foreign traders no longer needed to gain administrative approval for individual activities. And third, SOEs monopolies on trade in petroleum, grain, chemical fertilisers, cotton, sugar and edible oil were partially revoked.[17]

The 2004 Trade Law in itself generated the need for a range of other administrative reforms by different bureaucratic agencies to ensure that they themselves complied with the new law. It will take a long time for the legal administrative reforms to be completed, but in the process, we can hypothesise that there will be a shift in the balance of power within China. With the emphasis increasingly on a law based system – economically if not politically – then power should shift from the party as an institution to the state.

Meeting aims and objectives

Implementation and compliance

In addition to the ongoing process of reforming to become WTO compliant, signing the WTO agreement does not mean that everything will be implemented as originally intended. The question of compliance is not unique to China – all countries, even those in the developed world, face problems in fully liberalising in keeping with WTO requirements. In the Chinese case, there is a wary acceptance by much of the foreign business community dealing in or with China that policy reversals might have to occur if social stability is to be secured. For example, a survey of US companies operating in China found that most expected that the social costs of implementing the requirements would be so great that the Chinese would find it extremely difficult to implement all obligations. This was not so much a complaint by the respondents as a simple statement of fact (USGAO 2002). There also remains considerable reluctance in some parts of the bureaucracy to comply.[18] Any researcher who interviews Chinese officials and academics will be told that Long Yongtu and other negotiators were isolated from other political elites within China. The negotiations were 'closed' (Lai Hongyi 2001) in that a small group of leaders led the process without discussion with other domestic interested parties. The suggestion is that the process became a 'one-level game', with the need to come to an agreement with negotiating partners – the international game – overriding the need to ensure that the domestic Chinese constituents were happy with any concessions – the domestic game.

> the accession process was guided by a small number of top government leaders and that implementation relies on lower-level officials, many of whom oppose changes affecting their bureaucratic power base. (Murphy 2003)

Kynge (2002) argues that 'the regulatory agencies who often regard themselves as the protector of domestic companies rather than the regulator' have played a particularly important role in 'interpreting' WTO agreements in ways that allow more protection for domestic producers that was originally intended. This has resulted in 'a dense web of Chinese regulations' (Dougherty 2002) which in some cases has undermined the liberalising logic of the WTO agreement:

> China has started to release regulations to open up industries according to its obligations under the WTO. But often those regulations are accompanied by whole sets of new limitations that virtually reverse the promise of opening up. It is one page of opening up and fifteen pages of trying to reverse it (China Biz 2002)

According to Stratford (2002), this process entails 'legitimate (though unwelcome) exploitations of 'loopholes'', 'China's aggressive interpretations of ambiguous language', and 'blatant disregard for clear-cut obligations'.

A good example is the revisions to the Catalogue Guiding Foreign Investment in Industry that took place in 2002 and 2004 to make China's FDI regime WTO compliant.[19] These revisions entailed moving previously prohibited sectors to restricted, and moving the restrictions on some to make them encouraged. But the devil is in the detail. Many of those sectors that are now officially on the 'encouraged' list are in fact only encouraged with qualifications which in reality makes them restricted. And those that formally remain 'restricted' have restrictions placed on them that make operating in China more difficult than was expected at WTO entry. According to the annual Congressional-Executive Commission on China report in 2005:

> The Chinese government has also proposed and implemented new measures that appear to protect and promote domestic industry and disadvantage foreign business, sometimes in contravention of its WTO commitments. (CECC 2005: 99)

The list of unfair practices included denying foreign firms access to domestic marketing channels; imposing unreasonable requirements for technology transfer by foreign investors; discriminating against foreign companies in the allocation of major government projects; continuing to use the financial system as a means of channelling preferential loans from state banks; facilitating privileged access to listings on stock markets; providing tax relief to domestic producers; by giving domestic firms special access to land; and by funding the research and design (R&D) activities of Chinese firms through the official government budget. In preparing a submission to the US government calling for restrictions on Chinese steel imports, Price *et al* (2006: iv) added to this list the manipulation of raw material prices to provide cheap inputs, currency manipulation (more of this later); access to 'sophisticated facilities at low cost' in government funded development parks; and the conversion of debt to equity, debt forgiveness and lack of action to recover non-performing loans (thus freeing Chinese producers from historical debt burdens).

Intellectual Property Rights (IPR) abuses are not included on either of these two lists but are also a frequent cause of criticism.[20] Here, there is recognition that WTO entry has made a difference, and that the Chinese authorities have placed an emphasis on preventing IPR abuses. For example, legal changes have made it easier for foreign companies to use the Chinese courts to protect their IPR, and the government has established 50 IPR reporting centres to increase surveillance. But the acceptance that something has been done is heavily tempered by the general understanding that much more remains to be done. For the US Coordinator for International

Intellectual Property Enforcement, Chris Israel (2006: 3), poor IPR enforcement in China is a consequence of:

> lack of sufficient political will, corruption, local protectionism, mis-allocated resources and training, and a lack of effective public education regarding the economic and social impact of counterfeiting and piracy

with enforcement at the local level marked out as the single biggest problem. Here we return to the issue of local power holders identified in Chapter 2, and an understanding of the location of power within the Chinese state system. WTO entry might have been in part intended to use external pressure to enforce change on resistant local power holders, but this does not necessarily mean that they will comply. In a US congressional briefing paper, Morrison (2002) argued that 'Corruption and local protectionism are rampant in China, and gaining the cooperation of local officials and government bureaucrats that oversee various affected industries could prove difficult in the short run'. It might not be impossible for the central government to ensure compliance in the provinces, but it is a far from easy task.

Initial external observations of China's compliance record were prepared to accept a degree of hesitance and remained relatively positive. To be sure, there were calls for China to do more, but while the glass was not full, most portrayed it as being half full rather than half empty (USCBC 2002, USGAO 2002, Chan 2004). The first major sign of a reassessment was in July 2003, when US Secretary of Commerce, Donald Evans, issued a stinging attack on China's compliance record, complaining about the slow pace of reduction in trade barriers and government subsidies to domestic producers, and a lack of action over copyright infringement (Bloomberg 2003: 12). Evans' assistant, William Lash graded China at only a 'gentleman's C to a D+' grade on WTO implementation in 2003, while in the annual report to congress, the USTRO noted that implementation 'lost a significant amount of momentum' in 2003, and this could no longer just be put down to 'start up problems'. In January 2006, Deputy US trade representative Karan Bhatia (2006) suggested that China's track record of WTO compliance was 'remarkably mixed' and that:

> The United States will not hesitate, when appropriate, to use all tools at its disposal to ensure that China lives up to its commitments.... We

will continue to hold China accountable. That is our responsibility to the workers, farmers, and businesses here in the United States

When US Commerce Secretary Carlos Gutierrez (2006) commented that 'The bottom line is that our companies do not have their rightful access under the terms of China's WTO commitments' he went on to suggest that if things didn't improve 'it only strengthens those who want to build protectionist barriers around the U.S. market'.

Assuring market access

In combination, Bhatia's and Gutierrez's comments suggest that WTO entry has not resolved once and for all the issue of guaranteeing access to major markets. In fact, the continued growth of Chinese exports after WTO entry resulted in more trade conflicts, not less. In 2005, anti-dumping measures were imposed on US$8.9 billion dollars worth of exports – a 700 per cent increase on the previous year (*People's Daily* 2005e). For example, the large growth of textile exports to the EU meant that the Chinese quota for 2005 was completed half-way through the year. Although this was relatively quickly resolved by using part of the 2006 quota, the EU-China textile conflicts unsurprisingly re-emerged over the 2006 quota (the reason why the issue was dealt with so quickly in 2005 is dealt with in Chapter 5). There have been a number of other trade disputes with the EU over the import of 'unsafe' foodstuffs and cigarette lighters, with at least one Chinese trade official convinced that these were excuses to protect producers in the EU.

But the biggest and most important conflicts have been with the US. Despite WTO entry, trade relations in general, and with the USA in particular, have not been depoliticised. In some respects trade relations are now more politicised than before. Raising expectations that are then not met often raises more complaints than not having promised a different future in the first place. And in the case of Sino-US trade, the large growth in the trade relationship from an already high starting point at WTO entry has brought even closer focus on China. But while Sino-US trade relations remain very highly politicised, it is a different form of politicisation than before. It is not Chinese politics – human rights abuses and so on – that is the main issue now as it was during the MFN renewal debates outlined above. It is now US politics that is most important, and the political pressure that it generates for the US leadership to do something about the jobs that, it is often argued, are being lost in the US and being unfairly relocated to China.

For example, in calling for the introduction of restrictions on textile imports from China, Lindsey Graham, Republican Senator for South Carolina justified his calls by saying that, 'I have long maintained that China cheats on trade agreements. The practices of Chinese companies and the policies of the Chinese government are illegal and give them an unfair advantage' (Barboza 2003). As we shall see in Chapter 4, through foreign investment in China, often via intermediaries in East Asia, US companies themselves are actually the source of some of the textiles that Graham was complaining about. But the complexities of global production networks are probably not that relevant for the 270,000 textile and apparel workers, about a quarter of the US workforce in these sectors, that lost their jobs in the space of two years (Barboza 2003).

US producer groups unsuccessfully filed complaints to the US government asking for emergency protection from imports from China in a number of areas – bed springs, iron pipes, clothes hangers, wheelchair seat lifts, brake drums and so on. The government also rejected a petition from the American Federation of Labour to impose sanctions because China's repression of labour rights contravened Section 301 of the US Trade Law. This latter case seems to suggest that politics in China is still important in Sino-US trade disputes. Similarly, in their evidence to support a case against Chinese steel imports, Price *et al* (2006: 56–7) cite the US Department of State's (2005) report on Human Rights in China in support of its case. According to this report, production in China was aided by the lack of 'comprehensive' legislation relating to child labour, non-payment of wages, violation of maximum working hour regulations, poor enforcement of health and safety regulations, and the use of harmful materials in production. Whilst not wishing to suggest that anybody involved was unconcerned about what was happening in China itself, at least as significant here is the price advantage that such abuses gives to Chinese producers, and the unfair position this places them in vis-à-vis their US competitors. For example, in a petition to President Bush asking for action against Chinese imports, the AFLCIO and the Industrial Union Council argued that more than 727,000 U.S. jobs had been lost as a direct result of labour abuses in China. If these labour abuses were halted, they argued that the price of Chinese manufactured goods would rise by 12 to 77 per cent.[21]

The annual theatre of the MFN vote may have gone, but China remains an important part of political discourses in the US, particularly but not only in an election year. Although, other foreign policy issues ultimately became much more important, relations and particularly economic relations with China did form part of the Democratic campaign's criticisms of George W. Bush in late 2003 and 2004. For example, in June 2004, John Kerry responded to a US–China Economic and Security Review Commission Report by criticising the Bush administration for not standing up to Chinese violations of international law – particularly in relation to currency manipulation.

> America has lost millions of manufacturing jobs. Just yesterday, we learned that the trade deficit hit a new record. As the trade deficit with China has ballooned, President Bush has stood on the sidelines. He has failed to do anything to effectively address China's predatory currency manipulation, its violation of intellectual property rights and other unfair trade practices that violate its international obligations.[22]

As Alden and Harding (2004) argue citing the pro-free trade Chris Nelson, 'the issues of job loss and outsourcing have a resonance now that they haven't had before. And the Democrats have linked China in the minds of voters to those things'.

Whether anything would really have changed in a Kerry administration is something that we will never know. George Bush was not the first President to be criticised by opponents over China policy. The Clinton administration was similarly castigated by Republicans for being soft on China and ignoring US economic interests, not least when Bush himself was campaigning for the Presidency. But at the very least, we can note that notwithstanding (and partly because of) China's WTO entry, Sino-US trade relations have not been depoliticised and there remains considerable opposition in the US to China's 'unfair' and/or 'illegal' trade practices.

External pressure to liberalise

The above mentioned disputes aren't just about punishing China; they are also very much intended to pressure the Chinese authorities to further liberalise. In some respects, this is now easier than before, as the WTO dispute resolution mechanisms create a formal legalised means for other countries to continue to push for further reform over and above 'normal' bilateral dialogue and rhetoric. Or perhaps more correctly, the threat of the former adds weight to the latter.

Perhaps even more than IPR abuses, China's exchange rate policy has been the biggest source of external pressure to reform, though here the significance of WTO membership is less clear. From 1994 until July 2005 the RMB was pegged to the Dollar, and subsequently pegged to a basket which added the Yen and the Won to the Dollar. The new system allows the RMB to fluctuate by a maximum of 0.3 per cent of its value every day, and during the first year of the new system, the RMB appreciated by 3.8 per cent against the Dollar (*People's Daily* 2006c). There are widely fluctuating estimations of what the real exchange rate should be and how to calculate alternatives in the absence of a real market (Goldstein 2004). Before the introduction of the basket, the lowest estimate was 15 per cent, and the highest 100 per cent (China Currency Coalition 2004: 19), with 40 per cent the most often cited level. But the statistical uncertainty is in large respect less important than the political reality that 46 trade unions and producers associations have come together to form the China Currency Coalition to lobby the US government for punitive action against China, and that the US government blames China's unfair currency manipulation for at least part of the record US trade deficit in 2005 (Balls and Swan 2006).

China has become an increasingly large market for imports from the US, the EU and Japan – particularly after WTO entry. For example, between 2000 and 2003, U.S. exports to the world decreased by 9 per cent, but exports to China increased by 76 per cent (Freeman 2004). Nevertheless, the size of the Chinese trade surplus with the most important powers in the global political economy, the desire to gain greater access to the Chinese market and frustration at the perceived slow pace of liberalisation in China all combine to ensure that external actors will continue to pressure the Chinese leadership for further changes in the foreseeable future.

Given the extent of these criticisms, it is perhaps surprising that more hasn't been done to pressure China for further reform. But we should remember that it is not just Chinese companies that have benefited from the Chinese trade regime. In fact, foreign investment generates far more Chinese exports than domestic investment. Although some producers in the US and elsewhere are losing money because of production in China, many others are making more money than before because they have moved their production to China – an issue (and its implications) that will now be covered in detail in Chapters 4 and 5.

4
Beyond Bilateralism: What the Statistics Don't Tell Us

As we have seen in the Introduction, the growth of the Chinese economy in general, and the growth of Chinese exports in particular, have led to a growing strand of literature assessing the shifting balance of power in the global political economy. But as also argued in the Introduction, considerations of power in the global political economy are often misguided because political analyses of economic relations still rely too strongly on conceptions of bilateral relations between nation states. By considering the nature of post-Fordist production and globalisation, different conceptions of the location of power emerge that are not necessarily territorially bound.

As such, this Chapter will place a particular emphasis on *globalised* production networks built on the linkage between FDI and trade. This is not to say that what we might call 'domestic trade' undertaken by Chinese enterprises and the 'internationalisation of China' (Zweig 2002) is unimportant – far from it. But trying to interpret China's position in the global political economy by just looking at bilateral relationships between national units provides, at best, only partial answers. So this Chapter attempts to go beyond the bilateral by disaggregating or de-nationalising (or perhaps even de-bilateralising) international investment and trade relationships.

To a large degree, the implications of this mode of analysis are left to the discussion of Chinese power in the global political economy in Chapter 5, and the negative domestic consequences of reform in Chapter 6. Underlying the analysis that will follow in these two chapters are two arguments that link back to the different conceptions of spaces that formed the last section of Chapter 2, and which are both based on the hypothesis that international economic integration can generate the fragmentation of the national economic space. The first is the idea that those parts of China that are heavily engaged in international economic relations now have more in common with the East Asian regional economic space than they do with the domestic Chinese economic space. The second also conceives of globalised production networks becoming disembodied from the national economic space. But rather than thinking in 'territorial' terms, places a greater emphasis on the role of non-state actors in 'commodity driven production networks' and 'contract manufacturing enterprises (CMEs)' that are either transnational or supranational in nature.

Interpreting the growth of trade

Lies, damn lies and statistics again

Interpreting the political significance of investment and trade figures is never easy. If we focus on bilateral relations between two national territories, then we will never be able to come to coherent conclusions, because global production increasingly involves more than two national jurisdictions. But while there are generic methodological issues, China presents a number of distinct complications.

First, there is the issue of trade fraud and smuggling. As Chinese producers can claim a 15 per cent VAT rebate for exports, there is an incentive for producers to overstate the value of exports, or even to totally fabricate exports and sell them at home instead. For example, in the first half of 2000, claims for export rebates claims increased by 185 per cent – a figure that was more than 4 times higher than the actual value of provincial exports (*Taipei Times* 2001). Conversely, much trade (usually imports) goes unreported because of smuggling. The highest profile case uncovered to date in Fujian Province suggest that between 1996 and the first half of 1999, provincial officials conspired to smuggle more than 4.5 million tons of refined oil, more than 450,000 tons of vegetable oil, more than three million cases of cigarettes, 3,588 automobiles and large amounts of raw materials for manufacturing Western medicines, chemicals, textiles, and electro-mechanical goods, with the total value of US$6.38 billion (*People's Daily* 2001a).[1]

Even more problematic is the continuing role of Hong Kong as a transit point for Chinese imports and exports, which makes studying bilateral figures all but useless in trying to determine the real importance of other states for Chinese trade. Hong Kong's position as a link between China and the world has declined slightly in recent years as trade has followed investment further north along the Chinese coast to Shanghai, Dalian and so on. Nevertheless, it remains a key element of China's trade regime – and a dominant element in Hong Kong's evolving position as a global city as the sheer fact that Hong Kong's trade to GDP rate is around 259 per cent perhaps indicates. According to statistics collected by the Hong Kong Customs and Excise Department, the value of Hong Kong's re-exports grew from US$535 billion US$13,270 billion in the decade before China's WTO entry – an average annual growth rate of 10 per cent.[2]

Thanks to the statistics collected in Hong Kong we do have some ability to disaggregate Chinese trade that passes through Hong Kong and work out the real direction of trade. According to Hong Kong customs statistics, the percentage of re-exports to imports in 2001 was 84.65 per cent, with the percentage for consumer goods reaching 105.01 per cent. Hanson and Feenstra (2001: 2) calculate that between 1988 and 1998, just over half of all Chinese exports were routed through Hong Kong. But even with the relatively sophisticated date available in Hong Kong, it is still difficult to get precise figures. For example, goods that are re-exported through Hong Kong from Taiwan often themselves originate in third countries, or are subsequently re-exported from Taiwan to other destinations. This issue is closely related to Taiwan's position in global production chains – a matter we will return to later in this Chapter.

There is the additional problem of calculating the value of that trade and the Chinese component of that value. A key issue is the extent to which goods in transit through Hong Kong are classified as Chinese re-exports or not. The goods should be counted as re-exports if nothing has happened whilst in Hong Kong that has 'changed permanently the shape, nature, form or utility of the basic materials used in manufacture'. Whilst this seems fairly clear (though a bit vague at the edges) it provides the basis for considerable bilateral friction over the extent of China's trade surplus as Chinese customs statistics value the goods as they leave China, and importers value the goods as they arrive at their market. Hong Kong's continuing position as a link between China and the world means that shipping and insurance costs, or minor additions such as packaging, can be added in Hong Kong without changing the status from a re-export to a Hong Kong export. Moreover, if a company in Hong Kong is acting as an intermediate in the production chain (more of this later) it might simply change the price of the good. For example, if the Hong Kong company has been contracted to produce at US$1 per item, but subcontracts to produce at 75 cents per item in China, then the price of the good increased in Hong Kong but it still counts as a Chinese re-export.

Such value added can be considerable. Hanson and Feenstra (2001: 2) calculate that the average value added whilst in Hong Kong was 24 per cent of the value of the good, accounting for 10 per cent of Hong Kong's GDP. Chinese researchers, however, have suggested that goods in transit through Hong Kong typically have around 40 per cent value added between leaving China and arriving at their final destination. In the case of toys and textiles, the subsequent value added even exceeds 100 per cent – a disparity which is largely a consequence of transportation costs from Hong Kong to the final market.

This is not just of statistical interest, as these statistics have been used to support one stance or the other in numerous disputes over Chinese trade policies (and in particular, the consequences of China's trade surplus). As Feenstra *et al* (1998: 1) noted:

> It is quite incredible that while the negotiations of China's accession to the World Trade Organization (WTO) are greatly influenced by the deficit that the United States runs in its trade with China, the actual size of the US–China bilateral trade deficit is not actually known!

For example, according to US official estimates, the US–China trade imbalance in 1998 was around US$57 billion while Chinese official data showed an imbalance of 'only' US$21 billion. 1998 is taken as the example year here as it was the year used by Feng and Liu (1999) to recalculated Sino-American trade by taking into account the difference between Free On Board (FOB) and Cost Insurance and Freight (CIF) prices, re-exports through Hong Kong, and smuggling. They concluded that the Sino-US trade imbalance in 1998 was around US$35 billion – almost (but not quite) half-way between the Chinese and American figures, which still leaves billions of dollars unaccounted for.

The headline figures

So with these caveats in mind, what can we say about the growth of Chinese trade? Perhaps most simply, in 1978 it was rare to find Chinese-made goods on sale in the West. China was not a major trading nation, and what it did trade in was overwhelmingly primary produce with other developing nations. From 1978–2005 China's 'Trade volume increased by 70 times, the share of trade in GDP increased five-fold, and the country's share in world trade increased from 0.8 per cent to 7.7 per cent' (Min Zhao 2006: 4) leaving China as the world's third biggest importer and exporter (merchandise trade).

Chinese exports are dominated by trade with OECD countries, with manufactured goods accounting for 90 per cent of these exports. Like many developing states, textiles, apparel and footwear for a long time dominated China's export profile, but more recently hi-tech exports – particularly in computer related industries – have taken an increasingly significant role.

As we have seen, calculating China's real direction of trade statistics is an imprecise science, but after factoring in re-exports through Hong Kong and assessing the time-period from 1996 to 2005, then we can say that *roughly* 30 per cent of all exports from China ended up in the USA, around 26 per cent in Japan, and around 16 per cent in the EU. Exports to these major markets account for almost all of China's overall trade surplus. Notably, China runs trade deficits with the rest of East Asia which supplies components used in the production of exports.

The investment-trade nexus

China became the second biggest recipient of FDI in the world after the United States in the 1990s, and FDI has grown more than 20-fold since the beginning of reform period. In 2002, China actually surpassed the US as the world's major recipient of non-stocks and shares FDI reaching US$60 billion in 2005. Cumulative FDI in China in the reform period exceeded US$620 billion at the start of 2006, and China accounts for something like 20 per cent of global FDI in developing countries.

Yet more statistical problems

As with the study of Chinese trade, there are a number of methodological problems in studying the politics of FDI in China. For example, there are two sets of figures for FDI – contracted and utilised. As contracted FDI may flow into China over a number of years – or not actually flow into China at all – using actually utilised FDI figures provides the best basis for year-on-year comparisons. Furthermore, it is generally accepted that FDI figures for China overstate the real extent of 'foreign' investment due to the significance of 'round tripping'. This refers to the process of domestic Chinese actors investing in Hong Kong (often through a shell company) to re-invest in China to take advantage of the preferential treatment offered to foreign investors that will be outlined below.[3] There is a considerable literature on the importance of round-tripping in FDI into China. But the very nature of the process makes it difficult to be exact about its extent. Both Lardy's (1995: 1067)

and Harrold and Lall's (1993: 24) studies put the figure at 25 per cent of all investment in 1992, while Huang (1998) comes up with a figure of 23 per cent for the same year, with two possible higher estimates of 36 and 49 per cent.
  More recent figures are even more difficult to find consensus over. Bhaskaran (2003) suggested a figure of around 25 per cent in his 2003 paper for Deutsche Bank, while Wu *et al* (2002: 102) argue that the figure is likely to be 'much higher':

> the Hong Kong-based Political and Economic Risk Consultancy (PERC) concluded in December 2001 that out of the US$100 billion FDI to China and Hong Kong in 2000, probably only US$36 billion were real FDI, with most of that going to China

The highest estimates for round tripping can be found in Indian sources, where there has been considerable debate as to why China has done so much better than India in attracting FDI. Subramanian (2002) suggests that the figure for round-tripping FDI in China is as high as 50 per cent of all FDI.[4] However, it seems likely that these figures are derived from a misreading of the World Bank (2002: 41) *Global Development Finance* report for 2002, which reported that 50 per cent of all FDI from Hong Kong into China was round-tripping investment, not 50 per cent of all investment. Nevertheless, the 50 per cent figure does tally with Geng Xiao's (2005: 21) top end estimates, although he considers a figure of 40 per cent to be more realistic.
  We also need to be aware of the rather opaque statistics on capital flight from China. Theoretically, the authorities can manipulate interest rates without concern for the level of rates elsewhere. Controls on currency transactions and lack of full convertibility mean that capital should not leave China simply because Chinese interest rates are lower than elsewhere. However, in practice this has proved not to be the case, and considerable amounts of money have flown out of China (Ding Jianping 1998, Wu and Tang 2000, Gunter 1996, 2004). In some cases, enterprises exploit rules and regulations – for example, manipulating the timing of inward and outward remittances and debt repayments to ensure that capital stays in higher yielding foreign accounts as long as possible. In other cases, individuals and enterprises simply act illegally – by making unauthorised outward investment, faking payment requests for expenses supposedly owed oversees,[5] faking import invoices to show higher prices than were actually paid, and through straightforward smuggling (Zhao Linghua 1999).

As this capital flight is illegal, it is not surprisingly impossible to come to firm conclusions about its significance. The high-point of such capital flight was from 1997–9, when speculation was rife about a possible devaluation of the RMB. Calculations of the extent of capital flight during this era range from a high of almost US$90 billion to a low of US$53 billion.[6] If we accept the lower figure, then this is still around 30 per cent of all capital inflows into China during the same period (CD 2002), while Yang and Tyers (2000: 5) suggest that there was a net outflow of capital from China from 1996–8 in the region of US$30 billion. Concern at the extent of capital flight 'when the stability of the yuan and hence, the credibility of the central government, was perceived to be in danger' resulted in the introduction of new restrictions on currency transactions in 1998 that appeared at first to stem the flow (Wu and Tang 2000: 63). But Gunter (2004: 74) argues that largely through mis-invoicing of trade, capital flight soon recommenced and even increased. Writing in 2004, he argued that 'accumulated PRC capital flight since 1984 is approximately US$923 billion with almost half of this total occurring in the last 5 years'. Whatever the true extent, the issue of capital flight shows that even in a relatively closed financial system with strong controls over currency flows and convertibility, China cannot act in isolation and simply ignore the wider international context (Yu Yongding 1999: 11).

So perhaps foreign investment has been less important for capital accumulation and growth than the headline figures seem to suggest. And perhaps illegal capital flight means that potential domestic sources of investment capital have instead been diverted elsewhere. Nevertheless, the importance of foreign investment as a source of Chinese economic growth, and in particular, export growth is still an extremely significant element of China's re-engagement with the global economy. And perhaps the biggest methodological problem of all is trying to identify where investment into China actually originates.

Type of investment

FDI into China takes two forms – market accessing investment and investment for export production. The latter dominates FDI into China, accounting for at least two-thirds of cumulative FDI. Initially at least, WTO entry did little to alter this imbalance – not least because the liberalisation of key domestic sectors did not take place overnight. It was not until after the 11th December 2004 deadline for liberalisation that foreign investment significantly increased in the banking, tourism, commerce, hospitals and education sectors. And even then, export based investment continued to outstrip market accessing investment. FIEs account for over half of all Chinese exports – 58.3 per cent in 2005. If we add domestic Chinese producers who produce under contract for export using foreign components, then close to 70 per cent of all of Chinese exports are made by or for foreign companies. Typically, the value added within China is relatively low in these export oriented FIEs which rely primarily on imported supplies – an issue that has important implications that are dealt with in detail in Chapter 5.

In 2005, there was a surge of US$12 billion worth of foreign capital into the financial services sector – figures that do not appear in Chinese FDI statistics, but which would count for around 20 per cent of the total if they did.[7] While banking, insurance and securities promises to be an increasingly important destination for FDI, it has historically been very low – not least because the Chinese authorities have previously passed legislation to make it difficult or impossible. Cumulative investment in the tertiary sector as a whole has accounted for around 24 to 28 per cent of the total, with investment in the primary sector for around 5 per cent. So unlike the experience of China's East Asian neighbours, the vast majority of money has been used to manufacture goods and very little to speculate on potential economic futures (though real estate investment is the main target of FDI in the tertiary sector). Within the manufacturing sector itself, the single biggest reason has been to produce textiles, apparel, footwear, toys, and electronic goods to export to other markets.

Initially, foreign investors were forced into working with Chinese partners in either Equity or Contract Joint Ventures (JVs).[8] At the end of 2005, around 65 per cent of cumulative FDI had taken the form of contractual or equity JVs with Chinese companies. However, WFOEs became increasingly popular in the 1990s, becoming the single largest form of new investment in 1998, and the dominant form (accounting for over half of contracted investment) in 2000. In 2005, WFOEs accounted for just over two thirds of the actually established new foreign investments, and 73 per cent of newly approved investments (at the expense of both equity and contractual joint ventures). It seems that one of the few reasons for investing in a JV is because of restrictions stipulated in the Catalogue (outlined in the previous Chapter) that insist on JV operations, and to discourage investors from choosing WFOEs wherever possible.

Determinants of investment

The determinants of FDI vary depending on whether investors are trying to access the Chinese market, or use China as an export production platform. For market-based investment, the main determinant is the size of the Chinese economy, and the prospects for future developments. While market-based investors can and do make profits in China, for the majority, the decision is whether the *potential* of China in the future is worth putting up with the current obstacles that prevent full and free access to the domestic economy. As the SmithKline Beecham company argued, 'China's size today is not the truly significant fact; it is what it could become that is important' (FAC 2000: appendix 27) – a potential that many in the business community hoped would be unlocked by China's entry into the WTO. According to the Worldwatch State of the world report, China's 'consumer class' encompassed around 240 million people, with 169 million in the market for at least some imported top brand names.[9] However, the sheer geographic size of China combined with an underdeveloped (though developing) infrastructure, makes it difficult (if not impossible) to produce in one part of China and expect to sell to the whole country. The soft drinks market is one area where foreign firms have emerged as leading players, and it is notable that Pepsi operates out of 13 different factories while Coca Cola has 24 bottling joint-ventures allowing them to have a truly national impact.

For export based investors, the determinants of investment are rather straightforward, and are divided into 'push' and 'pull' factors. The push factors are effectively the rising production costs (primarily labour and land) elsewhere, and particularly in other East Asian states. In addition, the importance of the US market for exporters meant that relative exchange rates and bypassing US quotas also acted as a push factor for Japanese exporters (Cumings 1987). In terms of pull factors, Gill (2000) argues that the capitalist global economy has a disciplining impact on policy makers. By this he means that the desire to attract and retain investment forces policy makers into adopting liberalising policies that suit the interests of private actors in the global political economy:

> disciplinary neo-liberalism is connected to what I call the three 'C's' of the power of capital. It involves the ways that public policy has been redefined so that governments seek to prove their credibility,

and the consistency of their policies according to the criterion of the confidence of investors

In addition to the legal changes and the changing ideational basis of Chinese polity outlined elsewhere in this book, we should note that the Chinese regulatory framework provides considerable incentives to attract investors – tax rebates for exporters, tax free status for imported components, quick customs clearance and so on.

More specifically, the literature on FDI emphasises a number of specific pull factors. The single most important is an abundant supply of cheap labour. For example, most of the Japanese textile industry has been moved to China, where average manufacturing wages are three per cent of comparable Japanese manufacturing wages (Coutts 2003: 2). The rapid surge of Korean FDI to China in 2003 was similarly typically explained by an average 90 per cent saving compared to Korean wages. Furthermore, once one producer moved, then others argue that they simply have to follow if they are going to stay competitive (Song Jung-a 2003). The UK shoe manufacturer, Doctor Martins, relocated its production from the UK to China, where workers got US$100 a month (plus accommodation) compared to US$1,960 in the UK, and also worked over 50 per cent longer each week (Roberts and Kynge 2003: 21). Labour costs in China are also lower than in many other exporting economies. On an index where US hourly wage rates equal 100, then average rates in Brazil and Mexico are 12 compared to just 3 in China (Banister 2005: 83). Average manufacturing wages in China were only 58 per cent of Thai wages in 2003 (Coutts 2003: 2) with only Vietnamese workers able to undercut their Chinese counterparts in most sectors (Tongzon 2005).

Start-up costs are low in China, and land is cheap and discounted. In addition, Cheng and Kwan (2000) point to the importance of a physical infrastructure that facilitates the quick and easy flow of components into China and finished goods out. In this respect, the Chinese government (both local and national) has spent huge amounts of money facilitating international economic interaction. Tseng and Zebregs (2002) also pointed to the importance of 'scale effects' – in essence, the greater the amount of investment, then the greater the confidence of others to invest. Jiang Xiaoyuan (2003) has also demonstrated how once a specific industry has been established in an area, then others will follow to take advantage of the existing support for that industry. What is particularly notable in the Chinese case is that such clustering is built not only on the type of industry, but also the nationality of the investor (ie: Taiwanese computer firms in Dongguan).[10] For Zhang Honglin (2002), while low labour costs are the main determinant of deciding whether to invest in China or not, the decision on where to invest in China is based more on cultural background and specific incentives offered by local governments rather than comparative wage rates within China.

Location of investment

Almost 90 per cent of cumulative FDI since 1978 has gone to China's coastal provinces. Statistics from the Ministry of Commerce show that FDI in Guangdong, Jiangsu and Shanghai alone accounted for roughly half the national total from 2000–5. Guangdong Province has been the single biggest recipient, though its share of investment has declined as more FDI has moved to other coastal areas such as Shanghai and Liaoning.

There is also uneven distribution within individual provinces. For example, 58 per cent of all FDI in Liaoning Province goes to Dalian Municipality, and within Guangdong Province, investment is heavily concentrated on the Pearl River Delta. Only four provinces (Shanghai, Jiangsu, Fujian, and Shandong – plus of course, Guangdong itself) received more FDI than Shenzhen alone. This uneven share of provincial FDI is also reflected in the uneven distribution of exports. Guangdong has accounted for around 44 per cent of FIE exports, Shanghai 12 and Jiangsu 11. Add on Fujian, Shandong, Tianjin, Liaoning and Zhejiang Provinces, and the coastal provinces account for 95 per cent of the national total.

One of the explanations for the importance of Guangdong, particularly in the early years of reform, was the migration of Hong Kong's manufacturing capacity across the border into China. As with the case of the migration of productive capacity across the US-Mexican border from San Diego to Tijuana, this process is often referred to as metropolitan or growth 'spillover' or 'extended metropolis' (Chia and Lee 1993: 236).

After the initial boom of investment into Guangdong, and notwithstanding its continuing importance, there has been an increasing spread of FDI to other parts of coastal China. There has been an explosion of different types of zones intended to attract foreign investment with different degrees of ability to provide concessions to attract investors.

Bonded and Free Trade Zones (13)

Often located around major seaports. Companies registered in bonded or 'free trade' zones are exempt from complex customs regulations and tariffs and value-added taxes; they also enjoy a series of preferential access to foreign exchange. It is only when goods, products, or raw materials enter non-bonded areas from the bonded zones that the transactions are classified as imports or exports, and customs duties and VAT are imposed. Particularly important in the processing trade as the speed of clearing customs etc for both imports and exports is much quicker than elsewhere. FIEs are generally subject to a 50 per cent reduction on enterprise income tax. Companies with a term of operation greater than 10 years are eligible for an income tax exemption for the first two profitable years followed by a 50 per cent reduction for the following three years.

Hainan Yangpu Economic and Technological Development Zone

Although officially one of the National level development zones (and most sources will give the figure as 35 to include Hainan), the Yangpu Zone is in the unique position of being a combined special zone, economic development zone, bonded zone, and port zone.

Economic and Technological Development Zones (34)

National level development zones established by State Council fiat to attract investment in nationally strategic areas. Designed to act as 'growth poles' for the national economy as a whole. These zones have received massive central government investment, particularly in infrastructure projects (and particularly the construction or upgrading of ports). The Zone authorities have the right to approve investment projects of up to US$30 million without approval from a higher authority. Many contain 'zones within zones' – special industrial parks for specific industries, areas with preferential incentives, or special zones for investment from specific countries. For example, the Fuzhou zone contains the Fuzhou Hi-tech Industrial Park, the Fuzhou Bonded Zone, and the Fuzhou Taiwan Merchant Investment Zone. The zones can also be experimental – for example, over 90 per cent enterprises in the Wenzhou development zone are private enterprises. Some zones specialize in specific industries or sectors (eg: automobile industry in Wuhan). The zones offer various fiscal incentives for investors.

Regional Development Zones (133)

Regional development zones are created by provincial or municipal governments, and offer a number of incentives for investors such as rebates on local taxes, waiving of fees for facilities for certain levels of investment, and so on. Incentives are usually differentiated for different types of investment based on factors such as size, if they take over loss-making domestic enterprises, local development strategy and so on. It is not uncommon for one city to have more than one such zone (Shanghai has nine), which often compete with each other as well as other province's zones for investment.

> *Border Economic Cooperation Zones (13)*
> Established by State Council fiat in 1992 (Erlianhaote in 1993) to facilitate cross-border trade eg: the Heihe Border Zone links Heihe City in Heilongjiang with Blagoveshchensk across the river in the Russian Federation. Primarily concerned with developing infrastructure to facilitate trade, though Erlianhaote Sino-Mongolia Zone has been designated a free-trade area.

Sources of investment

FDI from 'the west' has increased in recent years, not least since China's WTO entry – perhaps most notably from the EU and the US (around six per cent per annum increases for each. Nevertheless, a dominant theme throughout the literature on FDI in China is the significance of investment that comes from the rest of Asia in general, and from 'Chinese Asia' in particular. Houde and Lee (2000: 7) calculate that between 1993 and 1998, Hong Kong provided over half of all investment into China, Taiwan nearly 8 per cent, and Singapore around 4.5 per cent. Charles Wolf (2002: 134) takes ethnicity rather than nation state as the basis of analysis and calculates that 'two-thirds [of all investment has] come from 'overseas' Chinese, especially overseas Chinese in Taiwan, Hong Kong, and Southeast Asia.'. If we add in investment from Japan, then the cumulative figure for Asia as a whole rises to nearly 80 per cent, with Europe and North America each accounting for between seven and nine per cent depending on which figures are used.

Regional(ist) perspectives

Not surprisingly, the extent of Chinese and Asian investment in China, combined with the concomitant trade flows, has led many to deploy regional perspectives of economic integration – and quite rightly so. There are perhaps three major sub-groups within this literature. First, there is a strand of literature that emphasises the importance of links between Chinese expatriate businesses in the Chinese diaspora and investment into China. This literature concentrates on the 'bamboo networks' (Huntington 1996: 170, Weidenbaum and Hughes 1996) that link Chinese Family Businesses (CFBs) to China's growing international economic relations (Haley, Tan and Haley 1998). This literature was largely developed to explain to an American audience why US companies had faired relatively poorly in comparison to Asian companies in accessing China. The emphasis here is on cultural ties between ethnic Chinese across Asia and the Chinese 'homeland' – ties of loyalty and trust, cultural understanding, common language, and also closer ties with government officials than those afforded to non-Chinese. Furthermore, this network creates linkages between CFBs across the region (not just between the CFBs and China) expanding into trans-regional conglomerates (Rauch and Trindade 2002).

The second strand of literature emphasises the emergence of an integrated economy spanning national boundaries of 'Chinese' states – Macao, Hong Kong, Taiwan and the PRC. While Huntington (1996: 170) used the phrase 'Greater China and its co-prosperity sphere' to define this process, most analysts steer clear of the notion of co-prosperity (with its connotations of military power and colonisation related to the Japanese effort of the 1930s) and stick with 'Greater China'. Even then, the term 'Greater China' remains a contested one with no clearly accepted understanding. Not least, there is the question of whether this integrated economy includes all of China, or just those coastal provinces that dominate China's international economic relations. Even then, some argue that the low level of economic interaction between China's 'internationalised' provinces suggest that there is not a single region, but a number of overlapping sub or micro regions.

It is for this reason that Naughton's (1997) framework provides the most efficacious understanding of Greater China – primarily because he eschews a definitive definition and instead deploys a fluid multilevel approach. At the lowest level, there is a Greater China circle which covers the most intense level of integration – that between Hong Kong and the Pearl River Delta of Guangdong (which accounts for over half of all investment in the province). The second level of integration covers the most internationalised provinces of China (Guangdong and Fujian), Hong Kong and Taiwan. The highest level circle, which has yet to see full integration, could comprise of the three Chinese economies in total.

Naughton further avoids the flaw of isolating 'Chinese integration' from the East Asian regional economy as a whole. And it is the focus on East Asian regional integration that constitutes the third major subgroup within the literature that takes East Asian regionalisation as the focus of attention. Often building on Akamatsu's (1962) 'flying geese' model of regional economic integration,[11] these approaches are perhaps best summarised by Cumings' assertion in 1987 that:

> it is misleading to assess the industrialization pattern in any one of these countries: such an approach misses, through a fallacy of disag-

gregation, the fundamental unity and integrity of the regional effort in this century. (Cumings 1987: 46)

The model suggests that as the lead goose (Japan) develops, it will shed off outdated and unprofitable industries to neighbouring states with lower production costs. Rather than produce at home, they will produce overseas and import the finished goods back into the domestic economy. Thanks to the influx of investment, these lower cost states will subsequently develop to the point where they too shed off unprofitable industries to even lower cost states. The whole cycle then repeats itself eventually leading to development for all and regional economic integration built on investment and trade (Kwan 1994: 93).

It is the promise of development for all that makes the model such an attractive one – if not for academic analysts, then regional policy makers themselves. In this respect, it represents something like the promise of the trickle down theory writ large, and justifies the emphasis on low cost production for 'foreigners' for developing state elites in the region. The 'model' of Korean and Taiwanese development had a strong pull for other leaders in the region – most notably in China – and also for many of the developing states within ASEAN. Before the 1997 crises, liberalisation and the adoption of export oriented strategies appeared to be the blueprint for development and helped spawn the concept that this century would be 'the Pacific Century'. Furthermore, it provides an attractive justifying model for leaders in the core states (essentially Japan). Hatch (1998) argues that official enthusiasm for the flying geese model has become the quasi-official ideology of the Japanese government 'justifying Japan's ongoing role as the economic hegemon of Asia'.

The model might be appealing. It also 'attempts to introduce dynamism into traditional, otherwise static, trade theory' (Hatch 1998), and avoids some of the flaws of using simple bilateral trade and investment figures in considering the major external actors and interests in China's opening to the global economy. It is also true that rising production costs in Taiwan and South Korea, two of the original recipients of outward investment from Japan, did lead to a relocation of investment to lower cost production sites including China.

But the model is too simplistic, and contains three major flaws. First, it assumes that trade and investment is contained within the participating economies. For example, Kwan (1994) builds his model on country A shedding production to country B, and then re-importing the goods into the domestic market of country A. But the reality is that much of the production that is 'passed down' to lower cost sites is not to create re-imports into the investor country, but to generate re-exports to other markets – most notably, the United States. So although rising land and labour costs played important roles in generating outward investment from first Japan, and later, South Korea, Taiwan and Hong Kong, so too did comparative exchange rates with the US dollar. In an attempt to reduce the trade deficit with Japan, the US government negotiated an appreciation of the Japanese Yen against the dollar in the Plaza Accord of 1985. As this made Japanese exports less competitive, many producers moved to Taiwan and South Korea, not only because of lower production costs, but also to take advantage of their exchange rate relations with the US. However these currencies in their turn also subsequently appreciated against the dollar as a result of growing trade imbalances and American economic diplomacy (Funabashi 1988, Bernard 1991).

The second major flaw is that the model assumes that whole industries are passed down the chain from country to country. But in reality, Japanese companies have only shod the labour intensive (ie: not profitable in Japan) element of production, and kept the production of profitable high tech components, control over brand naming and marketing, and R&D, within Japan. For Bernard and Ravenhill (1995), Crone (1993) and perhaps most forcefully, Hatch and Yamamura (1996), while this process has generated growth in the region, it has also created asymmetric interdependence. So rather than creating a unified regional economy with development for all, the pattern of investment and trade has instead created asymmetric development and technological dependence on Japan.

Finally, the model assumes that individual economies will become developed and rich before investment moves on down the chain to the next developing goose. But while this might have been the case with development of the original NICs, it has not subsequently been the case for other developing states in South East Asia. What the model misses is the competitive nature of development in the region. Rather than wait for Malaysia, Thailand, Indonesia and others to develop before it was their turn for investment, Chinese authorities have competed with these developing states for the same investment to produce the same goods for export to the same markets.

Tax havens

Working out the real source of investment into China was always problematic given the complications of investment routed through

Hong Kong from elsewhere. From 1998 it became even more difficult as the share of investment from Latin America increased to exceed investment from North America and also from Europe. Almost all of this Latin American investment comes from the British Virgin Islands, (now the second largest investor in China) and the Cayman Islands (now eighth) and to a lesser extent the Bahamas. With Western Samoa as the tenth biggest investor in 2005, the obvious starting place for explaining this investment is in their fiscal regimes.

The very nature of this type of investment makes it difficult to know where it originates – particularly when combined with strong privacy laws. Wu *et al* (2002: 102) point to the significance of Hong Kong companies, noting that 'the number of companies in Hong Kong that are incorporated in Bermuda and the Cayman Islands jumped 5.2 times from 178 in 1990 to 924 in 2000'. Other data, supported by interviews in the region, emphasises the role of Taiwanese firms. Like their Hong Kong counterparts, Taiwanese firms do this to benefit from advantageous tax regimes. But they also face government restrictions on investment in the mainland, which incorporating in tax havens allows them to ignore. Even when governments place restrictions on the actions of non-state economic actors, there are many ways in which these restrictions can be bypassed. After China, the British Virgin Islands and Cayman Islands rank second and third respectively as the biggest recipients of Taiwanese outward investment. It is instructive that British Virgin Isles are now the largest source of inward investment into Taiwan itself. As foreign companies pay lower corporate tax rates in Taiwan than domestic firms, it appears that, as with China, there is considerable recycling of investment in Taiwan. This suggests that Asian investment in general, and that from Hong Kong and Taiwan in particular, is more significant than recent bilateral figures suggest. For example, official Chinese figures put investment from Taiwan at around US$48 billion in the decade to 2000. By comparison, Taiwanese officials came out with a figure of US$70 billion by including investment routed through third places (Roberts, Einhorn with Webb 2001), and using slightly different data, Smith (2002) suggests that by including investment from the tax havens, the real figure was in excess of US$100 billion.

While we can have a pretty good guess at where the investment is really coming from the truth is that we don't really know. So while Wu *et al* (2002: 102) can point to the growing number of Hong Kong companies operating via tax havens, they acknowledge that 'this is still a lower-bound estimate of the number of tax haven companies in Hong Kong because such data for the British Virgin Islands are unavailable'.

And while Smith (2002) can come to a rough estimate of how much investment has gone across the Taiwan Straits, 'the real level of Taiwanese investment in China is unknown'.

The de-territorialisation of production and investment

Regional perspectives are clearly important. China's insertion into the global economy owed much to extant process of regional integration based on the investment-trade nexus. And this insertion has had important consequences for other regional states. But there are two issues that we need to consider alongside these regional perspectives, relating to the use of the nation state as the unit of analysis. The first is the question of whether China is integrated, or only parts of China (defined either by geography or sector). This issue has important consequences for the way that we think about the implications of insertion into the global economy for China's domestic political economy, and will be dealt with in detail in Chapter 6.

The second is the extent to which analyses based on conceptions of bilateral relations between nation states/economies misses the salience of extra-regional dynamics and processes. Jack Hou (2002: 1) perhaps provides the most extreme interpretation of this approach:

Much like the tropical forests of the Amazon River Basin, Asia is almost a complete ecosystem economically speaking....Just as it is hopeless for any individual biologist to unravel the interdependencies of the Amazon ecosystem, it is impossible for any economists to fully characterize the multilateral trade/investment relationship between the Asian economies.

Just as the literature on Greater China can run the risk of ignoring the importance of other East Asian regional actors in 'Chinese' integration, so the literature on East Asian integration should avoid the flaw of ignoring extra-regional actors and interests. As Camilleri (2000: 101) argues:

The East Asian division of labour was the outcome of a competitive dynamic, whose logic becomes apparent when placed in the context of a rapidly globalizing world economy

This is not to deny the importance of regionalisation, but to suggest that regionalisation and globalisation are symbiotic processes, and that processes of regionalisation are themselves often dependent on global processes. In order to move towards a more complete understanding of the process and implications of China's insertion into the global political economy, we need to consider 'what is produced, how it is produced, and how the products are exchanged' (Engels 1970). In a world of post-Fordist production:

> capitalism today...entails the detailed disaggregation of stages of production and consumption across national boundaries, under the organizational structure of densely networked firms or enterprises'.
> (Gereffi, Korzeniewicz and Korzeniewicz 1994: 1)

OEM production and industry standards

Original Equipment Manufacturing (OEM) was first used to refer to companies that put their own brand name on components produced by another company under a special agreement with the original manufacturer. Thus, for example, Mitsumi is one of the world's biggest producers of CD-ROM drives, rewriters and drivers that are used by numerous PC manufacturers. Whilst original OEM producers tended not to use the name of their components suppliers in the products, the situation has changed in some areas with the establishment of industrial standard leaders. In the computer industry, Intel has established a reputation as producing the best processors, and individual PC makers want to advertise the fact that they are using Intel components as a guarantee of the quality of their machines. Indeed, without the Windows operating system and Intel processors, it is all but impossible to gain a foothold in the PC market. As such, Microsoft and Intel can effectively control access to the PC market without producing PCs themselves through control of industry standards – a phenomenon that has been dubbed 'Wintelism' (Borrus and Zysman 1997, 1998).

OEM production is particularly important in IT industries, and in the production of hi-tech consumer goods – the fastest growing area of investment into China, and of exports from China. Perhaps the most relevant example for this study is the Taiwanese computer industry. Borrus (1995), Borrus and Zysman (1997, 1998) and Sturgeon (1997) all argue to different degrees that the US electronics industry altered its global strategy in the 1990s in response to challenges from Asia. Rather than simply competing with Asian producers, they instead created networks with Asian producers. The US companies concentrated on developing the key components required for production through innovation, research and development and brand marketing, largely leaving the production of the computers themselves to companies in East Asia. They did not need to own these companies as control of industry standards in high-tech and high value added sections of the production process ensured their continued dominance and profitability.

Around 70 per cent of all computer related goods produced by Taiwanese firms are based on OEM contracts with foreign firms – almost all from the US and Japan (Sasuga 2004). These Taiwanese computer companies themselves have embraced this changing manufacturing structure and located themselves as key links in the production chain. At a 'higher' level, they sign OEM agreements to produce computers using foreign technology and operating platforms – almost entirely with Japanese and US companies. At a 'lower' level, they have outsourced the low-tech and low value added elements of production to maintain cost efficiency (Chen Chunlai 2002). Nearly three quarters of China's computer related products are produced by Taiwanese companies, which are themselves dependent on OEM contracts with Japanese and US companies (Sasuga 2004). As such, these Taiwanese invested factories in China represent the end stage of a production process that spans the most industrialised global economies such as the USA and Japan, intermediate states such as Taiwan, and developing states like China. Bilateral investment figures will show Taiwanese investment in China. As the key components are sourced outside China, usually in Taiwan and Singapore and often exported to China via Hong Kong, one set of trade figures will show a Chinese deficit with regional states and suggest intra-Asian and/or Greater China economic integration. But another set of trade figures will show Chinese exports to the major markets of the developed world, suggesting for some at least increased Chinese economic power in the global system.

Foreign indirect investment

Extra regional actors also have a disguised involvement in the Chinese economy as foreign indirect investment takes place through subsidiary offices within East Asia, and in particular in Hong Kong. This is particularly important in considering the importance of Japanese investment in China, which Cheung and Wong (2000) argue is massively underestimated because of the practice of investing in China via regional offices. For example, Sanyo's business operations in China are managed and invested through Sanyo's subsidiary companies located in Hong Kong. Although sorting through the statistics is an inexact science, Matsuzaki (1997) has estimated that about 80 per cent of Japanese FDI in Hong Kong is subsequently reinvested in Guangdong, appearing first as Japanese investment into Hong Kong, and subsequently as a Hong Kong investment into China.[12]

In 2005, Hong Kong was the host to 3,798 overseas companies' regional offices or headquarters. Although US companies are the largest representatives, Japanese companies come a close second (Hong Kong SAR Census and Statistics Department 2005). Of course, not all of these companies are in Hong Kong just to access China, and not all of them will be sources of 'Hong Kong' investment. But what we can say is that Hong Kong remains an important platform for third party investment into China which is not revealed by looking at the official investment statistics.

Sub-contracted investment

It becomes even more difficult to calculate the real extent of non-Chinese investment in China when we consider the extent of sub-contracted FDI. Here, third country investors do not invest in China either directly or through regional offices, but instead sub-contract production to investment and/or management companies within the East Asia region itself. Such investment has been a major element in non-Asian involvement in China in textiles, clothing and shoes, toys, and more recently, electronics.

For example, the Pou-Chen company (known as Bao Cheng in China) based in Taiwan produces 15 per cent of the world's sport shoes in its factories in China. But instead of bearing the Pou-Chen brand name, the shoes are made for Nike, Reebok, New Balance, Adidas, Timberland, Asics, Puma, Hi-Tec, Lotto, LA Gear, Mitre and others. Notably, Pou Chen has been increasing activities in Vietnam since 2000 in order to spread risk and to keep production prices down (Li Qiang 2002). Whilst Pou Chen is a special case given its global market share, consumers in the West can purchase goods across a range of areas which will carry a non-Asian brand name and the 'Made in China' stamp, but where bilateral figures will show an Asian investment in China. Another type of sub-contracting is where the third country company sub-contracts to a regional intermediary, which then produces in China on a contract basis. In these cases, no investment will be recorded as the transactions are on a processing fee basis, even further disguising the original investors' involvement in the Chinese economy. Major investment companies such as the Swire Group and the Jardine Matheson Group have long acted as intermediaries between China and the global economy. Perhaps less well known are the plethora of Hong Kong owned companies such as Li and Fung, which act as intermediaries in the global supply chain. More recently, Taiwanese companies have also developed such an intermediary role in accessing China through companies such as Pou-Chen, BenQ and Hon Hai Precision Industry (Luthje 2002).

There are three main reasons why these intermediary companies have established themselves as a link between foreign producers and China. First, Rodrik (1997: 46) has noted a tendency to sub-contract to countries with poor labour standards rather than invest there directly. This assertion is supported by interviews with what must remain an un-named intermediary company in Hong Kong. Certain US based companies, which again must remain un-named, use sub-contracting through Hong Kong because they feared that being associated with sweat-shop production would severely damage their image (and therefore sales) at home. They can genuinely argue that they don't invest in sweat-shops – but it does not necessarily mean that products carrying their brand names are not produced in sweat shops.

Second, the intermediary companies themselves market themselves as matchmakers with specialist expertise and specialist knowledge of China – technical, cultural and linguistic (Hanson and Feenstra 2001). But it is not just a matter of having the correct connections in China. Many of these intermediary companies take responsibility for the entire production process, and not just the manufacturing element in China. As global supply chain manufacturers, they need to convince investors that they can provide all the raw materials and components needed to produce the specified good to the standards set by the investor company.

This is partly because of the third reason – the flexibility it creates for 'demand-responsive reflexive' producers (Hamilton 1999: 60). In effect, this means that many companies don't want to run their own factories and employ permanent staff who will still want paying or redundancy payments if demand falls. Much easier to let the burden of employment fall on others instead, particularly if they are operating in economies with rather laxer employment conditions. An increasing number of major multinational companies simply do not produce anything themselves anymore. As Chen Chunlai notes (2002: 251):

> Many brand marketers .... tend to concentrate their core competencies on brand-name resources and R&D, whilst outsourcing the remainder of the value chain. As a result, former vertically integrated multinationals are increasingly becoming hollowed-out corporations.[13]

They are variously referred to as 'manufacturers without factories' (Hamilton and Waters 1995), 'turn-key production networks' (Sturgeon 1997), 'global flagship networks' (Ernst 2001) and 'virtual corporations' (Davidow and Malone 1992).[14] Although different approaches point to different features, they share a basic understanding that Fordist production process based on horizontal integration have given way to vertical integration between core companies and their production affiliates, suppliers and sub-contractors. Notably, this vertical integration takes place across national boundaries, with different stages of the production process located in the most financially advantageous location.

The production process is often no longer controlled by the core company at all. Rather than operate through formal affiliates, production is placed in the hands of specialised companies. This is not a new phenomenon – major sportswear companies such as Nike have long been corporations without factories. But Luthje (2002) argues that it is becoming ever more significant in global production, particularly in the IT industry. He points to the growing significance of five major CMEs of North American origin which lay a pivotal role in the production of consumer electronics – Solectron, Flextronics, SCI, and Jabil Circuits from the USA, and Celestica from Canada. As Chen Chunlai (2002: 251) notes:

> unlike the more traditional manufacturers and multinationals, [CMEs] do not make their own brand-name products, instead deploying global networks with fast-response capabilities to provide production and other (mainly logistics) services to brand marketers.

As China has become the 'world's outsourcer of first resort' (Roach 2002), it has become engaged in this global division of production – typically at the low tech and low value added processing stage. But although the major CMEs are North American in origin, they typically operate in China through regional affiliates. Singapore Flextronics, for example, invests in China on behalf of Microsoft, Motorola, Dell, Palm and Sony Erickson. In all these cases, the 'Made in China' brand will appear on the good – a good which carries a non-Chinese brand name, but the investment and trade figures will show inter-Asian trade and investment.

Implications: globalised production and national based perspectives

The most obvious implication of the importance of de-territorialised globalised production for this study is that it is simply not possible to make meaningful generalisations by simply analysing bilateral investment figures. When considering Chinese trade figures, the flaws of taking simple bilateral approaches have long been accepted due to the role of Hong Kong as a link between China and the global economy. But assessments of investment still largely accept the figures and build their analysis on bilateral data. What this Chapter hopefully shows is that such bilateralism overemphasises the significance of 'Chinese' investment in China, and underplays the role of extra regional actors – and extra-'Chinese' and/or Asian actors in particular.

The prima facie evidence suggests that US companies have been much more engaged with the Chinese economy than the investment and trade figures suggest – albeit through third party actors. The evidence also suggests that Japanese companies have been even more important than might appear at first sight. But a logical conclusion is that it is almost impossible to gauge the full extent of this involvement due to the fragmented nature of production and investment. Virtually the only way of being sure is to trace the production processes involved for each specific good – a task that is likely to defeat all but the most fanatical academic.

If the role of extra regional actors is greater than most analyses suggest, where does this leave those understandings that emphasise culture and the linkages between different Chinese populations in China's global re-engagement? While investment based on ties of cultural loyalty might have been important in the early period of China's opening, the cultural dimension now plays something of a mediating role between China and the global economy. Witness, for example, the way that CMEs in Hong Kong and Taiwan deliberately market themselves as having the knowledge and the contacts – the *guanxi* – that are so important for doing business in China (and which are dealt with in slightly more detail in Chapter 6).

We also need to take care not to construct 'closed' conceptions of regional interaction. Economic integration based on investment and trade is taking place between China (more correctly, coastal China), Hong Kong and Taiwan. But this Greater China regional integration is largely predicated on wider processes, actors and interests. Economic integration in East Asia beyond Greater China is also taking place, and the regional economy is being restructured by Chinese growth, but again these processes are largely dependent on external markets, and the production strategies of external companies (Breslin 2004). It is not a case of the East Asian regional economy rising as a challenge to the US as some would suggest, but rather a case of US economic actors being inextricably interlinked with the regional economy itself.

It also suggests that the locus of power in the global political economy may not have shifted as far as it appears at first sight. Investment from Japan, the US and Europe is an important driver of Chinese export growth, and the above analysis suggests that it is ultimately even more important than what blunt bilateral figures suggest. Much of this investment is predicated on demand from the same three markets. As such, the key issue to be addressed in the following chapter, is whether China has the economic power that some suggest, whether more power is located in advanced industrial economies than the rise of China suggests, or whether nation states are where power is located in the first place.

5
Interpreting Chinese 'Power' in the Global Political Economy

In Chapter 1, I argued that conceptions of Chinese power vary depending on what approaches are deployed to studying China. Approaches that emphasise the importance of commodity driven production networks like the previous Chapter will generate very different conclusions from those that instead focus on states as the unit of interaction, and states as the unit of analysis. Where you are writing from (or for) appears to be an important determinant of conclusions. This is partly because different analytical approaches dominate in different parts of the world – but that is not the only reason. Within East Asia, the growth of the Chinese economy has already had a profound impact on both the structure of the regional political economy, and on the developmental trajectories of individual regional states. The significance of China is clear and present (though whether significance equates to power is a different matter), and the final section of this Chapter will discuss how China's re-engagement with the global economy has helped reconfigure the East Asian regional economy (and the economies of individual regional states as well).

The conception of China as a threat is also much more evident in the US than it is in Europe, and the majority of the literature predicting a future Chinese superpower challenging US power emerges from writers based in the US, largely intended to influence US policy makers. So before going on to question the basis of many understandings of Chinese economic power, the Chapter begins by considering the debates over whether to engage or to contain China – a debate that still persists (particularly in the US) despite the conviction of many observers that this dichotomous debate has become obsolete.

Coping with Chinese power? To engage or contain

In discussing why this was the case with colleague based in the US, they replied that Europeans have yet to fully understand the real challenge that China poses. Maybe so, but I contend that there are two other important considerations. The first is that the vote over whether to extend MFN to China discussed in detail in Chapter 3 provided an annual focus for considering China's position – both real and potential – that had no corollary in Europe. The second relates to conceptions of the nature of US rather than Chinese power. Perhaps the reason that there appears to be greater concern in the US about the rise of China is that nobody else has the ability to do anything about China's rise. For example, when the UK Foreign Affairs Committee (FAC) debated UK relations with China in 2000, the debate over whether to engage or contain China was a non-debate. There was an acceptance that 'Our influence can only be at the margins (FAC 2000: para 108)', and that the UK simply did not have the ability to have any considerable impact on what happened in China. It was not a case of engaging or containing, but how best to engage to benefit UK commercial interests in China and to have some influence on the gradual evolution of 'positive' social and political change in China.

Why engage?

UK policy towards China conforms with the broad engagement approach that is at the heart of most countries' contemporary China policies. To varying degrees, five broad justifications are deployed to defend engagement (or for justifying why there is little point in pressing China too hard on domestic political reform). First, there is the cultural argument that China really is different and should be judged against different standards of government and governance. For cultural relativists, the emphasis is on the different philosophical, cultural and historical contexts of China and the West. For material relativists, China is still a very poor developing country where socio-economic rights must take the priority over political rights for some time to come. Providing basic standards of living and maintaining stability is all that we can expect from a country like China at the moment.[1] Perhaps not surprisingly, this is an argument that is often proposed by the Chinese authorities themselves.

Second, there is an argument that rather than weakening China's authoritarian leadership, 'megaphone diplomacy and grand gestures' (FAC 2000: Section 76) will instead strengthen it. Nationalism has replaced socialism as the de facto legitimating ideology of the CCP, and containment strategies give it the opportunity to play up to its nationalist constituency – to portray an aggressive West attempting to stop China from developing and attaining its rightful place in the world. Nor is this just an issue of elite manipulation of popular opinion. If anything, the Chinese leadership struggles to keep a lid on popular anti-western nationalism, as epitomised by the popularity of a number of nationalist books in recent years railing against the West in general (and American hegemony in particular).

Third, there is the argument that the growth of the Chinese economy means that it is simply too important an opportunity to miss. Part of the job of diplomacy always has been to promote national economic interests, and the commercial opportunities that China's rise offer means that it is in the best interests of governments to do what they can to help promote domestic commercial interests. This is an issue of such importance that it will be dealt with in detail later in this Chapter.

Fourth, there is the liberal approach that engaging China is the best way of gradually promoting positive political and social changes in China towards the ultimate goal of liberal democracy. Rather than external actors pushing for direct change, this approach instead sees the international context as creating a domestic Chinese environment that will generate pressures for change. This is achieved by a slow process of locking China in to a system of international norms via a dense network of international interactions. As Wang and Deng (1999: 7) put it:

> International enmeshment facilitates China's social learning in terms of the values, norms and principles, and rules of the international system and adds China's stakes in the existing institutions and order. China's worldview and definition of national interests can be transformed toward greater compatibility with the rest of the world through transnational activities and networks, including tourism, academic and cultural exchanges, and commercial ties.

An understanding that was often asserted in the run up to China's WTO entry in 2001.

Fifth, there is the argument that whether we like it or not, we have to deal with the China that we have. China is effectively too big and too important to be contained (or to risk a containment policy). It has the world's largest population, a large and growing economy, it is a nuclear power, and a major contributor to global environmental issues. China also has one of the permanent seats on the International Labour Organisation board, and of course is a permanent member of the UN Security Council. As such, we have an interest for our own security in managing China's global role through engagement (Kristof 2003).

Why contain?

For sceptics, while there is evidence that engaging China results in economic gains for the engagers, there is no evidence at all this is resulting in 'positive' political and social change within China itself. On the contrary, representatives from the Free Tibet Campaign and Amnesty International have argued that the human rights situation in China had severely deteriorated in the late 1990s, just as China's international economic engagement took on a new momentum (FAC 2000: questions 181–223). US Republican Senator Frank Wolf (2003) has similarly argued that 'since PNTR has passed, there is even more evidence about China's gross human rights violations [and] religious persecution'.[2] These arguments support de Bary's (1997) less than approving definition of constructive engagement as 'doing business with China while sidelining human rights (and getting little in return from the People's Republic for this gesture of restraint)'.

There remains a group of writers who suggest that the West should be doing all that it can to contain China and prevent its rise. For proponents of this view, the West (which usually means the US) has no interest in speeding along the rise of the Chinese superpower by drawing it into international society. Rather, the US should be building a strategic alliance with Japan in an attempt to contain China, and promote India's development as an alternative pole to Chinese power in Asia. At the very least, China's engagement must be accompanied by significant concessions by the Chinese in return for anything given to them by the West (such as market access). Proponents of this view are often those same people who predict the inevitable rise of China and the inevitable conflict with the US noted at the beginning of the introduction to this book.

A redundant debate?

Kagan (2005) has added a sixth reason why pushing China to reform is at best pointless. He argues that 'the idea that we can manage China's rise is comforting because it gives us a sense of control and mastery, and of paternalistic superiority'. The lesson of history is this will not be possible, and 'we need to understand that the nature of China's rise will be determined largely by the Chinese and not by us'. Kagan's position suggests that the debate over whether to engage or contain China is pointless because there is nothing we can do. From a different position, Australian Foreign Minister Alexander Downer (1997) suggested even before China's WTO entry that China is already so 'deeply engaged' to make the debate 'irrelevant'.

While most observers seem to agree with one or other of these reasons (or a combination of them) for making the dichotomous debate redundant, it has not been put to rest. As we saw in the introduction, new books continue to be published calling for something to be done to stop China before it's too late to stop military conflict (Menges 2005, Babbin and Timperlake 2006). For people like Frank Wolf (2003) the West should not be engaging 'a brutal regime' but using whatever means possible to force change. Worse still, by engaging China economically, and facilitating the growth of the Chinese economy through international economic relations, the US and the West in general might actually be strengthening the power of the authoritarian CCP leadership. The debate is still ongoing in the US administration, with officials like Robert Zoellick urging further engagement in opposition to Rumsfeld's tendency towards pushing containment. Paul Wolfowitz who served as George W Bush's Deputy Secretary of Defence, had earlier compared China's rise to Germany's, noting that the former's sense of grievance at mistreatment by Japan and the West is even deeper than German dissatisfaction, and it was up to the US to prevent a future world conflict by

> using our current position of unprecedented strength and influence – not single-handedly, but within the framework of our impressive and equally unprecedented set of alliances – to affect the shape of the world (Wolfowitz 1997: 8).

Wolf's comments were made as part of an unsuccessful campaign to revoke the China's PNTR status in 2003. A similar petition was made by Byron Dorgan and Lindsey Graham in 2006, pointing to the growth of the US trade deficit with China from US$83 billion in 2001 to US$202 billion in 2005. According to Dorgan:

> The Chinese have engaged in labor abuses, intellectual property theft and piracy, currency manipulation, and unfair barriers against U.S. exports. Americans cannot, and should not be asked to, compete under these circumstances[3]

Understandings of the nature of China's economic power, then, and its impact on the US – though not just the US – are crucial for determining not just how China is perceived, but for how policy towards China should be formulated.

The nature of Chinese economic power

This book is primarily concerned with China's global economic role, and does not cover China's military threat in any detail at all. But it would be remiss to not even mention the argument that the rise of China as an economic power will facilitate the expansion of China's military capabilities. Military modernisation requires finances, and, if new equipment is to be bought from overseas, hard currency (Christensen 2006: 96). While the Chinese fiscal machinery remains relatively inefficient in capturing the benefits of economic growth to fund central government initiatives, China's insertion into the global economy has increased the finances available for military modernisation. There is still a very long way to go before China has a military force that has the command and communications infrastructure and the other hi tech means of modern warfare to provide a credible challenge to existing global military powers. But the strategy of locating increasing numbers of mid-range ballistic missiles in the Nanjing Military Region across the straits from Taiwan points to an area where economic reform and growth – and not least growth generated by insertion into the global economy – has resulted in an increased ability to project military power should China's political leaders deem it necessary.

Resource security and diplomacy

More important for this study is the extent to which the international economic order is being influenced by Chinese economic growth. What happens in the Chinese economy already has a significant impact on the global economy as a whole. Heilig (1999) asked 'Can China feed itself' – and although the final conclusion was, 'yes', it was only yes if a number of key policy changes were implemented. Even then, population growth, urbanisation, changing dietary preferences and declining yields as a result of chronic environmental degradation suggest increasing Chinese demand for agricultural goods that will have an impact on global prices (Smil 2004) – for Brown (1995) in the (very) long term, China's agricultural prices will become the world's agricultural prices.

In the longer term, the demand for oil and other raw material could be even more significant with competition over access to energy resources threatening to destabilise East Asia (Calder 1997). China became a net importer of oil in 1993 and overtook Japan to come second only to the US in the league table of oil importers in 2003, with consumption of 6.5 million barrels per day – roughly double the 1993 figure. Just under half of all oil consumption was imported in 2005, and according to the US Energy Information Administration, increased demand from China accounted for about 40 per cent of the increase in global demand from 2001–4 and was the main cause of increased oil prices.[4] We should note, however, that Chinese sources claim that the China factor is over-exaggerated, pointing to the relationship between supply and prices, and noting that oil prices reached a new record high of US$70 a barrel in 2005 – a year in which Chinese oil imports actually decreased (Fu Jing 2006). Chinese demand for other materials has similarly increased, impacting on not just the distribution, but also the price of key commodities. For example, in 2004, world steel prices rose dramatically, largely as a result of increased Chinese imports. At the same time, the decision to cut coke exports and to retain coke for domestic use in the steel industry, led to coke prices rising from US$120 a ton in 2003 to US$450 a ton in 2004.

Whilst these analyses point to the importance and significance of Chinese economic growth for the global political economy, the relationship between significance and power is not clear cut. From a Chinese viewpoint, it is difficult to see where the power actually is – China might have the ability to increase global prices, but as Chinese importers have to pay these higher prices, it's hardly a beneficial power if it's a power at all. Looking from the inside out, China is not powerful, but at best vulnerable and at worst, weak. The issue of energy security become increasingly important for Chinese policy makers in the 1990s (Zha Daojiong 1999, Downs 2000: Chapter 3), even before the Iraq invasion highlighted the relationship between energy and more traditionally defined concepts of security (Wang Zhengyi 2004). At the time of writing, China sourced over half of its imports from Organisation of the Petroleum Exporting Countries (OPEC) countries, and nearly two thirds of all oil imports pass through the Straits of Malacca.

But external observers note that notwithstanding these insecurities, the ability of other states to guarantee their own energy security in the long term is being undermined by the speed at which Chinese companies are buying control of supplies across the world. In addition, when China National Offshore Oil Corporation tried to buy the US gas and oil company Unocal in 2005, it was not just national pride that concerned many in the US. There was also a feeling that the free market was being distorted by a state owned company with access to cheap loans provided for political more than economic reasons, and underwritten by the state which frequently writes off the bad debts of strategic companies. The fact that a Chinese company was trying to take over a US company in a strategic industry might have been enough on its own to rouse sufficient protests to stop the transaction – the claims that Chinese companies don't adhere to the rules of free market competition was merely an added irritation.

Nor are external observers simply concerned with economic implications. Another key issue is the extent to which the international *political* order is being influenced by Chinese economic growth. The dominant concern in the short to medium term is China's position within the Asian region, and the impact of Chinese growth on the regional order will be dealt with in detail below. But beyond regional relations, there is unease that the search for energy and other raw material supplies will provide another means by which Chinese interests will come to dominate global agendas, challenging the global initiatives of the US (Ebel 2005). It is not just Chinese commercial relations with the Middle East and the states of the former Soviet Union that are important – though the long term implications for access to energy resources clearly are – but that new consensuses and even alliances will emerge that alter the strategic balance of power. Alliances that are partly built on the need to establish warm political relations to facilitate economic objectives, but also partly built on a shared concern about US power in the unipolar global order, and a shared opposition to the dominance of dominant norms and values.

If anything, this challenge to the existing political order is even more apparent in the renewed emphasis on building relations with African and Latin American states. Again, commercial interests are driving this process, with oil alone accounting for around 60 per cent of Chinese imports from Africa.[5] Both are also becoming important markets for those Chinese exports that fail to find buyers in the more lucrative markets of the West and there is some concern that cheap Chinese imports will swamp domestic markets and drive local producers out of business. Chinese companies are also winning government contracts in these regions that they would probably not be in contention for in other parts of the world. In addition, both regions have also become important destinations for Chinese outward investment with Latin America accounting for nearly half of the total in 2004 (Jiang Wenran 2006: 3). The vast majority of this investment is to be used to buy into energy related companies (particularly in Latin America) and the trend is likely to be ever upwards in the future.

When Chinese officials seek to establish economic ties with African and Latin American states, they bring with them no political condition-alities to economic relations relating to democratisation and improved human rights. This new Chinese resource diplomacy, then, provides an alternative economic partner with no political strings attached for mar-ginalised states (such as Zimbabwe) and those that reluctantly respond to US political initiatives because of economic dependence, providing a new challenge to the hegemon's attempts to construct a global liberal order that serves the US national interest (Zweig and Bi 2005).

As will be discussed shortly, the way that China has re-engaged with the global economy has had a huge impact on the rest of East Asia, and on the political economy of the region as a whole. However, whilst the US remains the dominant economic partner for both regions, it is in the realm of relations with what used to be called the Third World that China may well come to be even more significant in the coming years though increased trade and investment relationships. China may not be a direct threat to the existing powers in the global political eco-nomy, but its growing importance for Latin America and Africa could provide an important indirect challenge.

Market power

In developing his conception of the 'new constitutionalism' Gill argues that the US government uses the structural power of the size of its market to force change on other countries while not reciprocating with corresponding liberalisation of the US economy in order to benefit US based economic interests. As noted in Chapter 3, this conception in part explains why Chinese elites wanted to join the WTO, and also why Chinese negotiators accepted the terms on which entry was approved. The structural power of the US market (in terms of market access) certainly appears to have trumped the structure power of the Chinese market in WTO entry negotiations. Here, the question is whether we can think in terms of the Chinese market having structural power, even if it is less structural power than markets elsewhere.

The idea of the China market has influenced attitudes and policy towards China for many years. The delegation sent by King George III to China at the end of the 18th century to establish freer trade was in part to extract resources from China, but also in part to access what was even then a potentially lucrative and closed economy. Over two centuries later, the lure of tapping the 'last untapped market on earth' (Studwell 2003) remains an important consideration for policy makers – not least because the Chinese authorities' ability to ration access to the Chinese market has certainly provided a powerful bargaining tool in dealing with individual companies and countries. As we have seen in Chapter 3, even after China's WTO entry, many foreign companies still find their ambitions in China thwarted by the interventions of Chinese officials at both the national and local level.

The growth of the domestic Chinese economy has been important in securing new markets and profits for some companies. But as noted in Chapter 4, it is what the Chinese economy might become – its potential – that still dominates much commercial consideration and government policy. When President Clinton thought about not renewing MFN as he had suggested during his campaign, 300 corporate leaders asked the President not to obstruct the 'large potential benefits' (Bernstein and Dicker 1994: 44–5) of extending MFN to China in 1993 (Roden 2000: 87). Similarly, in the Parliamentary report on UK relations with China in 2000, submissions from individual business groups and business organisations typically pointed that government support was essential to help UK companies tap the potential of the Chinese market (FAC 2000)

> A good bilateral relationship at the political level is very important for doing business in China – and probably more important in the case of China than most other countries, simply because the role of the state and the government is so big.[6]

In the US case, if MFN were not to be renewed, then US companies would not be eligible for export credit and investment guarantees from the US government. For major corporations like Boeing, Chrysler, and General Motors, these guarantees were essential for their growing relationship with China. Given that EU states in particular were perceived as being less interested in Human Rights in China than developing commercial contacts, if the US took a moral stance, then US companies would simply lose out to their European competitors. In the UK case, in discussing whether UK policy disadvantages UK companies at the expense of European competitors, James Richards on behalf of Rolls Royce argued that:

> What is important for us, given the extremely competitive nature of the market in China and the fact that export credits are available for

our competitors, is that we should be no worse off, that we should receive equivalent treatment, because without it our business in China would certainly be undermined.[7]

In addition, there is the argument that the perceived nationality of a foreign company can influence market access depending on the Chinese authorities' perceptions of the 'home' country's political relationship with China. For example, when the US imposed trade sanctions on China as a result of the transfer of military technology to Pakistan, the Chinese aviation authorities switched from purchasing Boeing jets to the European Airbus – much to the annoyance of US authorities who felt that Europe should have held a common position with the US, rather than exploiting the situation for commercial benefit. There was also a strong belief in some quarters that UK companies failed to get contracts in China as a result of wrangles over the Hong Kong hand-over and the Chris Patten reforms.

The converse side is that if political relationships are warm between China and another national government, then private commercial interests associated with that country might benefit. This has led to concern that the potential of the market, and the need to help nationally based companies succeed in China, has resulted in wider change in diplomatic policy towards China. In the US, the extension of MFN to China under Clinton was similarly taken as a sign that commercial interests had led to the President abandoning his campaign pledge to link MFN to political and social change within China.

The UK parliamentary report was in large part commissioned because of fears that the UK government had decided to draw back on criticisms of China's human rights regime and had moved away from an ethical foreign policy in an attempt to help UK companies win contracts in China. In particular, there was considerable unease in the UK after Jiang Zemin's state visit to the UK in October 1999. Having been met by demonstrators in a visit to Switzerland in March 1999, Jiang Zemin criticised the Swiss leadership for failing to have a grip on its own country and was reported to have stated that Switzerland had lost a friend. On the UK visit, during which US$3.5 billion worth of commercial deals were signed, demonstrators were kept well away from the Chinese delegation through a massive police presence.

So in these respects, the Chinese market does appear to have structural power in the suggestion that diplomatic policy towards China is influenced by commercial decisions based on the need to secure competitive market access. Or more correctly, it is not the Chinese market as such, but a vision that has been constructed of what the Chinese market might become. So to a large extent, this vision of a future China impacts on the diplomatic initiatives of other countries towards China. As Cobbold and Bristow argued

> the perception in the West, that China provides a business opportunity which should not be missed, has given China more international leverage than it merits .... less attention should be paid by the Government to the optimistic predictions favoured by the business community and some government departments about China's future potential, and more to the statistics, the problems that China faces with its economy, its relative ability to influence developments internationally (FAC 2000: para 114).

Finance and production

China is also conceived as having the power to distort global finances. For example, at the end of 2005, China had US$8193 billion worth of foreign currency reserves – double the 2003 figure and second only to Japan (and this was after US$45 billion was spent on recapitalising state banks). Whilst this figure is noteworthy in itself, what China does with these reserves is even more significant. By buying US treasury bonds, China (and Japan) are effectively helping fund the US debt. Thus, there is a fear that the Chinese authorities hold the US economic fate in their hands. Should they suddenly sell all of these bonds, then economic logic suggests that this would lead to a rise in US interest rates, throwing US economic planning into turmoil. As Philip Segal (2003) says, China has the power to 'crash the US government bond market'.

But as Segal goes on to point out, while China might have the ability to cause a crash, a crash in the US would have a devastating impact on Chinese economic growth. With export growth the main engine of overall growth, and exports to the US a significant proportion of this growth, then triggering higher interest rates and currency realignment in the US and the rest of the developed world would have a disastrous impact on China's own economic fortunes. The theoretical power that is in the hands of Chinese financial elites remains largely constrained by domestic political considerations. Furthermore, Yu Yongding (2006) argues that such high foreign currency reserves not only act as a massive Chinese subsidy to the US every year, but also make it difficult for the Chinese government to control its own monetary policy.

Perhaps more important in terms of power over international finances is the Chinese government's ability to divert financial resources away from other developing states. For Huang (2003), the amount of FDI that has flooded into China should not be taken as a sign of Chinese power, but rather a sign of weakness reflecting the inability of domestic institutions to ration and distribute finances rationally for all the reasons which are outlined in Chapter 2 of this book. The focus here is not so much on the internal factors that Huang has dealt with in detail, but rather the extent to which the type of policies deployed to attract investment that were outlined in Chapter 3 translate into power over finance and production.

One of the oft used characteristics of a hegemon is dominance in a leading technological or economic sector. Hale and Hale (2003) have argued that China is 'leading the way' in key economic sectors, most notably textiles and more recently computer related equipment. But as the analysis in Chapter 4 suggests, and as Hale and Hale acknowledge, China's rise is very much dependent on external factors. The Chinese economy remains largely dependent on external demand and external supply of investment capital. If we think of those sectors where the 'Made in China' stamp is now commonplace throughout the world, then it is largely corporate decisions driven by understandings of market behaviour in core economies that have propelled Chinese exports.

China's export growth: who gets what?

The low level of value added in foreign invested export enterprises (briefly noted in the previous chapter) is the starting point for thinking about who benefits most from China's export growth, and what this means for understanding of Chinese productive power. 1998 was the first year that the value of exports from FIEs actually surpassed the value of their imports – though this is a very rough indicator as it includes all imports, not just those used to produce exports. Since then, imports as a percentage of exports found a level of sorts in the high 80s. For example, in 2005, the value of FIE imports was 87.2 per cent of the value of exports accounting for 58.5 per cent of total Chinese trade – and notably, both increased faster than the growth on 'domestic' imports and exports.[8] Imported components remain particularly important in hi-tech industries, which are the fastest growing export sectors with a particularly striking growth of FDI in computer related manufacturing for export. Only three of the top 20 FIE exporters are not in electronic related manufacturing. Although more of the supply chain is being located within China, the overwhelming majority of foreign producers in China continue to source their hi-tech components overseas – primarily from South East Asia, Taiwan and Japan but also from the US. For CMEs trying to attract contracts, emphasising the ability to produce at low cost in China is important; but so too is emphasising the ability to source high quality and reliable components from outside China. In addition, Lemoine and Unal-Kesenci (2004) note that the increased use of local content in FIEs is largely explained by FIEs sourcing from other FIEs in China rather than from domestically owned companies. They are trading more with each other than they are with the domestic economy.

The high value of import costs can partly be explained by transfer pricing. Despite considerable liberalisation, many foreign companies still face problems in repatriating profits made in China due to incomplete currency convertibility and the imposition of myriad ad hoc charges on the profits of FIEs. Furthermore, foreign investors would prefer to locate their profits in more fiscally advantageous localities – as one investor in the textile industry put it 'I don't want to make my profits in China – I want to make them in Hong Kong'.[9] Thus, many investors locate as much of their profits as possible in operations outside China by overcharging for imported components supplied by factories in other countries, usually routed through Hong Kong:

> there's no incentive for these exporting enterprises to leave any profit inside China. That means multinational corporations will buy from their Chinese factories at a price just enough to cover the cost and have all the profits assigned to their distribution companies elsewhere that have a much lower income-tax rate (CD 2004)

There is considerable concern within China at the loss of fiscal income through transfer pricing. Since the publication of the first comprehensive set of laws governing transfer pricing in 1998 (Circular 59), responsibility for investigating cases falls largely in the hands of the Anti-Tax Avoidance Division of the State Administration of Taxation. A further set of regulations was issued in 2004 (Circular 70), not so much because the original regulations were ineffective, but more because they had not widely been enforced. This was partly because of the low level of resources available – less than 3,000 personnel for the whole of the country dedicated to investigating tax avoidance issues, with the real job of on the ground supervision left to local tax bureau (Shu Wei 2004a). It is also partly because of lack of enforcement at this local level, where local authorities frequently decided to ignore the legal position so as not to discourage existing and potential investors (Shu Wei 2004b). As a result, further regulations issued in 2004 (Circular 143) moved the responsibility for investigating transfer pricing up from the county level to city level organisations (Shu Wei, 2004c). Nevertheless, whilst this has moved the chain of command higher, enforcement of government regulations is still largely dependent on local officials who do not have a particularly good track record in fully implementing central regulations across a wide range of policy issues.

Even taking transfer pricing into account, it is still a reality that much of China's export growth is driven not only by external demand and external supply of finances, but also by external supply of components and materials. It is also a reality that FIEs and those domestically invested companies producing for foreign buyers (and of course, Chinese workers) get remarkably little of the final price of the finished good. Jin Bei's (1997) research team found that in the mid 1990s, only three to four per cent of the retail value of shirts produced for Pierre Cardin went to the Chinese manufacturer in contract fees. A decade later, a *People's Daily* (2005c) report suggested that for each dollar paid for Chinese made designer clothes in the US, on average the Chinese manufacturers receive a mere 10 cents. Moreover, while average wages are increasing in China, there is evidence to suggest that the purchasing power of large companies like Wal-Mart combined with oversupply in China are actually driving down costs in some factories (and forcing some Chinese managers to break labour laws to produce on time and at price).[10] Fuller (2006) reports that the average profit margin for Chinese shoe and apparel producers has dropped from 10 per cent of their sell on price to about five per cent over the decade to 2006.

The fact that most of the benefits of FIE exports lie outside China is not lost on the Chinese leadership – particularly at times of increased tension with foreign partners over the size and implications of China's trade surplus. In 1997, the State Council (1997) produced a White Paper 'On Sino-US Trade Balance' using the example of Barbie Dolls to explain how the US deficit with China was really a deficit with region.[11] It is also an excellent example of how US based companies play a key role in promoting regional economic integration, and the extent to which the US trade deficit with China is in part at least generated by US companies.

At the time, individual Barbie dolls retailed in the US at around US$10 each, even though the unit import cost of each was a mere

US$2. Trade figures thus showed a US$2 export from China to the US (and a US$2 trade deficit with China). However, the raw materials for the plastics were imported into Taiwan from the Middle East, and the hair similarly exported to Taiwan from Japan. The goods were semi-finished in Taiwan, and only then exported to China by the Taiwanese sub-contractor for the final stages of production. The real value to the Chinese economy was a mere 35 cents, with the remainder of the US$2 either already accounted for in production costs outside China (65 cents) or in transportation costs (US$1).

Jin Bei (1997) argues that these goods should not be considered to be Chinese exports produced by 'the national industry' but 'para-domestically manufactured goods' that should be labelled and accounted in a different manner from real Chinese exports. Bilateral trade figures that only look at one stage of the relationship only show one part of a much longer chain of relations. For example, there was a sharp increase in investment from South Korea in 2003 which resulted in China accounting for roughly half of all Korean FDI (almost all of it in manufacturing industries). It also resulted in a 50 per cent increase in South Korean exports to China, surpassing the USA as South Korea's biggest trade partner for the first time (Brooke 2004). The rise in exports was partly a result of increased steel demand in China, but it was primarily a direct consequence of the growth of Korean investors sourcing their supplies from domestic Korean companies.

So these Korean exports to China along with exports from elsewhere in the region are largely disguised exports to Japan, the EU, and the US (where most of the finally assembled goods end up). Conversely, the US trade deficit with China is largely a disguised deficit with the region as a whole, and not just with China. Ross (1997: 48) noted that while the US trade deficit with China had increased between 1988 and 1997, the overall US deficit with Asia as a whole had not grown consider-ably.[12] What we see instead is China acting as the manufacturing conduit through which the regional deficit is processed (Hale and Hale 2003).

For Takashi, Hirofumi and Rüffer (2002: 3), 'Japanese exports to East Asia 'cause' significant inter-regional trade and ultimately exports to the US by East Asia'. As the Barbie example shows, so too have US com-panies generated inter-regional trade within East Asia in the supply chain, and ultimately Chinese exports to the US. So the loss of some of the manufacturing jobs in the US and some of the growing trade deficit with China is down to US companies. How much is not clear. The Chinese Foreign Minister, Li Zhaoxing (2003) suggested that 'more than half of the Chinese exports to the US are produced by foreign-funded enterprises in China, mostly US companies'. Wal-Mart alone imports 10 per cent of all Chinese imports to the US – equivalent in country terms to being China's fifth biggest export market.[13] But this does not include the forms of indirect investment through CMEs and intermediaries in Hong Kong and Taiwan outlined in the previous chapter, so the importance of the investment and production decisions of US companies in generating Chinese exports to the US will be even greater.

Nor do these figures include those domestically Chinese-funded enterprises that produce for single buyers – and in many ways rightly so. But in choosing to buy from China, rather than from domestic producers or from existing suppliers elsewhere, it is in the corporate strategy of major US companies that we find at least part of the reason for the growth of Chinese exports. It also leads us back to the question of who benefits most. One of the points of Li Zhaoxing's (2003) speech was that US consumers benefit hugely from the growth of Chinese exports in the form of continued low prices, and often lower in actual rather than just real prices compared to five years before. According to Morgan Stanley, buying US rather than Chinese made goods in 2005 would have increased prices by 0.5 per cent in 2005, and buying Chinese had saved US consumers US$600 billion in the preceding decade – more than China had received in FDI over the same period.[14] But Li's main emphasis was on the benefits accruing to not just the brand-owning producers, but to wholesalers, retailers, advertisers and so on that keep 90 per cent of the cost of designer clothes made in China (see also Fuller 2006).

National level analyses and globalised realities

Perhaps the first thing we should do in light of the discussion above is to return to the conclusion from the previous chapter and re-emphasise how problematic it is to draw political conclusions from bilateral investment and trade figures. Bilateral figures simply do not and cannot tell us anything about the realities of complex chains of relationships that characterise production in many sectors today. National level perspectives are also problematic in thinking of who gains (and who gains most). Competition from China is really resulting in job losses in the US, but it is often US companies that are reaping the rewards of China's growth through lower costs and increased profits, US consumers that benefit through lower costs, and share holders (including those with pension funds) in the west who benefit from increased corporate profitability.

The above section has focused on trade with and investment from the US. This is partly because of the importance of the US as an economic partner for China, but mainly because this is where most of the debate actually takes place. Nevertheless, the same comments could be made of China's investment and trade relations with other countries and regions. It is notable that when China's textile export quota with the EU for 2005 was met before half of the year was out, major retailers facing the possibility of empty shelves or more expensive replacements were at the fore of pressure to come to a quick agreement. Like their US counterparts, many Japanese workers have lost their jobs as Japanese companies increase profits by moving production (particularly in the textiles and apparel industries) to China. Many companies in Hong Kong and Taiwan have found new niches as intermediaries between China and the global economy whilst political leaders express concern about their economies becoming hollowed out and their increasing dependence on China (discussed in more detail below). Focusing on the nation state as the unit of analysis when it comes to considering competition, who wins and who loses, misses the point that it depends on which groups you are looking at within individual nation states.

The concept of China being the regional 'engine of growth' has become all but a mantra in analyses of East Asia. But China is not the engine of growth. It is a platform for production, but the real engine(s) are elsewhere. Investment into China and trade with China is driven by demand in Japan, Europe and most importantly, the US. While deliberations in China over whether or not to raise interest rates are important for regional investors and traders, what the Federal Reserve does in the US is ultimately more important in terms of regional trade and investment flows.

Globalised production, states and markets

So in many respects, economic power lies in the hands of non state actors in de-territorialised transnational production networks. But they do not act in isolation from political authorities, and Chinese state actors clearly had a crucial role in creating an economic environment that attracts such investment, often at the expense of other regional economies. It is not a matter of asking whether states or markets have power, but how they interact with each other.

If we think in terms of the state as a unitary actor rationally pursuing the national interest in a game of mercantilist competition, then it is difficult to reconcile an understanding of state power with notions of power located in transnational production networks. But if we think of the state as representing a sub-set of interests in the domestic sphere – either from a liberal or neo-Gramscian perspective – then the connection is much easier to make. Neoliberalism – as promoted by purposive state actors and international organisations – does not just exist in a political void. It is predicated on political and ideological preferences and, if not promoted by, certainly facilitated by the decisions of governments and international organisations (which also represent a subset of interests at the global level).

National and local governments across the world have implemented numerous policy initiatives to facilitate increased transnational economic relationships that have created the environment within which non-state actors can manoeuvre. For example, while Susan Strange (1996: 44–5) asserted that transnational corporations (TNCs) were key actors in the promotion of globalised production, she argued that:

> this has not happened entirely by accident. The shift from state authority to market authority has been in large part the result of state policies. It was not that the TNCs stole or purloined power from the government of states. It was handed to them on a plate – and, moreover, for 'reasons of state'

Strange went on to argue that even the US government could not contain the forces that it unleashed, and that even the world's most powerful government finds its actions constrained by the actions of TNCs. But this should not obscure the fact that the original liberalisation of the economic structure was based on political choice and decisions of governments that served the interests of a subset of national actors.

Strange's analysis was largely based on considerations of advanced industrialised economies, and particularly of the US and the UK. In this respect, we can perhaps think in terms of state actions that precipitated or initiated globalising forces. In the Chinese case, we can think in terms of recipients of globalising forces. The emphasis on economic performance as a key basis of legitimacy outline in Chapter 2 placed an emphasis on rapid capital accumulation. As with many other state developing countries, the best way of ensuring this rapid capital accumulation and economic growth increasingly came to be seen as insertion into the capitalist global economy. There is an ideational acceptance, albeit not necessarily explicitly stated, that dependence on the capitalist global economy is the best or at least the quickest way of promoting economic growth.

Locating parts of the Chinese economy as a low cost manufacturing site in global production chains might be a strange sort of power – particularly as it seems to entail the CCP overseeing what it once would have described as the exploitation of Chinese workers. It is a strategy that also requires state policies to be adapted to meet the requirements of largely external non-state economic actors. As such, 'Chinese' power here is shared with – perhaps better to say contingent on – the power of TNCs in the capitalist global political economy.

Reconfiguring the East Asian regional economy

Of all the different policies initiated to attract investment and to promote Chinese exports, perhaps the most widely debated is government manipulation of comparative exchange rates. As noted in Chapter 3, post WTO entry, complaints about the maintenance of currency controls have been a key source of Sino-US trade friction. But debates over the significance of currency manipulation far predates WTO entry, and for some observers the 1994 devaluation of the RMB was a pivotal moment in the reorganisation of the East Asian regional economy. For example, Makin (1997) and Bergsten (1997) both argue that it was the starting point for economic problems in many regional states that resulted in the financial crises. Devaluation made exporting from China so attractive that labour intensive production moved to China resulting in the ASEAN states losing out in the key US and Japanese export markets (Holst and Weiss 2004: 1256).

This is a contested analysis with Fernald, Edison and Loungani (1998: 2–3) and Wu *et al* (2002) finding no statistical evidence to support the case. But focusing on the region as a whole or even individual countries might be misguided. The Japan External Trade Organisation has disaggregated overall figures and analysed individual products. And these figures show that on a good by good basis, the rise in exports from China to the US and Japan of each commodity corresponds with a decline in exports of the same goods to the same markets from Malaysia, Thailand, Indonesia and the Philippines prior to 1997 (Hughes 1999).

China may not have caused the crisis, but the actions of Chinese elites certainly created a changed economic environment that other regional states had to (and perhaps failed to) respond to. In terms of Chinese power, perhaps the clearest and most immediate consequence of the way in which globalising state bureaucrats (Sklair 1995) have inserted China into the global economy is the reconfiguration of the regional economy. As in Latin America and Africa, there is some concern in the region that Chinese producer will gain a foothold in the region, undercutting domestic producers and potentially destroying some domestic sectors (Voon 1998). However, the biggest concerns relate to competition for investment to produce exports, and the idea that what once might have gone to Malaysia or Thailand or Indonesia is instead going to China, diverting not just finances but also jobs away from the region (Snitwongse 2003: 38).

> China is grabbing much of the new foreign investment in Asia, leaving its once-glittering neighbors – Thailand, South Korea, Singapore – with crumbs... Some Asian officials say they fear that Southeast Asia will be relegated to the role of supplier of food and raw materials to China in exchange for cheap manufactured goods (*New York Times* 2002)[15]

Much of what has been done in China has been inspired by the previous success of other regional states in attracting investment and promoting export-based growth. So ironically, those 'same historical forces' that helped generate growth in the region are now threatening growth in the region (Felker 2003: 255). Late developing states are now faced with an even later developer with even lower costs eroding their comparative advantage.

The investment-trade nexus in Asia is not a zero-sum game. However even those analysts who argue that the China threat to other regional states is exaggerated accept that what has happened in China has led to the diversion of investment and therefore trade (Wu *et al* 2002). Furthermore, its not just what China has done, but what China might do. China's entry into the WTO might have been greeted with optimism by those seeking to access the Chinese market, but was greeted with concern in the region that this might only further increase the diversion of investment from Southeast Asia to China (Braunstein and Epstein 2002: 2).

In reality, the impact of China on the region varies by country, and by types of economic activity within individual countries. Those who occupy 'higher' levels in the production chain in terms of technology, finances and services have been the main beneficiaries of China's rise (and WTO entry). By contrast, the closer a state's export profile approximates that of China, the greater the impact of Chinese growth (Kawai and Bhattasali 2001). Within these countries, workers will suffer in those areas where China increasingly has a price advantage in the key markets of the US, Japan and Europe. The textile and apparel sectors in the region have been hit hardest by Chinese growth, and are predicted to continue to suffer in the future (Ianchovichina, Sethaput and Min 2004). The challenge is most severe in the Philippines and Indonesia. To compound the problem, the jobs under threat in the Philippines are overwhelmingly in low skill sectors, where the new opportunities offered by China's rise require skilled workers, making an easy transition from one type of employed activity to another highly unlikely (Ianchovichina, Sethaput and Min 2004: 71). Felker (2003: 280) notes that the reduction in investment to ASEAN nations between 1996 and 2001 is almost all explained by what happened in Indonesia. Clearly, domestic issues in Indonesia did much to reduce its attractiveness for investors, but the concomitant attraction of China also played its part. Nearly a quarter of Indonesian exports are 'at risk' from Chinese competition (Ianchovichina, Sethaput and Min 2004: 69), and again the transition from competing with China to occupying a different level of the value chain seems unlikely.

Other regional states have begun to change the domestic economic structure and become a supplier to China rather than just a competitor. While Thai exports to the EU, Japan and the US have effectively 'stagnated' and 'labor-intensive manufactured exports shrunk', exports to China have increased – perhaps most notably of 'technology-intensive products' used in Chinese export oriented industries (World Bank 2003). Malaysian exports to China are also increasingly dominated by electrical components, chemicals, machinery parts, and petroleum and Indonesia's by processed oil and rubber – all materials or components that are in high demand in China's export oriented industries

So the implications of China's growth in part varies country by country based on relative levels of development. It also varies on a sector by sector and class basis. The biggest overall impact might be on Indonesia and the Philippines, but the jobs lost by workers in Japan, Hong Kong and South Korea as companies have moved production to China are just as real. And even where countries lose in aggregate terms, some companies and individuals have maintained if not increased market share and profits by moving production to China.

Of course, the national perspective remains important as it is the leaders who have to deal with the differential impact on a national level. The fact that companies in developed Asia are making profits from producing in China does not alter the fact that the domestic economy has become 'hollowed out', contributing to an economic recession and growing unemployment (Hornik 2002, Takeo 2002, Song

Jung-a 2003). While economic concerns loom large in most of the region, they are combined with political fears in Taiwan, where there is a real worry that economic dependence on the mainland will increase China's ability to force its will on Taiwan in political spheres. In an attempt to reduce this dependence, in 1993, Taiwan's economic minister, Chiang Pin-Kung announced a 'Go South' policy to encourage investors to look at South East Asia rather than China. A similar policy called 'No Haste, Be Patient' was introduced in 1996 in an attempt to slow the rate of investment on the mainland. Neither of these strategies have had a significant influence on the flow of investment from Taiwan to the PRC – quite simply because as with Hong Kong and Japan, producing in China makes more economic sense than either producing at home, or in other regional states.

The regional perspective also remains important (it's just that it should not be the only level of analysis). What has happened in China has already fundamentally altered production, investment and trade patterns in East Asia (even if the power to do this is not all 'China's'), and will continue to do so in the future. The regional dimension is also important in the form of the formal institutionalised relationship that China has developed with ASEAN, and the potential for further region building initiatives in the future.

China and East Asian regionalism

The increasingly proactive position towards fostering warmer regional relations and building functioning regional institutions reflects an important sea change in Chinese policy. This is partly because of the increasing emphasis placed on securing economic security outlined in Chapter 1, and the resulting recognition that working together to head off potential crises at a regional level is increasingly seen as being in China's own self-interest (Fewsmith 1999, Zha Daojiong 1999) – especially if such regional cooperation can mitigate the need to rely on the US dominated global financial institutions in times of crisis. In addition, ASEAN is no longer seen as necessarily a danger to China or Southeast Asia necessarily as an offshoot of US foreign policy. Shambaugh (2004: 67–8) points to the lack of condemnation from East Asian states (with the exception of Japan) to the Tiananmen killings as a key turning point in changing China's leaders' perceptions. Rather than acting as a regional branch of US foreign policy, ASEAN as an organisation and individual ASEAN state leaders instead decided to engage China at a time when international isolation was a real possibility.

Chinese 'monetary diplomacy' in the 1990s was also well received, further cementing the idea that engaging the region could well work to China's advantage – not just economically, but in classic realist conceptions of power balancing and the national interest. At worst, the region might be neutralised as a potential ally of the US hegemon – at best it might become part of an emerging alternative pole defending or even promoting a different set of values under Chinese leadership (Hund 2003, Cheng 2004). Furthermore, Chinese engagement could act to neutralise the potential of Japanese regional leadership (Desker 2004: 13). At a time when there was considerable discontent in the region against the terms of bailout conditions from the US dominated international financial institutions, and a feeling that this was in someway 'pay-back time' for Asia's previous economic success (Higgott 1998), there was ample space for a Chinese 'charm offensive' in Southeast Asia (Lautard 1999). Actually, simply not doing anything was enough to garner China significant goodwill. As a result of the rapid depreciation of many regional currencies, Chinese exports lost some of the price advantage that had been gained by the 1994 RMB devaluation sparking fears that China might devalue again and plunge the rest of the region into a further spiral of financial chaos. Not devaluing won considerable (and in many respects excessive) praise and helped promote the idea that China was a responsible economic actor. Snitwongse (2003: 38) also notes that

When it set up a bail-out fund and came to the assistance of the countries, such as Thailand, that were most affected by the 1997 economic crisis, China garnered the lion's share of appreciation from those countries – despite the fact that Japan provided them with significantly more money.

The monetary diplomacy of the late 1990s has been followed up by further attempts to engage the region. For example, China signed a 'Declaration on the Conduct of Parties in the South China Sea' in 2002,[16] and joined the ASEAN Treaty of Amity and Co-operation in Southeast Asia in 2003 while the 'Peaceful Rise of China' hypothesis first aired by Zheng Bijian at the 2003 Bo'ao Forum for Asia provides the theoretical justification of the continued charm offensive. China has shown that it is not only a force for peace and stability in the region, but the region as a whole can also benefit from the economic spillovers of Chinese growth. Far from being the threat to regional economic stability that some argued China's rise had already become in

1997, China's rise is the guarantee of regional economic stability and development:

> China's Peaceful Rise will further open its economy so that its population can serve as a growing market for the rest of the world, thus providing increased opportunities for – rather than posing a threat to – the international community (Zheng Bijian 2005: 24)

China's peaceful rise will benefit the world, but the rest of the region will benefit most (Ahn 2004).

A former Chinese diplomat in the region argues that increasing willingness to promote region wide bodies reflects China's transition to becoming a 'normal' state – a state that pursues its interests through dialogue and cooperation based on accepted norms, rather than through unilateral action based on a rejection of such norms. Others prefer to talk in terms of China deploying its 'soft power' to ensure regional dominance at the expense of the US and Japan (Nye 2005, Kurlantzick 2006). As 'normal states' also exercise 'soft power the two are not necessarily contradictory understandings, but while the former suggests a peaceful future, the latter carries (implicit at least) warnings of new challenges to come.

Although Kurlantzick (2006: 5) argues that the 'ASEAN-China free trade agreement, [is] possible only because of the appeal of China as an economic model', the real explanation seems to lie elsewhere. Ramo (2004) argues that China's leaders don't really need to try to persuade – China's sheer size and rapid growth simply means that others have no choice but to fall in line with their policy preferences. Heartfield (2005: 197) similarly uses a 'self-interested' argument suggesting that China's rise has been 'widely welcomed' because it has at least taken the sting out of the regional impact of recession in Japan. Shambaugh (2004/5: 76) adds a little liberal theory to this pragmatism by claiming that the best way of dealing with China 'is to entangle the dragon in as many ways as possible'.

Even though there is disagreement over why the relationship is developing, there is a growing consensus that a closer relationship with China is all but an inevitable component of ASEANs future. This shared conception of the integrated nature of the East Asian economy is reflected in the already increasingly institutionalised nature of relations within the East Asian region of production. For example, ASEAN Plus Three (APT) meetings have created a formal process through which China joins with Japan and South Korea in dialogue and consultation with ASEAN. China is also a participant in the Chiang Mai Initiative which allows signatory states to borrow US dollars from other members' reserves to buy their own currency in the event of 1997 style speculative attacks.

China has embraced moves beyond financial regionalism towards trade based regionalism in the proposals to create an ASEAN-China Free Trade Area (ACFTA). First proposed at the Manila summit in 1999, the ACFTA initiative took on a new impetus with the signing of the Framework Agreement on ASEAN-China Comprehensive Economic Cooperation at the Eighth ASEAN Summit Meeting in Cambodia in 2002. ACFTA is conceived as a dual speed process, with initial common tariff reduction to be completed by 2006, and a full free trade area in place by 2013, intended to act as a spur to intra-regional investment and to increase access to the Chinese market for ASEAN producers – though the other side of the same coin is a fear that it might also lead to a new influx of Chinese imports.

The focus on China perhaps underestimates the residual significance of Japan as both a regional actor and a determinant of future developments in regional institutions and organisations (Stubbs 2002, Hennock 2001). Neither should we forget the importance of extra-regional economies in facilitating economic integration in East Asia, suggesting that regional elites will have to take the opinions of elites in the US and elsewhere very seriously if they move towards a more formal regional grouping. But this short discussion of China's engagement with Southeast Asia (and vice versa) nevertheless points to a growing self-awareness within China of China's importance to the region. Notwithstanding the argument that Chinese power is still overstated, and the danger of overlooking the power of TNCs and other extra regional actors in promoting Chinese growth, it also reflects the recognition in Southeast Asia that:

> China still looms very large over Asia, and is a global economic force to be reckoned with. ASEAN will have to engage China both as a competitor and a partner – an intricate relationship that has to be managed prudently (Wu *et al* 2002: 110).

6
The Domestic Context: Stretching the Social Fabric?

China's insertion into the global economy has brought a tremendous transformation to the domestic economy. Annual average growth rates of around 8 per cent would have been unattainable without the FDI-trade linkage, it has created jobs, and those areas engaged in export production have the highest per capita GNP rates. It may be true that imported components are still a major part of foreign invested exports, but nevertheless, FDI has upgraded skills, raised factor productivity, increased technology transfer and encouraged reform of domestic Chinese industries (Houde and Lee 2000). In this light, it's perhaps not surprising that the word 'miracle' has frequently followed the words 'Chinese economic' in numerous press reports and commentaries in recent years.

But as noted in Chapter 1, the vision of a vibrant economy with miraculous growth sits uneasily with many of those who study the domestic situation in China – not least researchers and policy analysts within China itself. Whilst acknowledging that economic reform and participation in the global economy has raised the living standards of millions of Chinese, there is a strand of literature that points to the many economic problems that still need to be resolved. For example, Fan Gang (2002: 3), one of the best known Chinese economists outside China notes that:

> One of the characteristics of China, then, is that there is a plurality of problems. China is both a developing country and a transitional economy and the problems of both categories are interwoven and mutually restricting, making them very complicated. All this, together with a population of 1.3 billion and a vast territory, has easily made China no. 1 in the world in terms of bad debts, unemployment, the

number of laidoff workers, and probably also the income gap problem – one of the worst, if not the worst, in the world. As one comes to realize the difficulty of China's problems, it becomes evident that they cannot be solved in a short period of time

At the heart of Fan Gang's analysis is the concept of a double transition – the fact that the industrial revolution and the transition from a largely rural-agricultural economy is occurring not so much alongside, but as a key part of, the transition from a socialist state-planned and owned economy. Or perhaps put another way, it is not just that the largely rural-agricultural base of the economy is changing, but that the old urban-industrial economy is also changing – is being *'unmade'* – to allow that transition to occur. Furthermore, the creation of a capitalist market economy is occurring at a more rapid pace than was the case in either Europe or America, and on a scale that has never been seen before.[1] Take the economic dislocations associated with the transition from socialism in the former Soviet Union and Eastern Europe; add them to (or perhaps multiply them by) the economic dislocations associated with urbanisation and the industrial revolution in, for example, Great Britain; multiply them by a factor that takes into account the size of China (in more than one way) and it is not surprising that reform has generated economic and social dislocations that will not be easily resolved.

That China has many problems, then, and that they are not swiftly resolvable is something that should not surprise us. As the extent of these problems is already well known for students of domestic Chinese politics, economics and society, I did consider whether there was any point in repeating them here. This uncertainty was compounded by Zheng Shiping's (2003: 51) warning that:

> Laundry-listing many dangers that the Chinese regime is facing without spelling out how these dangers might be turned into opportunities gives the mistaken impression that the current regime in China is nearing collapse. Given so many serious crises, however, one needs to wonder why it hasn't collapsed already

and Guo Baogang's (2003: 2) assertion that such a focus on the negatives 'underestimates the ability of the regime to stay in power, and the ability of the CCP to adapt to the changing political environment'.

All that is written below should be read with these words of caution in mind. Nevertheless, I think it is important to acknowledge the extent of economic, social and political problems in this chapter for four main reasons. First, as noted in the introduction, outside the Chinese studies community the extent of these problems is not particularly well known. Even though there are accounts of these dislocations in the media, the dominant discourse – supported by many policy related publications – is of China's success, often in the context of thinking what this Chinese success means for the rest of the world. With the possible exception of China's environmental crisis, suggesting that China has problems and that the social and political order might not be wholly stable can still generate surprise amongst a non-specialist audience. Or perhaps more correctly, when prompted to think about the negative consequences of reform, they might not be a great surprise – but the prompting has to be made to overcome the default position.

Second, the literature that posits China's inevitable rise to global domination usually either simply ignores the domestic situation, or assumes a continued linear smooth progression to increased wealth built on (and in turn facilitating) continued political stability. Quite simply, I suggest that such an approach is flawed – and possibly in some cases, the domestic challenges in China are ignored as analysing them might lead to conclusions that do not support the preferred 'China threat' hypothesis.[2] In order to gain a more realistic and balanced understanding of China's place in the global political economy today and potentially tomorrow, we need to put the ontological separation of the domestic from the international aside, and at the very least consider those domestic factors that might shape China's global future.

The third reason for emphasising the negatives is because acknowledging the extent of the problems and seeking ways of dealing with them are an important part of both political discourse and policy within China itself. From the start of the reform process, considerations of (in)equity have always impacted on government policy, on intellectual evaluations of policy, and on mass responses to policy. Indeed, an argument can be made for explaining the 1989 demonstrations in Tiananmen Square as originally inspired more by disenchantment with the inequities of reform than by a real desire for democracy. But while concern with and research on the impact of inequality in particular remained important throughout the 1990s, its fair to say that the Hu Jintao-Wen Jiabao leadership has given a much higher profile to China's social and economic ills than their immediate predecessors, which has re-invigorated debates over the nature and efficacy of Chinese neo-liberalism.

Domestic debates and concerns bring us to the final reason. Whilst there may be members of the CCP who are concerned about inequality because they care about the people who are losing out, there is also concern that continued party rule might come to be challenged. Zheng Shiping (2003) and Guo Baogang (2003) might be right when they argue that the party is not about to lose control any time soon – but given the emphasis that the party has placed on what might happen if these problems are not resolved, we at least should focus on what strategies the party feels it needs to deploy to offset this threat. Crucially, we should also consider the extent to which these challenges in many respects reflect the party adapting to the changing class basis of its rule that was discussed in Chapter 1. As such, whilst this chapter does include something of a 'laundry list', its emphasis is on the fragmentation of Chinese society, and what this fragmentation means – what it means in terms of specific remedial policies, in terms of the force of ideas and ideologies that underpin these policies, and in terms of the basic building blocks of party rule in China. As established in the introduction, in attempting to rethink some of the dominant understandings of China in the populist international relations literature, this book at times tends to emphasise the negative consequences of reform that this literature sometimes overlooks. This tendency to accentuate the negative is strongest in this chapter, which should be read with this in mind.

Two final paragraphs of context setting are necessary here. Given that the focus of this study is on China and the global political economy, it would be valid to ask to what extent these challenges have an external dimension rather than simply resulting from domestic change; put another way, where is the global in all of this? The answer is partly that whatever the causes of these problems, their existence is important if they make us rethink some of the basic assumptions of at least some assessments/predictions of China's position in the global order. The answer is also partly that the external dimension is important in exacerbating problems that perhaps have their origins in the domestic realm – for example, the extent to which the concentration of FDI in China's coastal provinces compounds existing regional inequalities. These issues will be dealt with in detail in the final section of this chapter.

But the answer is also partly because, as argued in Chapter 1, in ideational terms at least the separation between the global and the local is largely a false dichotomy. In particular, the adoption of the ideology of the market and neoliberalism undermines conceptions of the national and international as separate spheres. While it is certainly true that China has far from a totally 'free market' and that neoliberalism is challenged – both in terms of policy and ideational hegemony – Wang Hui (2004) argues that neoliberalism has been the main topic of intellectual debate since 1997 for supporters and detractors alike. For Wang and other 'New Left' thinkers, it is not that reform has yet to *solve* all of these problems, or even that reform has *exacerbated* existing problems; neoliberalism is the *cause* of the problems. Notwithstanding the dualistic nature of government policy and the dualistic investment regime outlined in Chapter 3, debates over ideas ensure that attempting to make a neat separation between the domestic and the international is a flawed endeavour.

A laundry list of negatives and challenges

The political economy of the environment

In assessing the different negative consequences of reform and potential challenges to social and political stability, it is difficult to do much more than scrape the surface of each item on the laundry list. Each of the different issues considered below is worthy of a single study in itself – and each has been the subject of (often more than one) such study. But perhaps of all the different subjects of attention that will follow, the one that is hardest to deal with in a short space is the extent of environmental degradation – an issue that is arguably the single biggest negative consequence of reform and the biggest challenge to China's future in the long term (Economy 2004).[3] It is also perhaps China's biggest challenge to the world. Air and water born pollution impact on China's neighbours (predominantly going eastwards to Korea and Japan, though the poisoning of the Songhua River in 2005 was an important example of northern flows into Russia). Whilst very low in per capita terms, in aggregate contribution of carbon dioxide, greenhouse gases and other emissions, China comes either first or second in league tables of the world's worst polluters.

Myriad reports from Chinese and international agencies point to a depressing array of environmental problems – many of which Vaclav Smil (1993) argued were already irreversible in the early 1990s. Deforestation; degradation of land; pollution and overuse of water supplies; acid rain; poor and declining air quality; all are acute problems in China resulting in a similarly large and equally depressing array of human consequences from declining quality of life to millions of deaths each year.

The causes of China's environmental problems are myriad. They are in part a historical legacy of the Maoist conception that mankind could master nature and harness it for the greater good of China. The deforestation and poor land use associated with this revolutionary period continue in some parts of China today, where residual poverty and the need to scrape a living off the land can result in an abuse of that land (and in the long term a decreasing ability to scrape a living off it). State control and planning also resulted in energy and raw materials being almost free resources – more correctly, extremely cheap resources – supplied to enterprises that were more concerned with reaching production targets than ensuring environmentally sound consumption. And while these poverty and planning related causes of environmental problems persist, they coexist alongside the problems associated with growth, and increasing consumer culture, increased wealth and the emerging quasi-capitalist economy.[4]

China's insertion into the global economy has also played its part. On a positive note, some foreign investors have introduced the best techniques, philosophies and technologies into their operations in China. It might be the case that new production is taking place in China producing new waste and making new demands for resources, but new green production is better than the alternative. Unfortunately the alternative is also present in China in the abundance, with some foreign invested enterprises exhibiting little concern for their environmental impact. Investors from East Asia are most often suspected as caring least for the environment, and some at least are thought to have moved to China to avoid increasingly strict (and fully implemented) environmental regulations elsewhere in the region. Production in China is heavily energy intensive, using three times the global average to produce US$1 of GDP; not only more than in the West – around seven times more energy used to produce the same amount of industrial output – but even more so than other export oriented developing economies – around twice as much as in Indonesia (Bremner and Carey 2005). Furthermore, around 70 per cent of all energy in China comes from burning coal, most of it unwashed and therefore not only highly heat inefficient, but also highly polluting.

It's important to keep some balance. One of the biggest problems in terms of energy use and efficiency is the duplication of production discussed in Chapter 2 and the role of local governments as key determinants of what economic activity is carried out where. Nevertheless, Chinese companies and FIEs producing exports are in many respects causing environmental problems in China on behalf of consumers and companies elsewhere. The price of the final commodities might be kept low, but the impact on the global environmental commons is much worse than if production took place elsewhere (particularly when production is transferred from more advanced 'cleaner' production sites in the West).

Environmental awareness is increasing rapidly. In April 2005, the central government inaugurated the All China Environment Federation, and gave it a grant of RMB1.29 million to support its work in protecting environmental rights – a relatively small sum and far from enough to carry out the federations work. But is important as 'it is the first time that the central government has given financial support to a project by an non-governmental organization' (Qin Chuan 2005). At the time of writing, around a quarter of a million Chinese were members of nearly 3,000 environmentally related NGOs – 80 per cent of them under 30 and 90 per cent holding a university degree (Li Fangchao 2006).

Although these environmental NGOs are still relatively small in number, and most of them lack the financial resources and personnel to meet their own objectives, the environment is one arena where the CCP is prepared to allow NGOs at least some political presence. And it is notable that only a fifth of these organisations are formally registered with the Ministry of Civil Affairs (via a sponsoring organisation), leaving the vast majority of them operating in (at best) a semi-licit manner. Crucially, these groups are not opposed to the continuation of party rule, or challenging the party for political power. The vast majority are very small, and focus on local issues. Rather than being in opposition to the party, they share the aims and objectives of the central party leadership, providing a form of surveillance on environmental issues that local governments cannot be relied on to provide. In this respect, environmental NGOs are filling a political space at the local level in alliance with the central leadership to act as a check and balance on the power of local governments that not only regulate the local economy (and often own it in one way or another) but also exercise effective control over local environmental planning bureaux.

Environmental problems are also increasingly having negative economic consequences (rather than just negative environmental consequences). In 2004, the State Environmental Planning Agency moved to introduce a 'green GDP' to deflate the size of the economy to take into account the amount of economic activity that had been achieved by degrading the environment (defined as what was taken out in terms of water and other resources used and land degraded, and what was put in in terms of various forms of pollution). In Shanxi Province, the single biggest provincial provider of Chinese coal and one of the pilot provinces for developing the green index, an initial test calculation for 2002 reduced provincial GDP by 44 per cent. Using the same method, provincial growth for 2002 was reduced from 11.7 to less than one per cent – and a single per cent growth rate per annum was thought to be an accurate green deflated figure for much of the previous two decades (Hu Yong 2005).

The new index appears to have faced considerable resistance from some local leaders who feared that their promotion prospects could be damaged if the index drastically lowered their local economic growth record (*People's Daily* 2004b). It also proved extremely difficult to find a workable methodology that was acceptable to both the environmental and statistical agencies, and the Green index appeared to be abandoned (at the very least put on hold) in the spring of 2006. But at least it promoted the message that there are often very severe prices to pay for maintaining high growth rates, and is a reflection of the higher profile that the Chinese leadership now gives to environmental issues. This awareness is to some extent at least a consequence of the recognition that environmental issues are not simply important in their own right, but that they are already undermining long term economic objectives. It's not just the push for economic growth is environmentally unsustainable, but that it is not economically sustainable either. Quite apart from resource implications or the increased costs associated with the above mentioned health problems, continued environmental degradation is expected to reduce crop yields, reduce (or remove) fish stocks, corrode equipment and buildings, and exacerbate weather related crises (flooding and droughts).

The possibility of environmentally related economic decline is most urgent for the 100 million in China living just above the Chinese denominated poverty line. For these people, not just floods and droughts but also the declining fertility of land and the loss of food and extra incomes from dead rivers threaten to reverse the transition from poverty. As is the case across the world, it is the already vulnerable that face the biggest and most immediate environmental challenges to subsistence and existence – which brings us to a brief discussion of the continuing challenge of reducing poverty in China.

Poverty (and poverty reduction)

As noted in the introduction, trying to interpret statistics in China is always problematic. The task becomes even more problematic when the issue of which exchange rate to use is added to the equation – and even more problematic still when there are different definitional benchmarks to judge the different figures against. Trying to work out how many Chinese still live in poverty in China is a classic case in point.

Even though the World Bank seems to provide a straightforward definition of US$1 a day, how much US$1 a day actually is in China depends on which calculation of the value of the RMB you use. If you take the World Bank calculation of PPPs, then US$1 a day in 2002 equated to RMB879 per annum. On a pure exchange rate level, US$1 a day would equate to RMB3,018 and hence generate a much greater number of rural Chinese living in poverty. But to complicate matters even further, Chinese figures on rural poverty use a lower income per capita figure based on a survey of the income needed to achieve a basic standard of living in 1985 with the original base figure of RMB206 reassessed in light of inflation each year. Keeping 2002 as a base year for ease of comparison, this Chinese figure was RMB627 or 71 per cent of the PPP US$1 a day figure, which the ADB (2004: 4) considered to be 'a very low poverty line compared to international practice and only represents a basic level of survival'. When the number of rural Chinese that Chinese statistics consider to be above the poverty line but still 'poor' are added to those officially in poverty, the result is close to the PPP US$1 a day calculation, so perhaps it would be best just to stick with that!

So the number of rural Chinese living in poverty as defined by the Chinese authorities has dropped from 250 million in 1978 to around 25 million in 2006. A further 100 million or so live just above the poverty line, but are considered to be vulnerable to falling back into official poverty in the face of floods and/or prolonged droughts, or through a SARs-like health epidemic (CD 2005) – as happened when those living in poverty increased in 2003 largely as a result of natural disasters (Watts 2004). Using PPP US$1 per day calculation, the figure is closer to 90 million, with one source suggesting as many as 134 million in 2004,[5] and the CIA World Factbook suggesting 150 million in 2005.[6] In large parts of the countryside, corrupt excising of taxes and the imposition of ad hoc fees and charges by local authorities means that even those above the official poverty line are subsequently brought into financial hardship (Bernstein and Lu 2003). Liu, Rao and Hsiao (2003) have also shown that when expenses for medical care are taken off incomes to provide a closer like with like basis of comparison with earlier eras, then the percentage of the rural population living in poverty rises from 7.6 per cent to 10.6 per cent. To offset these problems, some analysts use consumption rather than income figures, which generate even higher figures in the region of 200 million. Notably, while Reddy and Minoiu (2005) have found a continued downward trend in poverty defined by income, both the ADB (2004) and Chen and Ravallion (2004a, 2004b) suggest that poverty reduction by consumption has at best levelled off and possibly even slightly reversed since the late 1990s.

But even though the specifics change depending on which figures you use,[7] the basic message remains the same. Economic reform has increased rural incomes pulling many millions out of poverty. Even if we take the higher US$1 a day figure for those still living in poverty, the decline from around 250 million in 1993 to less than 100 million today (with most of this reduction occurring between 1993 and 1996) is both dramatic and impressive. Nevertheless, the task is far from complete with around 10 per cent of the rural population very poor with a further 10 per cent vulnerable to sliding back into poverty.

The message also seems to be that urban poverty is on the increase – although it is even more difficult to reach consensus on the figures as there is no accepted Chinese definition of what the urban poverty line actually is. Individual municipalities set their own benchmark where Minimum Living Standard Scheme benefit payments kick in, and these vary significantly with poorer cities setting lower thresholds; for example, 'in 2000, Beijing's benefit line was 3,360 yuan per capita per annum whereas Chongqing set its line at 2,028 yuan'. (ADB 2004: 4–5). Around 7 per cent of the urban population (c.22 million people) qualify for these payments (ADB 2004: 4), but as almost all migrant workers are not currently eligible, this is only a very rough indicator. Regulations have been brought in to extend coverage to migrant workers, but according to a 2006 government survey published on Labour Day, these are almost never actually implemented by local governments (*People's Daily* 2006a). Solinger (2005: 3) started with an internal investigation on poverty, added on official estimates of the number of poor migrants in the towns and cities, and came up with a figure of 70 million urban poor and growing.

The number of migrants in the urban poor suggests that rural poverty has in some cases become urban poverty. While the growth of TVEs soaked up much of the surplus labour released from agricultural production in the 1980s, employment growth in TVEs slowed drastically in the second half of the 1990s (Johnson 1999, Jiang 2000) going into a 'clear tailspin' in 1997 (Wang Hui 2004: 47). It is widely accepted that around 120 million rural workers are without work for most of the year, though a figure of nearer 200 million has been mentioned in private in interviews. One of the more notable consequences of this increased rural unemployment is the growth in migration – both state sanctioned and supported, and illegal. Not surprisingly, China's poorest provinces are the major sources of migrant workers.[8] Neither is it surprising that many have made their way to the cities in search of jobs – rural unemployment is now very definitely an urban issue.

The growth of unemployment

Urban poverty is also increasing as a result of the transition from state planning and ownership towards a more market efficient basis for economic activity. The official urban unemployment rate has typically remained around four per cent. But there is a difference between different types of people who are not working in Chinese statistics. Although the Chinese authorities are moving to unify calculations of unemployed (*shi ye*) and laid off (*xia gang*) workers, most Chinese unemployment statistics will not count those that are laid off – and workers can be laid off for up to three years before they count as officially unemployed. While urban unemployment increased by about 8 per cent per annum in the 1990s, the number of laid off workers increased by around 40 per cent a year. Two thirds of these laid off workers were from SOEs – and, as with all things in contemporary China, there are large geographic variations. In essence, the old industrial bases have both the highest levels of unemployment and the highest levels of laid off workers – 14.2 per cent of the pay-roll in Liaoning, 13.8 per cent in Heilongjiang, 11.2 per cent in Hunan and so on.[9]

In addition, the officially 'unemployed' does not include men over the age of 50 and women over 45 or those who have migrated to the cities and are thus not registered as formally urban dwellers. Indeed, the statistics are so unreliable that Solinger (2001) suggests that it is impossible to come to an accurate figure for urban unemployment in China. So we can only make an educated guess, and based on calculations made by Hu Angang at the Chinese Academy of Social Sciences, John Giles' work on unemployment data,[10] and interviews with officials and academics, a figure of 15 per cent is towards the top end of estimates, but not a totally unrealistic assessment of the urban situation. Wolf *et al* (2003) factored in migrant workers, workers in enterprises that have stopped production but have not yet been formally laid off and the rural unemployed and came up with an unemployment figure of 23 per cent in 1999, with 16 per cent of the urban workforce and one in four of the rural workforce effectively unemployed under various different terms. Chen An (2002: 58) uses a similar wide definition of unemployment to reach a 'staggering' figure of 27.8 per cent in 2000.

To make matters worse, China has yet to make the full transition from the workplace delivered welfare of the socialist system to other forms of welfare delivery. And for Ding Kang (2004) the establishment of an effective welfare system has become more important as a result of WTO entry. This understanding was reflected in the forward to the 2004 White Paper on Social Security, which noted that:

> To establish and improve a social security system corresponding to the level of economic development is a logical requirement for co-ordinated economic and social development. It is also an important guarantee for the social stability and the long-term political stability of a country (State Council 2004)

But as the White Paper also noted:

> China is the biggest developing country with a large population in the world, and its economic base is weak and the development between regions and between town and country is unbalanced. Establishing a sound social security system in China is an extremely arduous task

This 'arduous task' began with a number of local experiments with unemployment benefits first introduced in 1986. From the outset, the reforms displayed a massive 'urban bias' (Duckett 2003) with a primary goal of preventing social instability in industrial centres. For example, in 1998 the government introduced the 'three guarantees' of a basic level of subsistence – but only for those laid off from SOEs and urban residents. Even those in the urban sector covered by the system can only claim benefits for a maximum of two years if they have been paying premiums for at least ten years,[11] but this limited support is better than the absence of government support that is the reality for the majority of the Chinese population. Similarly, medical and old age insurance is limited to 109 and 155 million people respectively in urban areas.

As we shall see in the last section of this chapter, the Hu-Wen leadership have placed a greater emphasis on rural poverty, and more money is being spent on the countryside. Experiments in extending social security in rural areas have also been extended – but even by the best estimates, only cover about a tenth of the rural population. Nor does it typically cover those in the collective sector (Duckett 2004: 170), or migrant workers (though reforms announced in 2005 promise to bring migrant workers under the social security umbrella in the near future).

Corruption

The above examples point to the costs of reform and those who have felt the main brunt of these losses. As will be discussed in more detail below, China's leaders take the possibility of these losers challenging party rule very seriously. They are also aware that discontent might also emerge as a result of the popular perception that party members have been the main beneficiaries of reform, and the apparently endemic state of corruption in contemporary China. As Chen An (2003: 148) puts it:

> from the populace's viewpoint the widening income gap among social classes has resulted less from market mechanisms and more from the two related factors, namely political corruption and the prevalence of business cheating. Economic 'upstarts' have acquired their wealth through collusion with corrupt bureaucratic power or have taken advantage of market chaos to practice illegal or immoral businesses with impunity

Identifying the extent of the problem is hugely problematic as we only have the data that the Chinese authorities release, and this data is only based on the cases that they have uncovered. In money terms, the US-China Security Review Commission (2002) argued that China has 'the largest dollar amount of corruption of any other country in the world'.[12] Jiang Zemin gave an indication of the size of the problem when he announced that up to 20 per cent of the official budget was going missing every year as a result of corruption in 2000, while the National Audit Association calculate that a tenth of the government's specific poverty alleviation spending 'goes missing' (Watts 2004). Hu Angang's (2002: 44) forensic investigation found that the economic losses caused by corruption averaged nearly 15 per cent of GDP from 1999 to 2001. Hu identified 10 major causes of such financial loss: bribery; falsifying invoices; evasion of customs duties: illegal charges levied by monopoly industries: tax evasion (by faking losses to avoid liabilities); embezzlement of public investment; illegal capital flight; the sort of insider privatisation discussed in Chapter 2; arbitrary and ad hoc fees charged by public institutions; and what he terms 'corruption in financial industry' (Hu Angang 2002).

In terms of the people involved, Zheng Shiping (2003: 51–2) notes that:

> During a 15-year period from 1987 to 2002, the CCP disciplinary commissions and the state supervision agencies had investigated a total of 2.42 million cases of corruption and other forms of disciplinary violation. Among those who were penalized, 64,996 were officials at the level of county magistrate/division chief; 5,452 at the level of prefecture commissioner/bureau chief; and 286 at the level of provincial governor/central minister.

In 2003, official figures showed that 130,000 cases of corruption had been investigated involving the misuse or embezzlement of US$8 billion worth of funds. But as Hu Angang (2000) argues that only one in every five of corrupt officials at the county level or below ever get caught, this is probably just the tip of a very large iceberg.

The Chinese authorities are well aware of the issue and the potential consequences of allowing corruption to continue unchecked. In 1997, Jiang Zemin was reported as saying that corruption will 'bury the party, the regime and the modernization program if it is left unchecked' (Zheng Shiping 1997: 5). Despite targeting corruption as a key task of the party and the government, six years later in his final speech as Communist Party leader at the 16th Party Congress in November 2002, Jiang Zemin was still making startlingly similar comments:

> To combat and prevent corruption resolutely is a major political task of the whole Party. If we do not crack down on corruption, the flesh-and-blood ties between the Party and the people will suffer a lot and the Party will be in danger of losing its ruling position, or possibly heading for self-destruction

Yet despite the fact that fighting corruption has been on the top (or near the top) of the list of work to do in every government work report for over a decade, there are few signs that the situation is improving.

The persistence of corruption is sometimes explained in cultural terms – indeed, it is difficult to go far into any writing on how to do business in China without coming across the concept of *guanxi*. Often simply translated as 'relationships', *guanxi* more correctly refers to informal relationships between individuals that result in the distribution of rewards and resources. Based on a conception of reciprocity and obligation between individuals that share a bond of allegiance (for example, education or birth place), a *guanxi* relationship is one where exchange is expected to take place, but not necessarily equal exchange. An interconnected set of *guanxi* relationships creates a *guanxiwang* – a social network of insiders with the ability to distribute scarce resources and rewards to other members of the network.

Guanxi is typically conceived as being something uniquely Chinese that has its origins in traditional Chinese society and philosophy. But while it is distinctly 'Chinese' it does not seem particularly unique when compared to patterns of patrimonialism and neo-patrimonialism in many parts of the world – or either to networks of insiders that operate within the business cultures of developed states. And, I would argue, it is a culture as currently practiced that has been generated by the system of distribution in modern China, rather than by Confucian values. It is, more than anything, a consequence of the political economy of socialism *and* the political economy of the retreat from socialism (Kwong 1997).

During the years of state planning, personal relationships often proved to be the only way of getting hold of extremely scarce goods and resources that were often unattainable through the formal planning and distribution system. *Guanxi* acted as a means of overcoming the defects of the planning system, and also provided forms of compensation to party-state officials that were not available through formal mechanisms. As noted in Chapter 2, one of the key sources of power in the emerging Chinese capitalist system is the opaque nature of decision making, and the privileged knowledge insiders have of market conditions (and the state's policies towards the market). The lack of transparency resulted in party-state elites capturing many of the benefits of market reform. For He Qinglian (2000) it was simply inevitable that state actors who remained as gate keepers, knowledge keepers and allocators in the market would use their positions to generate private wealth, arguing that there have been three main phases of official corruption. Before 1995, corruption was largely individually based, with officials working on their own for personal gain, or with a small group of colleagues. 1995 to 1998, saw the emergence of a new large-scale organised corruption into organised illegal activities. After 1998, corruption became fully institutionalised with established arrangement within institutions such as the People's Liberation Army (PLA), the banking system and local and provincial governments (He Qinglian 2000).

The type of market economy that has been introduced, and its relationship with the state, creates the environment in which corruption can flourish in many different ways (Ting Gong 1997, Chen An 2002). As Fan and Grossman (2001) argue, it facilitates the 'transformation of the typical government official from being an unproductive political entrepreneur, to being a productive economic entrepreneur'. Furthermore, those officials who are most able to act corruptly are often the same people charged with preventing it:

> The government is not only the maker of the rules of the game, but also the sportsman competing in the game and the referee for the game at the same time (Guo Yong and Hu Angang 2004: 272).

For Walder (2004: 207–8), a repetition of the Russian model of corrupt privatisation in China is unlikely. Nevertheless, he argues that managing the consequences of privatisation over the long term (not just the initial process, but the longer term regulation of newly privatised enterprises) could be the key determinant of the party's political future:

> The question facing China is whether it will be able to transfer ownership in ways that prevent widespread corruption and theft of state assets. Central Europe and the Baltics show that this can be done; Russia and the Ukraine show the dangers of rapid and poorly regulated privatisation. A Russian-style process holds two distinct dangers for China: widespread opposition, likely to emerge even within the Party itself, arising from a perception that the elite is plundering state assets under cover of dictatorship; and defection of members of the elite into the private sector (or abroad, taking assets with them).

The process of insertion into the global economy also provided an opportunity for corruption to pay – though of course nobody forced the people involved to act corruptly. The maintenance of higher domestic prices for some goods above global market prices placed a premium on illegally importing these commodities outside the formal trading system. In Xiamen, the Yanhua group smuggled US$9.5 billion goods into China tax free using naval ships to escort smuggled goods and diverting the attention of already bribed customs officials through the development of special brothels. The project included the local Chief of police, head of customs, and provincial foreign trade authorities, and resulted in seven executions and 200 other convictions. The dualist trade regime also provides an incentive for corruption. With tax rebates paid for exports, but not for domestically consumed goods, then faking exports to gain tax rebates is very profitable. So too is illegal capital outflow bypassing stringent currency controls to take advantage of higher interest rates paid elsewhere.

The job of dealing with corruption is in the hands of the Ministry of Supervision, the Party's Central Discipline Inspection Commission, and the Chinese Procuratorate anti-corruption offices. Whilst Prime Minister, Zhu Rongji was not averse to administering ad hoc justice including sacking a factory boss on the spot for wearing a Rolex watch that he couldn't afford on his official salary. However, there is weak bureaucratic control over the implementation of anti-corruption policies because of the concentration of power in local governments where corrupt officials are often the final arbiters of their own judicial fate. In addition, as civil society organisations are under administrative oversight and control, they cannot always act as effective societal watchdogs against the abuse of power. High profile anti-corruption campaigns run the risk of actually undermining party power if they only highlight the extent of the problem without fundamentally dealing with the causes of the problem. Separating political decisions and power from economic power might not end all corruption, but without a fundamental restructuring of the relationship between political power and the emerging market economy, corruption will still have fertile ground in which to flourish.

Corruption undermines popular faith in the party in a number of ways. On one level, high profile cases such as those briefly outlined above provide highly visible examples of how party state leaders are using their positions to obtain personal wealth. On another level, perhaps more destabilising in the long term, many Chinese bear witness to almost daily cases of small time corruption 'demoralizing and destabilizing society and politics' (Lu Xiaobo 2000: 273). Perhaps the most important of these is the illegal excising of fees and taxes noted above – most notably in the countryside (Bernstein and Lu 2003, Wedeman 1997). Protests at the actions of local rural officials have been one of the main causes of the growth of civil unrest in China in recent years. In one of the most serious (that has been reported) security forces were needed to quell a riot in Yuntang in Jiangxi Province in April 2001, reportedly wounding 20 demonstrators and killing two

(Pomfret 2001). Not surprisingly, transferring ad hoc fees to more transparent taxes is one of the key central government strategies for reducing rural discontent. But as Ray Yep (2004) and Chou (2006) both point out, the financial burdens on local governments mean that they cannot often cover their costs if they stick to the official fiscal structure, and raising extra budgetary revenue through licences and fees can be out of necessity rather than out of corrupt greed.

Divided China

In its 1987 report on 'China 2020', the World Bank (1988) noted a startling rise in the gini coefficient from 0.288 in 1981 to 0.388 in 1995 – probably the highest rise in inequality of any country over that period. Since then, the figure has continued to rise, reaching an official rate of around 0.46 in 2004, though Hsu (2002) argues that if you add in illegal and unofficial income that doesn't show up in the official date, the figure was already more than 0.56 in 2001. If we accept official figures, then China ranks 5th in the list of most unequal economies, whereas Hsu's (2002) calculations puts China behind only South Africa and Brazil. What this means in practice is that the richest 20 per cent earn half of all income in China, with the poorest 20 per cent earning 4.7 per cent. Notably, wealth is highly concentrated at the top end of this richest quintile, with the richest 10 per cent earning 45 per cent of all income (and the poorest 10 per cent earning 1.4 per cent of the total).

Although the income gap between those living in China's coastal provinces and the rest of the country continues to grow, the main determinant of income level remains the urban-rural divide. The income of the average urban dweller is over three times more than their rural counterpart, and is even higher when non-income benefits (that most rural residents have to pay for out of their net income) is taken into account. Li Peilin suggests that once non-income benefits are included into the equation then the average urban dweller earns six times more than their rural counterpart (Chai Mi 2004). But in reality, there isn't an average urban or rural dweller. In the countryside, for example, the less dependent the individual is on agricultural production for their income, then the richer they are. Farmers in the richer coastal provinces with easy access to major urban centres also earn more than those doing similar work in other parts of the country – the richest earning perhaps as much as four times more than China's poorest farmers in Guizhou Province (visiting the rural population in parts of Zhejiang Province for example, does not exactly entail visiting China's poor). Within the urban population, there are also vast differences depending on geography, levels of education, the specific industry worked in, and so on.

Fragile China?

According to the Central Party School, the extent of inequality has reached the 'yellow alert' level – if it is not dealt with, then inequality will reach a 'red alert' level threatening serious political disorder by 2008 (*People's Daily* 2005d). This understanding is not just based on the idea that political instability becomes more likely once the gini coefficient reaches 0.40. It is also based on the growth of civil unrest in China. For example, the officially reported number of labour disputes increase over fivefold in the decade to 2002 from 28,000 to 181,000 (Guo Baogang 2003: 15). Official reports of the overall number of what is called 'mass incidents' were suspended in 1999, when the figure was 32,000 (Tanner 2004). In 2005, the Minister of Public Security suggested that three and a quarter million people had been involved in 74,000 incidents in 2004, with 'public order disturbances' rising to 87,000 the following year (McGregor 2006). Chung, Lai and Xia (2006) have worked through a number of different sources to arrive at a best estimate of incidents from 1993 to 2005 suggesting a doubling from 2000 to 2005 alone.

There are many causes of this social unrest, but not surprisingly, they almost all have their roots in protests by groups that feel that economic reform has served them less than well. For example, the closure of SOEs, and in particular, the subsequent non-payment of benefits, have been particularly important in those areas that used to be the heartland of the old planned economy:

> Police in Liaoning Province on the border with North Korea claimed a stunning 9,559 incidents involving more than 863,000 people between January 2000 and September 2002 – an average of almost 10 incidents involving 90 people each day for nearly three years.' (Tanner 2004)

The extent of rural taxes, the way they are collected, and the ad hoc fees charged by many local authorities in rural China have probably been the major overall cause of disturbances. More recently, ad hoc land seizures by local governments, where peasants have simply been thrown off the land with either minor or no compensation has been a major source of violent unrest.[13]

These demonstrations are typically targeted at the failings of local governments and are 'remedial in nature and hence do not constitute a direct and fundamental challenge to the legitimacy of the regime' (Yep 2002: 5). They are isolated events that can usually be dealt with by a response to the issue that has generated the discontent. For Blecher (2002: 286), it is not the number of strikes and demonstrations that is surprising, but the fact that there has not been a 'co-ordinated challenge in the face of the fundamental transformations that have so profoundly afflicted so many workers and that threaten so many more'. In answering his own conundrum, Blecher argues that those who are losing out might be unhappy with their own specific situation, but accept the overall logic of the need to reform and the ideological hegemony of the market. Thus, protests, when they emerge, are about making the system work better for them, rather than challenging the system. This assessment is shared by Lau (1997: 46):

> ideologically, most labour-oriented activists accept the logic of the regime's reforms, with many seeing a private capitalist market economy as 'just', to be tempered only by a 'humanitarian quality of competition'.

But Blecher accepts that this does not preclude the emergence of a counter-hegemonic project, and there is a fear amongst China's elites that wider social issues such as the gap between the rich and poor – between winners and perceived losers – might lead to further problems in the future that cannot be dealt with by addressing the specific issue at hand (Kang Xiaoguang 2002).

Class (re)formation

Of course, other states have survived intact despite the maintenance of high levels of inequality measured by the gini coefficient (and by other measurements as well). But even though the challenge to party rule from a violent uprising by the dispossessed might be unlikely, there is a recognition that a fundamental reorganisation of the class basis of Chinese society is under way, and that this inevitably impacts on the nature of party rule – a reorganisation that is extremely fluid and far from complete. These changes have been recognised within China for quite some time.[14] Of particular note are the two long reports on the stratification of Chinese society produced by Lu Xueyi's research team in the department of sociology at the Chinese Academy of Social Sciences (CASS) (Lu Xueyi 2002, 2004). Whilst CASS is not just a mouthpiece of the government, the production of these two volumes (which both received wide press attention in China) and other work on growing inequality suggests that the research interests of CASS members coincides with the concerns of top Chinese leaders. In the two reports, Lu *et al* divide the social structure into ten broad groups, each of which can be subdivided into smaller sub groups.

(1)   state and social management (*guojia yu shehui guanli*)
(2)   economic management (*jingli*)
(3)   private enterprise owners (*siying quanyezhu*)
(4)   specialised technological personnel (*zhuanye jishu renyuan*)
(5)   administrative personnel (*banshi renyuan*)
(6)   individual industrial and business households (*geti gongshanghu*)
(7)   business service personnel (*shangye fuwu renyuan*)
(8)   (business) workers (*shangye gongren*)
(9)   agricultural workers (*nongye laodongzhe*)
(10) urban unemployed (literally urban without work to include laid off workers), unemployed and 'semi' unemployed personnel (*chengshi wuye, shiye he ban shiye renyuan*).

Notably, the report uses the definition of *jieceng* or social strata, rather than class (*jieji*) – partly because of the 'not good' connotation of 'class' in China (Lu Xueyi 2002: 6) and instead grouped the population by occupation. Given the harsh treatment of those categorised as bad class elements in the Cultural Revolution, such a suspicion of 'class' as the basis of societal stratification is highly understandable.

The rejection of a notion of the relationship to the means of production as a basis of stratification is also reflected in the emergence of conceptions of the new middle class (*zhongchan jieji*) in China. Four different criteria have been used to calculate the size of the Chinese middle class – occupation, income, spending power and life style, and self classification. Given the different criteria used, it is not surprising that analyses of the size of the Chinese middle class differ greatly. The highest figure is based on a survey of nearly 6,000 urban residents by CASS, which found that just under half now consider themselves to be in the middle class. A much smaller figure emerges from using income and spending power criteria. Here a good working definition of the middle class is 'a group of people with stable incomes, capable of purchasing private houses and cars, and can afford the costs of private education for children and vacation' (He Li 2003: 88)

Using this definition, then the middle class in China rose from 15 per cent in 1999 to around 19 per cent in 2003 (*People's Daily* 2004e). However, Li Chunling (2004) is highly sceptical of these findings, arguing that the high percentages emerging from research at CASS is a myth that has been used as a propaganda tool to laud the success of national economic strategy (Lian Yue and Xue Yong 2004).[15] Li argued that the methodology used skewed the findings to create the highest possible figure. For example, the income criteria for middle class in Beijing was only RMB10,000 a month (around US$2,090 at the time), ensuring that a quarter of the Beijing population were included. More important, while a relatively high percentage of the population surveyed fell into at least one criterion, a mere 4.1 per cent met all of the criteria. Furthermore, the urban bias in the survey means that you can not simply extrapolate from those surveyed to reach a national figure, and once this is taken into account, then Li concludes that only 2.8 per cent of the entire population – just over 35 million people – were really members of the middle class in 2004 (Chua 2004).

The concept of an authoritarian elite exaggerating the significance of the growth of a middle class does not sit easily with many understandings of political modernisation theory. Why would the CCP wish to exaggerate the size of the middle class which we might expect will be the social stratum that will increasingly demand greater political representation and challenge the party for political power in the future. There are perhaps three main reasons for this: the lack of homogeneity of new middle and bourgeois classes, the relationship between old and new classes, and the social contract between the Chinese state and the Chinese people.

Divided classes

Not least because the process of transformation is still very much ongoing, there is no solidity amongst emerging groups and it is difficult to identify 'a single identifiable social interest or propensity to action' (Goodman 1998: 40). Lau (1997: 46) points to an increasing heterogeneity within the working class as workers have been 'sectorized' into narrow interest based conflicts. For Solinger (2003: 949), the key is the creation of a new class of dispossessed ex-workers – the laid off and the unemployed – whose interests and identifications are very different from those still in work.

Despite the tendency for those Chinese surveyed by Lu Xueyi (2004) to categories themselves as middle class, there is also a self-acknowledgement that they are not part of a homogenous group. For example, in terms of the distribution of 'social resources', state and social administrators were considered to be the main beneficiaries, with private business owners in the second tier of the middle class and management personnel in the third. The majority of the self-identified middle class placed themselves in either the fourth or fifth of the ten strata and considered that they received a smaller share of resources than those in the top three tiers.[16] This self analysis echoes Hong Zhaohui's (2004: 25) categorisation of three separate groups in the broadly defined middle classes: 'new private entrepreneurs', urban professionals, and 'the managers, bureaucrats, and professionals' who service the capitalist classes.

Heberer focuses on the creation of identity – both in terms of a shared consciousness within the social stratum itself and in terms of external identification of them. He argues that larger and more success-ful entrepreneurs in China possess a 'striking group consciousness' (Heberer 2003: 64) including an awareness of their political power that distinguishes them from smaller and less successful groups of entrepre-neurs. Furthermore, they have become a 'strategic group' that works together with a clear plan to 'try to improve their chances of success through altering the context in which they operate' (Heberer 2003: 72).

Bai Shazhou (2004) also considers political influence, though focus-ing specifically on a tripartite division of capitalist classes rather than the broader conception of middle class. This generates a tripartite divi-sion of capitalist classes based on the nature of their political relation-ship with the party. 'Alliance Capitalists' are those that actively support the party and seek party membership in the ways outlined in Chapter 2. The second group and the numerically largest are the 'Deaf and Mute Type' who keep close to political powers to protect their own interests and will not challenge the party's monopoly on power. The third and smallest group is the 'Challenger Type' – capitalists who pursue a dangerous policy of criticising the regime from the outside, and are subject to periodic campaigns against them.

The party state and the new middle class

Bai's analysis draws us to the second explanation for the apparently state sanctioned exaggeration of the size of the Chinese middle class. As He Li (2003: 89) argues, the Chinese middle class differs from European understandings because it contains within it not only intel-lectuals, managers and professionals, but also 'middle and lower-level cadres under the payroll of the party-state'. The new middle class should not be seen as necessarily separate from the state as large sections of the middle class are state functionaries who benefit from the continued existence of authoritarian state power. Why should the middle class challenge the state for power when many of the middle class are part of the state apparatus and dependent on continued state power for their status. As such, expectations that an emerging middle class will challenge existing elites for political power need to be modified to take into account the symbiotic rather than confrontational relationship between authoritarian political elites and the emerging middle class.

Aspirations and legitimacy

As was shown in Chapter 2, the CCP has modified both its membership criteria and its basic understanding of who the party represents (and what the party is for). It has also adjusted the bases of legitimacy accordingly, promoting itself as the vehicle through which the Chinese people can attain the aspiration of a 'middle class' existence. In much the same way as Deng Xiaoping urged the Chinese to aspire to become 10,000 Yuan households at the start of the reform process, becoming part of the 'Middle Class' (sometimes translated in English language publications as 'middle income class') has become a state sponsored aspiration. For example, Jiang Zemin emphasised the party's goal of creating a *'xiaokang'* society. Whilst *xiaokang* and middle class have been used interchangeably, it is better understood as referring to the creation of a moderately well off society – 'less affluent than 'well-off' but better off than freedom from want' (Xinhua 2002).[17] Post Jiang, the Party has explicitly used the term 'middle class' rather than *xiaokang* in establishing its goals for societal change.[18] In essence, whether it be the creation of a *xiaokang* or middle class society, the party promises to provide a structure in which all citizens can become relatively well off if the people do not challenge the party for political power.

The party feels that it needs a large middle class to overcome the political problems that could emerge from the maintenance of a wide divide between different societal groups. A social structure with a small but very wealthy elite, a slightly bigger but still relatively small middle income class, and a massive base of poor and relatively poor is not considered to be politically stable. Thus, there is a desire – perhaps more correctly a perceived need – to alter the social structure to become more politically stable. The Chinese social structure is often described in China as being like an onion (*yangcongxing*) – it is multilayered with many different strata. The goal, as argued by Lu Xueyi (2004) is to construct an 'olive shaped' structure (*ganlanxing*) with a large middle class and a very small distribution at the top and the bottom (Wang Jinchang 2004).

The fourth generation, the 'new left', and new 'socialist' agendas

There has, then, been a resurgence in interest in the implication of class politics in China (Chen An 2003) – although not always explicitly using the language of class analysis. However, many 'new left' writers are more than happy to use the explicit language of class analysis. A recurring theme in the new left writing is that the adoption of neoliberalism and the move towards capitalism has allowed a small number of people either in or connected to the party to make massive economic gains. Inequality has rapidly increased, and many of the previous beneficiaries of the old state system – the peasants and the state-owned working class – have lost out as the party has formed new class alliances. Rather than being a dictatorship of the proletariat, the party leadership increasingly resembles an authoritarian executive leadership acting on behalf of the bourgeoisie (and in many respects, generating the bourgeoisie).[19] For Chen An (2003: 150):

> economic dependence upon the private sector has compelled the leadership to move to the right on the political spectrum and to bring its class orientation into line with its new developmental strategy

This characterisation of party rule has been made by party officials themselves. In 'How the Chinese Communist Party Should Lead the Capitalist Class' Lin Yanzhi argued that a capitalist class had been produced by the party, and was now seeking to take power by changing the character and class basis of the party (Wang Dan 2001). As Guo Baogang (2003: 15) argues, 'the foundation of the communist rule used to be based on a socialist social contract between the party-state and the working class. At the end of Jiang's tenure this contract was essentially non-existent'.

But post-Jiang, the new left agenda has been increasingly reflected in the rhetoric and at least some of the political objectives of the fourth generation of leaders under Hu Jintao and Wen Jiabao. They have also become increasingly critical of the previous leadership's neglect of disaffected groups, and an apparent belief that growth alone would eventually solve China's remaining developmental problems. According to a 2004 People's Daily editorial, this placed Chinese economic policy at a crossroads – go one way and China could have the prosperity in the long term of the USA and Europe, go the other and half the population would remain in poverty for many years suffering continued Latin American style economic crises. Just as Roosevelt's economic policies built on a budget deficit to provide relief for the poor avoided a potential structural crisis of the US economy in 1929, so China's leaders need to

> build a strong national industrial system to bring more people into economic activities. It requires us to complete reform to the investment system as soon as possible and kick off large-scale economic construction (*People's Daily* 2004d).

The editorial argued that the 16th Party Congress 'took a memorable turn in the process of China's economic advancement' by 'putting people first' – a 'political tactic successfully preventing China from falling into the pit of a Latin-American mode'. Without stating so explicitly, this suggests a distinct shift from what we might term the 'economic tactic' associated with the Premiership of Zhu Rongji of emphasising increased economic efficiency. It is an implicit recognition that the economic agenda of the previous leadership had not only failed to address the rise in inequality, but had contributed to increased societal stratification. It was time for politics to reassert itself over economics and for social justice to reassert itself over economic efficiency as the party's main task.

This strategy is part of a wider attempt by China's new generation of leaders to try to deal with the perceived down-side of the transition from socialism – to do something for the 'underprivileged areas and people left behind in the breakneck transition to free markets' (Hutzler 2003). To this end the leadership has moved to deal with some of the most immediate sources of rural discontent outlined above. The agricultural tax has been abolished, all ad hoc and opaque fees are supposed to have been transferred to more regularised and transparent taxes, and peasants are now supposed to have transferable 30-year land tenure to protect them from ad hoc seizures. But writing in 2006, Chi Lo argued that many local governments have simply ignored the 2003 Rural Land Contracting Law and 'many Chinese farmers have not got their 30-year rights, and only a small minority has heard of the law'.[20]

The leadership has also pledged to devote more government spending to the countryside and to 'build a socialist new countryside' (*jianshe shehuizhuyi xin nongcun*).[21] Yet the images that the word 'socialism' might generate when applied to rural reform in China are not reinforced by the details behind the headline. In his annual work report to the National People's Congress in March 2006, Wen Jiabao reported that the socialist countryside would be built over the next year by completing the abolition of the agricultural tax and phasing out of fees, more central and local government spending to ensure access to compulsory education and the long term eradication of all tuition fees, more investment in science and technology to introduce new crop strains and agricultural technology, the renovation and modernisation of hospitals and the creation of new contributory cooperative medical care systems (*People's Daily* 2006b). This new investment and the reduction of financial burdens on peasants are clearly significant and important – but it's not the rejection of liberalisation and reform that its title perhaps suggests.

In a similar vein, when the leadership announced that it would change the spatial focus of growth from the coast to the interior, many observers thought that this could only be achieved through stronger centralised planning (Goodman 2004a: 318). The drive to 'open the west' predates the Hu-Wen leadership, and was first announced by Jiang Zemin on Labour Day 1999, with the State Council 'Office of the Leading Group for Western Region Development' opening in 2000. This focus on the West after years of growth in coastal provinces resulted in lobbying from leaders from other areas, and the creation of the 'Northeast Office' in 2003,[22] and the adoption of the 'Rise of Central China' strategy. As with the focus on agricultural development, the Hu-Wen leadership have taken a pre-existing idea and given it more rhetorical force and organisational coherence.

And as with the socialist new countryside, the new strategy does not represent the rejection of liberalism that the rhetoric might suggest. Again, more budgetary resources are being devoted to projects away from the coast (particularly infrastructure and energy related projects) in much the same way that many governments across the world use budgetary revenues for development projects. Furthermore, one of the key strategies for promoting development away from the coast is to encourage foreign investment. By providing special incentives through the 'Catalogue of Priority Industries for Foreign Investment in the Central-Western Region' and not just allowing but in some cases encouraging foreign mergers and acquisitions of SOEs in the northeast, the regional development strategy in part entails more, rather than less, liberalisation (Breslin 2006).

The Hu-Wen leadership are well aware that party legitimacy will probably be undermined by an increasingly polarised society, and that the emerging market economy and the process of integration with the global economy have played their part on generating social and economic stratification. They also seem prepared to listen to (and sometimes give credence to) the more critical and negative assessments of neoliberalism. To this end, the 11th Five Year Outline Plan (technically now an Outline Programme rather than a Plan) changed the focus of government work from promoting growth to fostering harmonious sustainable and common development for all. It may well be the case that some liberalising reforms are slowed down as a result, and perhaps even at times de-liberalised through supplementary counter-measures. For example, Naughton (2005) argues that by establishing new rules governing the way in which SOEs are privatised, and by establishing more direct control over SOE budgets, SASAC has restored some of the direct control over the state sector that was supposedly lost when the state moved from state planning and ownership to regulation in 2003 (see Chapter 2 for more details). What this suggests is a more proactive approach to promoting preferred developmental projects and a desire to rebalance the relationship between the domestic and the globalised sectors of the economy. It also appears to be inspired by yet another attempt to reduce the ability of local governments to control local economies by restoring more control to central level agencies charged with developing macroeconomic policy. But it does not suggest a rejection of the market and reform *per se* – indeed, if local governments' control over local economies is reduced, then the overall extent of market intervention will actually decrease.

The downside of China and the global economy

China's insertion into the global economy during a period of domestic restructuring has had clear beneficial consequences for the Chinese leadership. The importance of the investment-trade nexus for overall growth has grown at times when the growth of the domestic economy has slowed. Two periods warrant special attention here. The first was when the then Premier Li Peng introduced an economic retrenchment campaign in the autumn of 1988. The second period between 1998 and 2003 saw the domestic economy in effective deflation. The declining profitability of TVEs combined with the restructuring of the SOE sector, and an attack on inflation after 1994 resulted in annual negative growth in retail and consumer price indexes. Massive government spending (both through a budget deficit and through directed lending via the banking system) helped maintain overall growth rates, but the major source of growth and in particular new jobs during this period was from foreign invested export industries. Insertion into the global economy thus allowed the government to ride the waves of domestic recession and restructuring relatively unscathed. Nevertheless, participation in the global economy has generated problems for China's leaders as they attempt to maintain social stability whilst restructuring the national economic base.

In some respects, it is the very success of the integrative strategy itself that has caused these problems (Lewis and Xue 2003). While the decision to join the WTO was ultimately made by Chinese leaders, China's economic successes played a key role in bringing foreign pressure to liberalise domestic sectors which is blamed by some in China for at least some of the negative consequences of reform. The massively disproportionate emphasis on China's coastal provinces in terms of investment and exports at the expense of the interior provinces has contributed to the growing regional inequalities. This has generated dissatisfaction from leaders in the interior at their relative neglect, and has provided a pull factor for those in the interior who are prepared to join the ranks of China's migrants.

For some Chinese observers – and not just from the new or even the old left – this has contributed to Chinese economic growth becoming too unbalanced and vulnerable. With growth so heavily dependent on foreign investment producing exports to foreign markets, China's development has become doubly dependent on factors outside China's control.[23] The argument that China has had too much FDI might be difficult to accept in those economies where investment and jobs have been lost as China grows. But as witnessed by the proposals to restrict some investment and to make tax breaks for others dependent on sourcing from domestic Chinese producers in August 2006, there is a recognition that less FDI that helps develop the domestic economy might be better than more FDI that simply imports, assembles and exports. The influential economist, Yu Yongding (2006), has argued that the dominance of the processing trade in Chinese FIEs means that the process of integration has not proved to be an effective way of promoting domestic industrial upgrading, and that the emphasis on attracting investment (or at least, investment for processing and assembly) should be overturned.

In addition, the extent to which growth is built on this investment-trade nexus has reduced Chinese leaders' autonomy to control their own economic affairs. Central leaders' freedom is partly constrained because the central government has largely devolved the ability to conduct international economic relations to local authorities and to the market – though much of the power devolved to the market has become lodged in the hands of the self-same local authorities. Reliance on external investment to generate an export boom means that external actors and interests have a profound impact on the Chinese economy. The uneven spatial division of international economic relations and the type of economic activity engaged in within China are largely a result of the interaction between the initiatives of local state actors, and the requirements of internationally mobile finance capital. The Chinese leadership might want to move the focus of investment to the West, and might want to change the nature of economic activity, but the reality of life in the global political economy is that governments alone cannot dictate what is produced, how it's produced or where it is produced. As Camilleri (2000: 66) has argued:

> The greater international division of labour with transnational corporations, evidenced in increasing intra-firm trade and investment flows, shows how the engine of industrial restructuring is increasingly driven by transnational objectives and strategies .... States will no doubt continue to perform a number of important administrative and legitimizing functions in the management of economic activity, but their ability to control, let alone plan, the industrial restructuring process is diminishing

A downside, or just not as positive as appears at first sight?

In considering economic regionalisation in East Asia, Bernard and Ravenhill (1995: 197) argued that 'foreign subsidiaries in Malaysia's EPZs were more integrated with Singapore's free-trade industrial sector than with the "local" industry'. Similar trends are identified by Heron and Payne (2002) in 'Caribbean America' where 'production sharing enclaves' have served to increase the involvement of the Caribbean apparel sectors in the US production system without generating horizontal linkages and integration within the apparel sectors in the Caribbean itself.

Writing just after the first big wave of FDI to produce exports, Lardy (1995: 1080) noted a similar isolation on export 'enclaves' from the rest of the domestic economy. In its extreme form, this can lead to what is termed 'technologyless growth', in that the technology base of the national economy is not advanced as economic growth occurs through the assembly of external productive forces, rather than domestic productive forces. As Hout and Lebreton (2003) argue:

> Unlike Japan a generation ago, which reinvented manufacturing through quality and continuous improvement, China is deinventing it by removing capital and reintroducing manual skill and handling on the plant floor.

Of course, wholly technologyless growth is a pure type which is not reflected in reality. The quantity and quality of technology transfer has increased, particularly since WTO entry as investors have increasingly exported machinery to China for use in export production, rather than simply exporting components. As Cheung and Lin (2004) have demonstrated, there are also clear spillover benefits in terms of innovation, research and development and technological upgrading in domestic Chinese companies that have a relationship with foreign funded enterprises. Domestic Chinese companies in the supply chain have also restructured their operations, reduced costs and increased quality in an attempt to develop a domestic source of components and other supplies for FIEs. In some sectors such as audio-visual consumer goods, the development of a domestic supply chain has occurred rather quickly.

Nevertheless, whilst domestic suppliers are gaining an ever greater role, at the time of writing, linkages between export oriented areas and sectors and the rest of the domestic national economy as a whole remain relatively weak or 'shallow' (Steinfeld 2004). At the very least, the level of technological and developmental spill-overs of export oriented growth are lower than the huge global FDI figures for China might suggest without investigation, and lower than what China's leaders hoped for when embarking on the reform process (Rosen 2003, Lemoine and Unal-Kesenci 2004).

There is also the question of what Brecher and Costello (2001) term a 'race to the bottom'. The proliferation of free trade and export zones across the world has seen significant competition for investment to produce export. As a result, there is now a competitive international environment with competitive devaluations, competitive tax holidays and so on. What this means is that growth is often occurring without the benefits of this growth being located within the local economy. As such, growth figures may often overestimate the real impact on the host locality and country from participating in export led projects. Such competition does not just occur between states. There is considerable competition within China to attract investment (Head and Ries 1996). This quote by Braunstein and Epstein (2002: 27) based on an interview with an official in Dalian aptly sums up the level of competition:

> We asked him, 'Who is your greatest competitor when it comes to trying to attract foreign investment?' expecting the answer to be Vietnam, or Malaysia or, perhaps, Beijing. But his answer startled us: 'Our biggest competitor is the export processing zone down the street.' Not only does one province or one town compete with another; but in China, there are numerous zones – export processing zones, high tech zones, industrial zones – all of which compete for foreign investment. The result is cut throat competition.

Whilst this competition used to be between coastal regions, we are now seeing the first signs of a move inwards as some toy and textile producers are taking advantage of better communications between the coast and, for example, Jiangxi Province, to move production to even lower cost sites – and of course, the transfer of production from the coast might be exactly what the central leadership wants, and government investment in new infrastructure projects have been essential in starting this westward trickle (Roberts 2005).

Competition to attract investment has led some to conclude that the benefits of FDI in terms of job creation, technology transfer, increases in fiscal revenues, development of management techniques and so on, has been at the expense of the exploitation of the Chinese work force (Chan 2001). Although regulations on minimum wage rates came into effect in 1993, the responsibility to set rates based on local conditions was left to individual local authorities, and compliance was largely voluntary. China's first national regulations on minimum wages were only introduced on 1st March 2004. Minimum wage rates are still set by local authorities 'in accordance with local conditions' with variations allowed within individual provincial level units. These variations should be based on 'minimum living cost, the urban resident consumption price index, social security and housing accumulation fund fees, average salary, economic development level and employment situation'. Although the national regulations do not set a maximum hourly working week, they do stipulate hourly as well as monthly minimum wages. In most of the FIEs in the Pearl River Delta in 2004, the minimum wage was RMB450 a month (c. US$54), though many enterprises will take off charges for living expenses, as workers live in dormitories at the factory and eat in factory canteens. Detailed investigations by Chinese labour watch reveal working conditions in FIEs that Anita Chan (1995) described as 'Dickensian' in 1995 had not noticeably improved a decade later. The list of issues uncovered include workers being paid as little as 33 cents an hour and unable to support their families; no provision of insurance or pension to workers who typically do not have access to welfare benefits if they are laid off, and simply have to return home; unrealistic production targets, largely resulting from intense competition for investment, leading to violations of the labour law which limits overtime to 36 hours a month (to as high as 86 hours a month);[24] and low health and safety standards. And the extent of unemployment and rural poverty outlined above means that there is no shortage of women waiting to be employed in FIEs if at all possible.

Of course, Chan and Zhu (2003: 561) are correct when they remind us that:

> management practices at workplaces in the PRC are no less authoritarian, disciplinary, and punitive than their counterparts in England in the period of the Industrial Revolution

though Kynge (2006) calculates that Chinese workers earn less in real terms than British workers did at a comparable stage of the industrial revolution. It is also true that remittances from workers to their families have been an important means of pulling families in the interior out of poverty (or near poverty). And as Fan Gang and Zhang Xiaojing (2003: 9–10) point out, its not just that FDI is an important source of employment, but that this employment is a crucial means of providing social stability. Given the very high capital flows into China, we might instinctively expect FIEs to be a major source of employment. While it has indeed been a key source of new jobs, FIEs still only employ around three per cent of the workforce – though this small percentage translates as just over 20 million actual jobs. Returning to the style of the introduction, then yes China has gained much from integration into the global political economy, but not as much as perhaps appears at first sight.

Conclusions

Writing about shades of grey is simply not as enticing as stark black or white predictions of impending chaos or more often impending power. Getting the message over to policy makers and into the collective popular conscience encourages rather exaggerated positions. But when it comes to writing about China the tendency to exaggerate is perhaps even stronger than usual. The world has been waiting and fearing China's rise since at least the eighteenth century and at last there seems to be evidence that it is happening. Add the speed of China's transition from virtual isolation to key player in the global political economy to the size of the Chinese population, multiply by vague concerns about 'communism' (and/or the impenetrable nature of Confucianism), and the result is a vision of a disciplined workforce mobilised behind an organised national effort to return China to a self perceived 'rightful' place of global dominance. Here is a new power that is 'different' – it doesn't share 'our' values and doesn't do things the way that 'we' do, with long held grievances about its past treatment and unresolved territorial claims that threaten regional and perhaps even global security. At the other extreme, once a specific understanding becomes dominant, the best way of challenging that understanding is by providing an equally stark alternative – impending collapse for example.

While it is very easy to see why the vision of China as rich and powerful has come about, it is built on only a partial vision of China that tells only one part of the story of the consequences of the transition from socialism. It can also lead to at best ineffective policy towards China. For example, if we think of China as rich, and China's environmental problems as a result of growing wealth and production, then we might develop policies designed to help China resolve these issue – but we might overlook the solutions to those environmental problems caused by residual poverty and underdevelopment. If we ignore the fact that China still has millions living in poverty, and increasing social dislocations in some areas, then we might come to conclusions about China's potential futures that assume away domestic politics.

The visions of China that focus on new wealth and power are built on strong and sometimes compelling evidence. By primarily attempting to puncture some of the hyperbole about China, this book has deliberately emphasised the down-side – or more correctly, the 'not as good as appears at first sight' side – of reform and opening. So it's probably worth re-iterating here the 'yes' side of the introduction. Yes, there have been many changes in China that have significantly improved the lives of millions of people, and yes China is an increasingly important element in the global political economy; what happens in China now really does have important implications for the rest of the global economy. However, given the tone of the analysis so far, it is not surprising and fitting that the main conclusions return to 'buts' of the introduction.

Importance, significance and power

As Chapters 4 and 5 hopefully showed, China's importance and significance does not automatically equate with power – or Chinese power at any rate. To be sure, domestic producers have played their part in promoting export growth (particularly the TVEs in the 1990s), but Chinese export growth remains largely driven by external demand and external supply of finances and resources aimed at meeting that external demand. This is particularly so in exports to Japan, the EU and the US. It is notable that while 'made in China' is now extremely familiar in these markets, Chinese brand names are not, with these exports instead carrying the names of leading non-Chinese producers, or the names of leading non-Chinese retail outlets. It is a different story altogether when considering Chinese exports to Africa, Latin America and much of East Asia. Here domestic Chinese producers are exporting own brand goods at prices that undercut local enterprises and in some cases threaten to wipe out domestic suppliers. So the impact and significance of Chinese exports very much depends on the extent to which external actors are involved in generating those exports, which in turn very much depends on comparative levels of development relative to China.

In short, more power in the global political economy resides now where it has done for a long time than the rise of China might suggest – in the markets and companies of the advanced industrialised economies. Whilst production processes (including employment at home) are clearly influenced by what has happened in China, TNCs and other companies from these economies have been able to respond in a manner that preserves their interests and utilises China's global re-engagement for their own benefit (which is of course partially passed on to consumers). China may not be as open a market as many western producers would like, but many western producers have nonetheless ensured that they have gained from China's opening – often indirectly through relations with CMEs and other intermediaries in globalised financial and production networks.

So while the volume of newsprint and bandwidth on the subject might suggest that the US is the greatest 'victim' of economic growth in China, I suggest that the reality is that while US workers might be losing, many US companies and consumers are not only gaining, but also generating this economic growth in the first place. The same is true to greater or lesser extents in the EU, and Japan, and other more developed East Asian economies that act as conduits supplying the Chinese economy with finances, services and components (for example, Hong Kong, Singapore, Macao, South Korea and Taiwan).

The impact of the China challenge is less easy to control or manage (or actually generate) in other parts of the world. Chinese growth and export growth in particular has had a fundamental (though differential) impact on individual East Asian economies, and the way that these economies interact with each other. Regional states are increasingly orienting their policies to fit into the new reality of regional relations, and China looms large in any consideration of the evolution of formal regional cooperation. China's relationship with Africa and Latin America is also hugely significant, and likely to become ever more so as diplomatic initiatives support commercial efforts to obtain raw materials (particularly energy resources). These new and burgeoning relationships will also increasingly be important beyond Latin America and Africa themselves both in terms of competitive access to resources, and in terms of providing an alternative pole to US hegemony (albeit a less powerful pole in an asymmetric global system). The warmth of Sino-Venezuelan relations is an excellent example of how Chinese investment and the Chinese market not only provide a commercial opportunity, but a diplomatic bulwark against US pressure.

In Africa and Latin America, China's state owned monopolies are investing huge amounts of money in securing rights to (usually jointly) explore oil fields and gain access to other types of resources. Chinese investment is also becoming increasingly significant in Southeast Asia and particularly in Laos, Thailand and Burma. Again, much of this is targeted at securing resources (though Chinese investment in manufacturing capacity in the region is also increasing) and in the case of Burma, comes with no democratising conditionalities. All available evidence suggests that the growth of Chinese outward investment will continue to grow, and it is reasonable to surmise that the main focus of this growth will be to gain access to resources, followed by a slower increase in investment in manufacturing capacity. So we can hypothesise that outward investment will become an important new element in the projection of Chinese economic power. We can also suggest that this will have most influence in East Asia, the former Soviet Union, Latin America, Africa, and the Middle East.

Growth and development

Whilst the manner of China's integration into the global political economy has been very successful in generating growth, the investment-trade nexus has not been anywhere near as successful in promoting long term and sustainable development for five key reasons (and I am only referring to the growth of FIEs here). First, notwithstanding the increased role for domestic Chinese companies in supplying processing industries, FDI has not resulted in a significant modernisation and upgrading of 'domestic' Chinese industries – certainly not as much as the gross figures might suggest and not as much as China's leaders expected when first establishing the open door policy. Second, while FIEs have created jobs, the vast majority have done little or nothing to raise the skills level of workers (and in some cases resulted in extensive human damage). Third, the financial benefits of this growth have not been captured by the state and used to promote long-term development programmes (though again I suppose I really mean nowhere near as much as the figures would suggest). This is partly because so much of the financial gains of export growth is distributed outside China, and partly because the incentives offered to attract and retain FDI by competing local authorities has lowered the potential tax take. This raises questions about China's 'state capacity' which I will return to below.

Much more tentatively, the fourth reason is that the 'success' of the growth strategy has perhaps allowed the government to pay less attention to rural development than might otherwise be the case. The young migrants from the countryside working in many FIEs have proved an important source of rural growth through the remissions that they send back home. In at least one programme designed to find new ways of alleviating poverty in rural southern China, the conclusion was to make it easier for workers to migrate to the coast. Export growth by FIEs has thus ameliorated rural poverty, but perhaps also freed policy makers from the need to develop sustainable long term programmes at the same time (up until recently at least).

Equally tentatively, the fifth reason is that the 'success' of FIEs in generating growth has established growth (rather than development) as the benchmark for measuring success. In an echo of the need to meet and surpass targets during Maoist campaigns, attaining expected growth figures, first established by the central government as a benchmark of success, has become a key objective for local governments. For local government officials seeking promotion, growth matters – and this means a focus on quantity rather than quality. To be fair, this exists outside the investment-trade nexus and is an important component of the focus on promoting (short term) growth as opposed to (long term) development across China. However, in export oriented economies, the focus on promoting growth exacerbates the tendency to offer incentives to investors to the point that some investment provide extraordinarily little to the Chinese economy. Furthermore, with growth in these areas dependent on investment, it makes it difficult to 'upgrade' to the type of FDI that does bring improved technology and skills and helps upgrade the domestic economy.

There is historical evidence to support this idea that the growth imperative has trumped the quality imperative during previous attempts to alter the nature of investment. For example, in 1995, the Shenzhen government decided that it was time to shift the focus of investment away from just low level processing and assembly to better quality high tech industries that would be more deeply embedded within the local economy. When incentives were removed, so the 'low quality' investment slowed (and moved to other parts of the Pearl River Delta where local authorities were happy to welcome them) but new money didn't replace it because investors didn't want to source from China. By the end of 1995, the Shenzhen government was reintroducing incentives for processing industries because growth targets could not be achieved without them. Similarly, a nationwide reduction of tax exemptions on imported goods for FIEs in 1996 was reversed in January 1998 in response to declining investment figures.

The above examples suggest that having located China as a low cost assembly site in an international division of labour, it is difficult to move on to a next higher stage if this does not conform with what investors want from China. In some areas, the supply chain is already changing from low skilled labour intensive assembly, and is utilising Chinese suppliers and also increasingly China's stock of well educated and qualified technicians, researchers and designers (technicians, researchers and designers who are much cheaper to employ than their western counterparts). This has not simply come about through teleological forces, but because Chinese policy makers have acknowledged the importance of investing in education and training and of promoting and supporting industrial restructuring. If people stand back and simply expect China to move to higher levels of the supply chain and to establish a foothold in the production of higher tech and higher value added exports because it happened before in Taiwan and South Korea, then it won't happen. Such a transition will require active intervention by governments (and the emerging private sector) at all levels and significant investment in training, education and high level research and design projects. As this is already taking place, then the prospects for China to really lead the way in the production (rather than assembly) of some commodities is already likely.

If the Chinese government is really committed to making the transition from low cost assembly, then people might need to be persuaded that its OK to accept slower investment and export growth and maybe even a reduction (at some point at least). This message seems to have been accepted by China's top leaders, but for Yu Yongding (2006) the message needs to be made clear and enforced at the local level as well:

> Preferential policies for exports should be cancelled. Preventative measures should be introduced to stop local governments competing for Foreign Direct Investment. The local government should also be banned from using the introduction of FDI as part of the political performance criteria for local officials.

So in many respects, achieving developmental objectives remains contingent on the acquiescence of local governments. It also depends to some extent on foreign investors. Even if it proves relatively easy to discourage low quality investment in the future, attracting alternative higher quality investment is far from a guaranteed certainly. For example, the ultimate success of the objective of developing the West in part depends on whether foreign investors want to invest in the West. And while the importance of getting components into China and finished goods to export markets remains a key priority of investors, then the strategy is likely to attract only few foreign investors.

Potential Chinese futures

The extent of the domestic problems outlined in Chapter 6 are well understood by China's top leaders who recognise that leadership positions (either individually or perhaps even collectively as the ruling party) might be under threat if these problems are not dealt with. To this end, policies designed to reduce inequality and to spread the social safety net to include more of the rural population and the currently often sidelined migrant population in the cities are highly sensible. So too is the recognition that economic growth needs to be rebalanced so that China depends more on domestic demand for domestic growth, reducing dependence on the global economy, and providing more domestic sources of endogenous growth. The central government is also keenly aware that growth alone will not provide what the government (and millions of people) want. The government must intervene to try to direct (if not control as it did in the past) economic activity to prevent further polarisation and increased social stratification.

All of this seems highly sensible, but is it easily attainable? Wang Shaoguang and Hu Angang (1993, 2001) have longed warned that China has weak 'state capacity' because even after the 1994 reforms the fiscal system is unable to secure what the state (or the central state) needs. The ongoing weakness of the financial sector discussed in detail in Chapter 2 doesn't help either (from a long term perspective, perhaps one of the greatest achievements of Chinese reformers will be if they manage to avoid a financial crisis that has appeared possible and at some points probable for much of the last decade). Here we have a leadership who, like their predecessors, have been continually unable to prevent corruption, and only slightly more successful in preventing local leaders using local financial resources to promote locally favoured enterprises almost irrespective of national goals, objectives and policies. This lack of state capacity is clearly hugely important in thinking about China's potential futures – particularly when added to the external constraints on the central state's ability to attain these objectives. Failure to do so could have a profound impact on how the political consequences of the transition from socialism pan out.

Economic and political transitions

When considering future political change in China, the focus is typically on the transition to democracy; if it is likely and if so when it will emerge. In particular, the emergence of a middle class and civil society are taken as signs that the transition from authoritarianism is on its way – even if the end point of liberal democracy may still be some way off. Of course, this view of an inevitable transition is challenged. There is a school of though that suggests that the emphasis on the middle class as agents of democratisation is misconceived. On one level, for some the European experience of democratisation does not travel easily to Asia, where the relationship between the state and society has evolved in a very different way. For example, Goodman (1998: 40) challenges the efficacy of modernisation theory as a predictive model for Chinese political evolution. Drawing from evidence from the rest of East Asia, he argues that:

> There has been little evidence of the political space and subsequent potential for conflict between the state and the middle classes which was a major source of the drive to democratization in the European experience.

Others argue that even in the European case, the role of the middle classes was much exaggerated, and the real roots of democratisation lie in action to prevent working class revolution.[1]

For the time being at least, the CCP leadership itself seem rather unconcerned about the rise of the middle class. On the contrary, they want to bring more Chinese into the ranks of the middle class or 'xiaokang society' to help cement their legitimacy by providing the people tangible economic gains (and by delivering on their promises). Instead, attention is focused on the potential challenges that might emerge from the dispossessed or at least the discontented. Those in the cities and the millions more in the countryside who have lost out in the process of the transition from socialism – or at the very least, don't feel that they have gained as much as they should have done whilst others prosper.

China has undergone and is still undergoing an incredible process of change – actually processes in the plural – on a massive scale. An agricultural revolution is in place alongside an industrial revolution and a de-industrialisation process in the shape of the transition from state ownership and socialism and a process of engagement with the capitalist global economy from relative isolation. A hugely uneven spatial pattern of growth is exacerbating other axes of inequality generating hugely different experiences, interests and demands. Class formation and reformulation is ongoing and all of this is occurring under the leadership of a ruling party that has effectively abandoned its ideology which was supposedly the very reason for its very existence, let alone its monopoly of political power. When you think of it this way, it is astonishing that the party has managed to stay in power and not been crushed by the weight of the social and political changes it has engendered.

Indeed, whilst it is possible to find support for the inevitable democratisation thesis from an investigation of contemporary China, it's perhaps easier to find evidence to support other theories of political change that suggest revolution rather than peaceful evolution to democracy. The functional explanation of revolution, for example, focuses on government failure to cope with a rapidly changing environment and to maintain equilibrium between the social environment of production on one hand, and the values and belief systems through which individuals orient their societal behaviour on the other. Crucially for Johnson (1966), the status quo equilibrium will always be challenged through changes in either the environment or values – through the emergence of new ideas and technologies, new and/or shifting modes of interaction with external groups, changing expectations and so on.

A government is successful it its task when it reorients policy to restore the balance and to ensure that the society's value system is in equilibrium with the mode of production and vice versa. Ideas and practices have to legitimate each other, and the task of government is to ensure that they do and always restore equilibrium. The oft used example here is trying to restore balance in a set of scales – if something is added, taken or changed on one side of the scales, then something has to be done in response to the other side to ensure that the balance is restored. So if either values or the environment changes, then the government has to respond to restore the balance. If both values and the environment changes as I suggest they have in China during the transition from socialism, then the task of restoring equilibrium becomes ever more difficult.

It becomes even more difficult if societal values fracture and diverge at the same time as the number of environmental changes rapidly increase and become more diverse in origin from not just domestic but also international sources. Moreover, in responding to one demand, the government may well adopt policies that act against the interests of other groups, leading to counter (and contradictory) demands for further action. It's not just that the government is unable to meet all the demands placed upon it, but in responding it generates new value or environmental changes that in themselves demand changes that generate changes and so on. As a result, existing societal divisions are likely to widen and harden as groups organise to represent their interests. In Johnson's (1966) functional model, the regime's failure to meet these different demands and to restore equilibrium leads to 'power deflation' as the population lose faith in the government's ability to meet their needs. It may continue to rule through the increased use of force to suppress dissent, but the government's authority has gone and societal divisions increase the potential for revolution.

Or consider Olson's (1963) challenge to the then developmental orthodoxy, and his assertion that development can easily be the cause of instability and conflict. As we have seen in the Chinese case, economic growth and development has generated new winners and losers with some of the previously relatively privileged becoming new losers. And what's more, its not just the losers who might become sources of political instability. For Gurr (1970), men rebel not because they are poor, but because their expectations have not been met. It is not absolute poverty and deprivation that is the source of revolution, but relative deprivation. As the livelihood of the population as a whole improves, as has clearly been the case in China, then Gurr argues that people will always want things to improve more quickly than is possible. Quick and significant improvement not only fails to sate expectations, but actually generates expectations of even greater and ever faster improvements in the future. Even though things are getting better, the gap between what the people expect and what the regime can deliver grows ever bigger, undermining popular faith in the legitimacy of the party. And if things stop improving and actually decline (even a temporary decline), then the gap between expectations and reality becomes a 'revolutionary gap' (Davies 1962). Or returning to Olson (1963), instability can occur if people are getting better off, but others are doing better – particularly if the comparator group is deemed to be benefiting unfairly.

We might suggest that this is likely to be so when the major beneficiaries of rapid change appear to the very same elites who are supposed to be looking after the interests of their citizens. As noted in

Chapter 6, to a large extent those new economic classes that are emerging from the transition from socialism have either emerged from within the existing power structure, or have been rapidly incorporated into it. They do not need to challenge the party for power because their connections with that authoritarian political system serves their interests. Of course the argument can be made that this is only a temporary situation, and as Chinese capitalism evolves – perhaps 'matures' – then the interests of the new economic and old political elites will diverge irrespective of their common heritage, resulting in pressures for these interests to be represented in a democratic political system. But a third alternative explanation for revolution might also be apposite here if the relationship between political elites and new economic elites might be considered to represent a new class rule in China. A class that not only regulates the economy to generate surplus for itself, but is also allied with others outside China to promote the neoliberal project in China to exploit Chinese workers in the pursuit of superprofits. And a class that utilises its levers of authoritarian rule to prevent the emergence of any challenges to its political position – either the peaceful evolution of democracy or more desperate violent popular protests.

It is notable that both structural and social psychological explanations of revolution say a lot about the causes of discontent, but less about what turns this discontent into an active political revolution. Furthermore, despite the firm convictions of some Marxists, the extent to which discontent needs to be led and mobilised into political action for the revolution to succeed has concerned many Marxist thinkers and political practitioners – amongst them, of course, many of the first generation PRC leaders. So I am not saying here that China is on the verge of a revolution. But I am saying that there are enormous challenges that Hu Jintao, Wen Jiabao and others recognise could ultimately lead to the end of CCP rule if they are mishandled. I am also saying that the apparently contradictory situation where an authoritarian leadership oversees economic liberalisation is not a contradiction at all. As New Left critics argue, political authoritarianism is essential for economic liberalism, as it prevents the emergence of the popular challenges to the ruling elites that some of the above approaches predict:

> neoliberalism, in truth, relies upon the strength of transnational and national policies and economies, and it depends upon a theory and discourse of economic formalism to establish its own hegemonic discourse. As such, its extrapolitical and antistate character is utterly

dependent upon its inherent links to the state. That is, in the absence of such a policy/state premise, neoliberalism would be incapable of concealing unemployment, the decline of social security, and the widening gap between rich and poor using the mystifications of a 'transitional period (Wang Hui 2004: 8)

Authoritarian illiberalism thus provides the political basis for economic liberalism to flourish and for class realignment to occur – even if this entails the occasional slight economic reversal to ensure continued political stability.

But most of all, I am saying that visions of Chinese future based on an analysis of Chinese politics look very different from those visions that ignore the domestic and instead just focus on the international sphere. So too do we find different interpretations and predictions from those who disaggregate power and interests in the global(ised) political economy and focus on actors other than the state on one hand, and those who focus on an aggregated actor called China as the unit of analysis in international economic relations on the other.

Afterword: The Global Crisis and China's Place in the Global Political Economy

This book was written and published before the onset of the global crisis – an event which it's fair to say has had more than some impact on China's role in the global political economy. And even though we are not yet in a position to make a full assessment of the impact and implications for China (for reasons that will be explained later), we can at least reflect on some of the consequences of the crisis and China's response to it.

As already noted in Chapter 6, there was a concern in some quarters that economic growth had become too dependent on exports (and investment) which made China vulnerable to shocks in the global economy. The exact importance of exports for growth has been challenged. Given the high levels of imported components in many Chinese exports (notably those produced by foreign invested enterprises) the *net* contribution to growth was much less than the headline figure. As a result, for Anderson (2007: 1) Chinese growth had become 'decoupled' from the global economy and as such, China's leaders had 'little to fear from a global demand slowdown'. For Cui and Syed (2007) this methodology underestimated the growing role for Chinese capital goods and components in exports. And as Dew et al. (2011) pointed out, export industries had considerable 'spillovers' in the domestic economy – for example, through infrastructure development to facilitate trade flows. Add this all together and export-related growth might have accounted for more than half of Chinese growth before the crisis (Akyüz 2010).

Whatever the true statistic we can say two things with relative certainty. First, China's leaders certainly acted as if exports had become too important, and had already started to try and move to a more 'balanced' growth model even before the crisis hit. Second, when the crisis did hit, it had a devastating impact on Chinese exports, and very quickly too. Exports in October 2008 showed a 21.9 per cent increase over the previous year. In November, there was a 2.2 per cent reduction – and things only got worse. By the end of 2009, exports were down 16 per cent on the previous year with around 20 million migrant workers thought to have lost their jobs during the downturn (Zhao and Liu 2010: 14).

Ding Xueliang (2010) argues that the crisis highlighted the 'chronic illness' of the Chinese model. For Yao Yang (2010), it signalled the 'end of the Beijing consensus'. And it is hard to find a dissenting voice now to the argument that the economy needs to be rebalanced with the growth of domestic (household) consumption as the main objective. But in the short term at least, the rebalancing that took place wasn't so much from exports and investment to consumption, but from exports to investment.

The speed at which China's leaders responded to the impact of the crisis was impressive – though it entailed overturning much of what they had been trying to do over the previous year. The headline event was the announcement of a RMB4 trillion stimulus package in November 2008. It later transpired that around a quarter of this had already been designated to help Sichuan Province recover from the devastating earthquake of May 2008, and of the remainder around half was to be spent on infrastructure and power projects, with money also earmarked for development projects (low income housing, rural development, health education and welfare), technological innovation and the promotion of green strategies (Naughton 2009).

Although half of this money was to come from central government coffers, this still left a large shortfall. The solution came through the expansion of new bank loans which doubled in 2009 to reach RMB9.6 trillion – or in other words the increase in new loans in 2009 was more than the overall stimulus plan (which was meant to be rolled out over two years). The figure for new loans in 2010 was *only* RMB7.96 trillion. Around a quarter of all bank loans went to households in 2009 and over a third in 2010. When combined with tax cuts and subsidies to encourage the sale of cars and consumer durables, domestic consumption accounted for around a third of overall net economic growth in 2009 (Yu 2010).

One of the underlying themes in the book was the importance of local governments as economic actors in China – and this importance was highlighted by the response to the crisis. Local governments across China used Local Investment Platform Companies (LIPCs) to borrow money (that they weren't allowed to directly borrow themselves) and invest in local infrastructure projects. Working out the exact amount that they borrowed and spent is a little tricky for the reasons outlined in the introduction to this book, but we can suggest that around half of the new loans that were lent in 2009 went on local governments' infrastructure projects via LIPCs, and that this was the single biggest reason that Chinese growth stood up despite the impact of the crisis and ultimately exceeded the 8 per cent target.

So far so good. But the reason that we cannot yet fully judge the Chinese response to the crisis is that the financial consequences of this stimulus will take a number of years to flow through the system. According to a survey by the Chinese Banking Regulatory Committee in 2010, most of the projects funded this way were not making enough money to even meet interest repayments, let alone to pay off the debt (Tobin 2012). And according to the National Audit Office, the combined debt of local governments and their LIPCs in 2010 was over RMB10 trillion, or roughly a quarter of GDP. Notably, this debt is not evenly spread with most of it held at the city and county levels (rather than by provinces) and the problems more severe in central and western China than on the coast.

Cheng Siwei (Bloomberg, 2011) has gone as far as to refer to this local government debt as the Chinese equivalent of the US subprime crisis. This is perhaps taking things too far – after all, China's central government is in a stronger financial position than its US counterpart was in 2008 to step in to bail out both local governments and banks if things get too bad. But it does suggest that the response to the crisis has not been cost free and that there are still problematic consequences that will need to be addressed down the line. And there are other related problematic issues as well.

Bank lending in 2009 saw a massive expansion of mortgages (Lardy 2012). At the same time, local governments increasingly turned to their control of land as a means of raising revenue – not selling land itself, but selling land use rights (Naughton 2010). Indeed, there was more than 100 per cent increase in income from land use rights in 2010 alone, leaving it as the single biggest source of income under local government's control (as opposed to money that is transferred to them from the centre) (MOF 2011). This often entails moving existing tenants on to sell the land use rights to higher bidders. They get compensated (or at least, should get compensated), but only at the price they paid and not its new going rate. Such 'land seizures' and related demolitions were said to account for 22 per cent of all mass protests in 2012, and were also at the heart of an 'uprising' that saw the effective overthrow of the local leadership in Wukan in December 2011.

One might think that the active supply of land by local governments across the country might result in prices dropping: but it hasn't. On the contrary, there has been a rush join in and benefit from rising prices. With depositors getting slim rewards in interests from the banks, investing in land and property development projects via various trust schemes has become a popular alternative. At the time of writing, there were signs that some of these projects were coming unstuck, and what look remarkably like bubbles in some parts of the country were beginning to deflate if not pop. So the problem here is if prices continue to rise, then buying property is going to be even more difficult than it already is in many cities. But if prices come down, then local governments will lose a key source of income and find it even harder to pay off debts. Investors are also likely to take a big hit. This could prove to be a difficult circle to square in the medium term.

Two other issues are worth a brief mention here. First, land seizures are not *just* about raising money for local governments. It's fair to say that some individual also benefit considerably, and complaints about land seizures are often intertwined with resentment about corruption. The opportunities for corruption created in the transition from socialism were considered in Chapter 6. Much attention is not surprisingly placed on high profile cases, such as the dismissal of Bo Xilai in 2012 in a case that included murder, sex and subsequently Bo's alleged hunger strike (Coonan 2013). But corruption goes much deeper than this. In the five years from 2008, the Chinese Chief Procurator was in charge of investigation of 30 officials at ministerial level or high and 13,000 at county level or above (Xinhua 2013). The fact that Xi Jinping placed fighting corruption as his first and major task when he came to power in 2012 is a clear indication that his predecessors' equally firm commitment to stamping it out hasn't worked. Indeed, we might suggest that the amount of money pumped into the economy in response to the crisis created new opportunities and incentives for corrupt officials.

Second, the banks did a good job in supporting the state's objectives when the crisis hit. But quite apart from the emergence of new debt, much of the old debt has not gone away. The way in which bad debts were taken off the banks' balance sheets and taken over by Asset Management Companies (AMCs) was discussed in Chapter 2. When the AMCs were first established, they were partly funded by selling bonds back to the banks themselves. These bonds were due for repayment in 2009. But as the debts had been bought at full value (rather than at a lower rate as is usually the case when this type of arrangement has happened elsewhere) and by definition were not highly attractive assets, the AMCs have been unable to recover enough money to cover their obligations (Martin 2012: 30). In response, the bonds were rolled over for another ten years (Walter and Howe 2011: 67), with the Ministry of Finance subsequently taking over responsibility for the interest payments of Cinda

– apparently from tax paid by the China Construction Bank. So what we see here is an interlocking set of financial relationships between the big banks and the AMCs that are underwritten by support from the People's Bank of China and the Ministry of Finance – sometimes the implicit expectation that the state will step in to ensure that things don't go wrong and sometimes very clear and explicit guarantees. What they do is essentially recycle guarantees to each other (Walter and Howe 2011). This is possible because of the stockpiles of money stored up elsewhere in the financial system. But perhaps more importantly, they can do it because people have confidence that they will do it! A quick look at the financial situation of the banks makes them look rather healthy. Delve a little deeper and consider the non-performing assets that they are technically traceable back to them and they look rather weaker.

On Chinese global power

In the conclusion to the book, it was suggested that 'outward investment will become an important new element in the projection of Chinese economic power'. This was akin to forecasting a light rain shower before a massive downpour (or actually, as the downpour was already starting). Much has subsequently been written about the growth of Chinese economic activity overseas – mostly in Africa and the rest of Asia but more recently also in Latin America and the Middle East. And indeed, even the European Union turned to China for help (without success) when money was needed to try and shore up the Eurozone. China has emerged not only as a potential major source of much needed investment, but also through the development of its own domestic demand, as a *potential* alternative to declining Western consumption. As the People's Daily (2010) rather proudly put it, China has become a 'stabilizer' of the global economy. It's fair to say that in light of these developments, conceptions of Chinese power today are somewhat different than when the manuscript was completed in 2006.

At a rather intangible level, the global crisis increased attention on whether there might be a 'China Model' that provides a better mode of development than the so-called "Washington Consensus". This might seem rather odd given the apparent consensus in China itself that there is a desperate need to move to a new mode of growth promotion, but this apparent contradiction can be reconciled by identifying how the China Model has come to be defined. On one level, it has become identified with an idea of strong state developmentalism – a state that can and does guide economic activity and can act decisively to mobilise the economy behind a national project when the need arises. But on another level, it is not what the China model *is* that's important as what it is *not*. China did not go in for neo-liberal 'shock therapy' liberalisation (accompanied by political democratisation) but instead experimentally and incrementally changed its old structure based on what leaders thought were in China's best interests at that time. So what the Chinese model suggests is do what is best for you, and don't be forced to do what others (in the West) tell you to do (Breslin 2011). And of course, many developing countries now have increased their ability to ignore the West, and China has emerged as a new source of markets and development-related loans.

The crisis also helped propel China ever closer to the core of global politics and attempts to reform global governance mechanisms. This has occurred both through cooperation with existing powers via membership of the G20 and reform of the IMF, and also the creation of new partnerships with developing states and emerging powers (for example, through the Forum on China Africa Cooperation, and membership of the BRICS). Chinese officials also seem to have become more confident in enunciating Chinese interests and objectives in two main ways. First, while Chinese officials remain committed to proving that China is a responsible great power, this does not mean that they are satisfied with the (liberal) norms that underpin the existing order, and the distribution of power within it. This dissatisfaction is articulated independently and also collectively with other dissatisfied powers (for example, in BRICS summits). But China's leaders seem to have no great appetite to use their economic power for anything other than serving what they perceive to be China's interests. So this dissatisfaction is moderated by a lack of desire to take on global leadership roles that might have domestic costs – for example, on environmental issues. And policy makers are well aware that China's developmental needs requires access to markets and resources that would be made more difficult to attain if China was to destabilise international relations and/or antagonise key players. So while it might be dissatisfied, it is what I called a 'responsible dissatisfied great power' (Breslin, 2010).

Second, there is a stronger confidence in asserting Chinese 'core interests' (核心利益 hexinliyi) defined as the 'state system and national security', 'sovereignty and territorial integrity' and 'the continued stable development of China's economy and society' (Swaine 2010: 4). These are areas that foreigners have no right in interfering at all – indeed, at times it seems as if foreigners don't even have the right to comment on. The fear in the West is that China might use its financial resources to damage Western economies. But the nuclear Mutually Assured Destruction of the Cold War has now been replaced by a form of Mutually Assured Economic Destruction and dumping dollar holdings, for example, to harm the USA would have detrimental economic consequences for China as well (Gagnon 2010). But as Drezner (2009) argues, China now has a significant economic deterrent to prevent others trying to pressure China for changing its policy on economics, human rights and politics, and maybe even territorial issues.

Despite oft-repeated claims of harmonious intent and global responsibility, the forceful claims to territory (and water) in the South and East China seas and a sense of Chinese 'triumphalism' (Shi 2013) has created friction with a number of China's regional neighbours, and the possibility of some form of conflict cannot be discounted. Yet it was the very concern that fear of the consequences of China's growth might result in an international environment that was not conducive to China getting what it wants economically that prompted the emphasis on why this would be a Peaceful Rise in the first place. This is, after all, a country where managing and promoting the national image – a preferred understanding of what China is and what it stands for – has been a major state strategy in recent years. Wang Jisi (2011) argues that the power shifts during the global crisis took China's leaders by surprise and that they are still coming to terms with their new global position. This includes a reluctance to take on more global leadership roles – particularly if they entail putting responsibility as a global actor ahead of domestic Chinese national interests (Shambaugh 2013). They face a difficult task in reconciling their international economic interests and attempts to promote a positive national image on one hand, with territorial claims and strong domestic nationalist sentiments on the other hand. In the long run, gaining more global power might prove easier than exercising it in effective and strategic ways.

References

Akyüz, Yılmaz (2010) 'Export Dependence and Sustainability of Growth in China and the East Asian Production Network', *Geneva South Centre Research Paper*, No.27.

Anderson, Jonathan (2007) 'Is China Export-Led?', *UBS Investment Research Asian Focus*, 26 September 2007. http://www.allroadsleadtochina.com/reports/prc_270907.pdf.

Bloomberg (2011) 'Local Government Debt Is China's Subprime'. Available at http://www.bloomberg.com/news/2011-09-16/local-government-debt-is-china-s-subprime-ex-lawmaker-says-1-.html, accessed 21 September 2011.

Breslin, Shaun (2010) 'China's Emerging Global Role: Dissatisfied Responsible Great Power', *Politics*, 30 (s1): 52–62.

Breslin, Shaun (2011) 'The 'China Model' and the Global Crisis: From Friedrich List to a Chinese Mode of Governance?', *International Affairs*, 87 (6): 1323–1343.

Coonan, Clifford (2013) 'Bo Xilai 'Goes on Hunger Strike' as Corruption Probe Drags on', *The Independent*, 21 February.

Cui Li and Syed, M. (2007) 'The Shifting Structure of China's Trade and Production', IMF Working Paper, No.07/214. Available at http://ssrn.com/abstract=1033207.

Dew, Ed., Martin, Jeremy, Giese, Julia and Zinna, Gabriele (2011) 'China's Changing Growth Pattern', *Bank of England Quarterly Bulletin*, 51 (1): 49–56.

Ding Xueliang (2010) 'Jingtizhongguomoshi de "manxingbing" ' (Watch Out for the "Chronic Illness" of the China Model)', *NanfangZhoumo (Southern Weekend)*, 9 December: 31.

Drezner, Daniel (2009) 'Bad Debts: Assessing China's Financial Influence in Great Power Politics', International Security, 34 (2), 7–45.

Gagnon, Joseph. (2010) 'China's Dollar Leverage Is an Exaggerated Threat', Peterson Institute, PetersonPerspectives Interviews on Current Topics. Available at http://www.piie.com/publications/interviews/pp20100218gagnon.pdf, accessed 5 June 2011.

Lardy, Nicholas (2012) *Sustaining China's Economic Growth after the Global Crisis*, (Peterson Institute for International Economics).

Martin, Michael (2012) 'China's Banking System: Issues for Congress' *Congressional Research Service Report* No. R42380 available at http://www.fas.org/sgp/crs/row/R42380.pdf, accessed 3 January 2013.

Ministry of Finance (MOF) (2011) 'Guanyu 2010 zhongyang he difang yusuan zhixing qingkuang yu 2011 nian zhongyang he difang yusuan can'an de baogao Report on the Implementation of the 2010 central and local budget and the draft budget for 2011)', Report to the National People's Congress, 17 March 2011 available at http://www.mof.gov.cn/zhengwuxinxi/caizhengxinwen/201103/t20110317_505087.html, accessed 6 August 2011.

Naughton, Barry. (2009) 'Understanding the Chinese Stimulus Package', *China Leadership Monitor*, (28): 1–12.

Naughton, Barry (2010) 'The Turning Point in Housing', *China Leadership Monitor*, No. 33: 1–10.

People's Daily (2010) 'China, "Stabilizer" of World Economy' People's Daily online, 2 February, available at http://english.people.com.cn/90001/90778/90862/6885538.html, accessed 2 February 2010.

Shambaugh, David (2013) *China Goes Global: The Partial Power* (New York: Oxford University Press).

Shi Yinhong (2013) ' "Triumphalism" and Decision Making in China's Asia Policy', *Economic and Political Studies*, 1 (1): 107–119.

Swaine, Michael (2010) 'China's Assertive Behavior, Part One: On "Core Interests" ', *China Leadership Monitor*, No. 34: 1–25.

Tobin, Damian (2012) 'The Anglo-Saxon Paradox: Corporate Governance Best Practices and the Reform Deficit in China's Banking Sector', *Journal of Chinese Economic and Business Studies*, 10 (2): 147–168.

Walter, Carl and Howe, Fraser (2011) *Red Capitalism: The Fragile Financial Foundation of China's Extraordinary Rise* (Singapore: John Wiley).

Wang Jisi (2011) 'China's Search for a Grand Strategy – A Rising Great Power Finds Its Way', *Foreign Affairs*, 90 (3): 68–79.

Xinhua (2013) 'China Investigates 30 Ministerial Level Officials within Five Years', *People's Daily Online*, 11 March, available at http://english.peopledaily.com.cn/90785/8161504.html, accessed 11 March 2011.

Yao Yang (2010) 'The End of the Beijing Consensus? Can China's Model of Authoritarian Growth Survive?', Foreign Affairs Online, 2 February. Available at http://www.foreignaffairs.com/articles/65947/the-end-of-the-beijing-consensus, accessed 5 March 2010.

Yu Yongding (2010) 'The Impact of the Global Financial Crisis on the Global Economy and China's Policy Responses', *Third World Network Working Paper*, No. 25.

Zhao Quansheng and Liu Guoli (2010) 'Managing the Challenges of Complex Interdependence: China and the United States in the Era of Globalization', *Asian Politics & Policy*, 2 (1): 1–23.

Notes

Introduction   China – Yes, But ...

1 Whiting (1995) also identified an 'aggressive nationalism' where an external enemy is identified that has to be dealt with for China's interests to be secured (something akin to an 'antagonistic contradiction' in Maoist terms).
2 Although Fishman (2005) thinks that China is on the way to becoming a superpower, one of his core arguments is that lower prices for US consumers and higher profits for US based companies is helping to create this superpower.
3 The Chinese currency is officially the Renminbi Yuan. Using the term Renminbi is akin to using Sterling, while Yuan is akin to pound or dollar.
4 The US Dollar, the Euro, the Japanese Yen and the Korean Won.
5 Reported on the Ministry of Commerce website, http://english.mofcom.gov.cn/aarticle/newsrelease/significantnews/200608/20060802833586.html, accessed 21 August 2006.

1   Studying China in an Era Of Globalisation

1 The single reference to any European state is three lines on the UK handover of Hong Kong.
2 For a very good overview of how this popular opinion was expressed in different ways by different groups, see Shen (2007).
3 'Sino-American Rivalry' (Chen Feng *et al* 1996) argued that US policy to contain China was doomed to fail in the face of a newly powerful and resurgent China. This was followed by the highly popular 'China Can say No (Song Qiang, Zhang Zangzang and Qiao Bian 1996) which railed against the US as the self-imposed imposer of international norms, and the self-imposed adjudicator of right and wrong. China was a great civilisation which should resist American hegemony and strive to exert itself over the global hegemon. In 1997, Liu Xiguang and Liu Kang (1997) produced 'Behind the Demonisation of China' which similarly argued that Western powers (essentially short-hand for the US), were trying to force western cultures and values on developing countries like China, through the expansion of western media into the developing world. China's Path Under the Shadow of Globalisation (Fang Ning, Wang Xiaodong and Song Qiang 1999) called for a much more aggressive (or at least assertive) response to any US attempt to harm China's interests. For a good overview of this literature, see des Forges and Luo (2001).
4 Though the division between the two is somewhat arbitrary. Fang Ning, for example, spans both sets of writers.
5 Wang Shaoguang (2003) perhaps goes further than most by more or less arguing that political theories and concepts developed outside China are

not applicable for studying China as they are not 'localised' or embedded within China's distinct social, political and historical context.

6   Cited in Zeng Huaguo (2006).

7   Not least because overseas institutions have provided scholarships to facilitate this overseas study. US based funding agencies have been particularly proactive in this area, but more recently, the EU-China Higher Education Cooperation Programme has facilitated greater exchange between Chinese and European institutions and scholars.

8   Whose work on globalisation predates the policy changes that Harris refers to.

9   See the special issue of World Economics and Politics (Various 2004).

10 Fewsmith (2001a) provides an excellent overview of the emergence of the New Left.

11 Though I also admit that I know the first three institutions better than others in China, so it might be a case of bias or uneven knowledge on my part.

12 A message that came over whilst I was working on a UNDP project in Vietnam in 2005.

13 Bundy's 1964 speech at John Hopkins, quoted in Diamond (1992: 10). This citation taken from Cumings (1997).

14 The subtitle of a special issue of the Third World Quarterly edited by Gills and Philip (1996a) which assessed how different embedded historical, political, social and 'cultural' contexts led to different developmental outcomes in developing states notwithstanding similar internationalising contexts. In particular, see Gills and Philip (1996b) for a conceptual overview, and Breslin (1996b) for a case study of China.

15 For example, See Holm and Sorensen (1995), Hurrell and Woods (1999) and Seligson and Passe-Smith (1998).

16 Thanks to Ian Taylor for pointing this out.

17 For example, Amsden, (1989), Chowdhury and Islam (1993), Cotton (1994), Haggard (1990), Johnson (1981, 1987), Wade (1990),

18 For example, Mittleman (1999), Hettne (1999), Hettne and Söderbaum (2000) and Schultz, Söderbaum, and Öjendal (2001).

19 Specifically, Cox (1981), Cox (1983) and Cox (1990).

20 See also Beeson (2001).

21 These were suggested in the original draft of the introduction to *Regionalism Across the North South Divide*, but not used in the final published draft.

2   The Transition from Socialism: An Embedded Socialist Compromise?

1   After being rehabilitated after the Cultural Revolution, Deng was blamed for orchestrating demonstrations in Tiananmen Square in April 1976 supporting the late Zhou Enlai and denouncing the Gang of Four.

2   A point made by David Goodman in my first doctoral supervisory meeting.

3   This quote is taken from Macfarquhar's (1996) analysis of the resolution. For details of the reassessment of Mao, see Goodman (1981).

4   Most clearly at the 6th Plenum of the 11th Central Committee with the 'Resolution on Party History' which accused Mao of negating inner party democracy.

5 With different types of 'control' depending on the level of shareholding. For definitions, see Holz (2003b).

6 They cite Wong (1988), Byrd (1990), and Che Jiahua and Qian Yingyi (1998a) as proponents of this view.

7 Citing Chang and Wang (1994), Li (1996), and Che Jiahua and Qian Yingyi (1998b).

8 Cited in Woo (1999: 46).

9 Zhu served as Vice Premier with responsibility for financial reform from 1994 to 1998, and as Premier from 1998 to 2003.

10 This is often associated with the 15th party congress in 1997, but was in fact first announced as party policy by the central committee in September 1995.

11 Quoted in China News Digest, 10th March 1996.

12 The China Business Review, March–April 1997.

13 State Statistical Bureau via China News Digest, 15 December 1996.

14 We need to read the reports on statistics with great care. Various reports all emanating from an original Xinhua report in March 2006 seemed to suggest that SOEs lost over RMB100 million as a sector in 2005. But a check on the statistics of the NSB suggests that this just refers to those that are losing money losing even more in 2005 than in 2004, and ignores the fact that those that are profitable were also more profitable in 2005 resulting in the sector as a whole being in the black.

15 All four received the same amount irrespective of the extent of bad debts in their area. See China News Digest, 7 November 1999.

16 Zeng was Chairman of the State Development Planning Commission. See China News Digest, 7 November 1999.

17 Private unpublished paper cited with author's permission.

18 Private unpublished paper cited with author's permission.

19 Or of course, they might not have been prepared to tell me.

20 Guangxi, Hainan, Liaoning, Shandong, Shanghai, Sichuan, and Zhejiang

21 Shanghai was allowed to keep so little of its locally collected revenue that complaints by local leaders eventually led to a change in its status allowing more money to be retained locally after 1987 (Wang Huning 1988b; Zhang Zhongli 1988). The revenue sharing system was also readjusted in 1988. For details see Wong, Heady and Wing (1995).

22 For a good overview of the 1994 tax reforms, see Bahl (1999).

23 Though they take different perspectives and use different methodologies and theories, these include Oi (1999), Montinola, Qian and Weingast (1996), Xu Chenggang and Zhuang Juzhong (1998) and Lin and Liu (2000).

24 Though Huang (1996) argues that the central authorities have had more power to control investment spending in the provinces than other authors suggest. The key for Huang is that despite economic decentralisation, there is still strong political integration between provincial and central leaders.

25 Bernstein and Lu (2003, chapter 4) also argue that is viewed as essential by local authorities to pay the salaries of the ever increasing number of local officials.

26 Young (2000: 1128) similarly refers to local 'fiefdoms'.

27 When the 11th Five Year Plan was announced in 2005, the term *jihua* or 'plan' was replaced by *guihua gangyao* or 'outline programme'.

28 And ranked China as less free in 2003 than before China joined the WTO in 2000. The only areas where China came out 'well' (by the heritage foundation criteria) was a 2 for the low level of fiscal burden, and 1 for monetary policy due to low levels of inflation. See http://cf.heritage.org/index/country.cfm?ID=30.0

29 The Asian Development Bank calculate that all of the 27 million new jobs created in the five years to the end of 2001 were in the private sector, and that for every 1% increase in the share of private employment, there is a corresponding increase of RMB164 ($20) in per capita GDP (ADB, 2003: 97).

30 Though Walder (2004) points out that this process is much smaller in scale than has been the case in the former Soviet Union.

31 For examples, see Dickson (2002), Unger and Chan (1995), Oi (1992) and Pearson (1997). Huchet and Richet (2002) provide an excellent overview of the different forms of corporate governance in contemporary China.

3   Re-engagement with the Global Economy

1 Not at the Third Plenum itself, but shortly afterwards. For details of the specifics see Ho and Huenemann (1984).

2 These were Xiamen in Fujian Province, and Zhuhai, Shantou, and Shenzhen in Guangdong. When Hainan Island was later separated from Guangdong to become a province in its own right, it was established as the fifth SEZ.

3 Unless indicated to the contrary, the trade data used in this paper all originates from sources that use figures from the PRC General Administration of Customs. These figures are lower than those estimates of non-Chinese agencies due to different accounting methods. While these figures might deflate the real value of exports by western standards, they are the only way of ensuring the use of common figures, and therefore making like-to-like comparisons.

4 See also Lardy (1998, 2002).

5 There is also a separate 'Catalogue of Encouraged Hi-tech Products for Foreign Investment' that lists 721 items where investment is encouraged to improve China's technological base.

6 Restrictions include the amount of factories or outlets an investor can own, an insistence on joint ownership with a foreign partner, a limited geographic scope of activity etc. For full details of the different restrictions and how they have changed over the years, see Breslin (2006a).

7 These issues and others were addressed in Yu, Zheng and Song (2000), one of the earliest Chinese collections on the potential impact of WTO entry.

8 For details of the technicalities involved in negotiating WTO entry, see Yang Guohua and Cheng Jin (2001).

9 Since the WTO replaced the GATT in 1995, none of the new members have been allowed to use the transitional periods after entry that were previously granted to developing countries.

10 For example, sector specific reservations were negotiated by Argentina, the European Union, Hungary, Mexico, Poland, the Slovak Republic and

Turkey. These reservations were largely related to exports of items of textiles, clothing, footwear, toys, ceramics and cigarette lighters. Mexico, which did not resolve its bilateral disputes with China, but agreed not to block accession, has 21 items on its reserved list. See WTO (2001).

11 It is notable that there is no mention of 'developing country' at all in the final accession document.

12 Email discussions with USTRO negotiator – cited with permission.

13 Reported by China News Digest, 10 December 1996.

14 The other nine were Taiwan, Hong Kong, Indonesia, India, South Korea, Mexico, Brazil and Argentina.

15 http://www.fas.usda.gov/itp/china/accession.html

16 This is quite apart from the terms of Section 201 of the US 1974 Trade Act which allows imports to the US to be restricted or blocked if US producers face an ill defined 'serious injury'. For details, see Breslin (2003: 220–3).

17 A percentage of trade in each commodity remained reserved for SOEs.

18 Its not just that there was opposition, initially at least there was considerable ignorance of what needed to be done. In February 2002, a leading trade official in what was then the SETC said that none of her staff understood what the implications would be for them – I had gone to the interview to ask what the WTO meant for the SETC and she asked me the exact same question.

19 The Catalogue was formally amended in 2004, but came into operation on 1 January 2005. As noted above, it was originally jointly produced by the State Development and Planning Commission, the SETC and the former Ministry of Foreign Trade and Economic Cooperation. After the administrative reform discussed in Chapter Two, the 2004 amendments were jointly issued by the new State Development and Reform Commission and the Ministry of Commerce.

20 The US Department of State has a web-page devoted to Chinese IPR issues. See http://usinfo.state.gov/ei/economic_issues/intellectual_property/ipr_china.html

21 From the AFLCIO website http://www.aflcio.org/issues/jobseconomy/global-economy/ExecSummary301.cfm

22 Kerry Statement on the U.S.–China Economic and Security Review Commission's Report http://www.johnkerry.com/pressroom/releases/pr_2004_0615b.html

4 Beyond Bilateralism: What the Statistics Don't Tell Us

1 The officials included the former Vice Minister of Public Security, the deputy Party secretary of Xiamen City, the vice mayor of Xiamen, the head and deputy head of the Xiamen Customs, the deputy director of the provincial public security department, the president and deputy president of Fujian Provincial Branch of the Bank of China; and the president of the Xiamen Municipal Branch of the Industrial and Commercial Bank of China.

2 With thanks to the Hong Kong Government Information Centre.

3 In addition to the sources cited below, see Tseng and Zebregs (2002), Gunter (1996) and Sicular (1998).

4 If this is true, then 'real' FDI as a percentage of GNP in China and India is roughly equal at 2 per cent and 1.7 per cent respectively (Financial Express 2002).

5 For example, patents, commissions, travel expenses, transportation and insurance.
6 It is perhaps worth noting that the lower estimate comes from the State Foreign Currency Administration which is responsible for preventing illegal capital flight.
7 See http://www.uschina.org/info/chops/2006/fdi.html
8 In Equity JVs the two sides pool investment capital in agreed proportions and share profits and loses in proportion to their equity stake. With contractual JVs, the Chinese partner provides land, factory building, and labour, while the foreign partner provides equipment, capital and technical expertise.
9 See http://www.worldwatch.org/node/3864
10 For details of industrial clustering in China, see Jiang Xiaoyuan (2003).
11 As one of the anonymous reviewers of this manuscript pointed out, it is not strictly speaking an integration model, but it is nevertheless a model that predicts an integrated regional economy.
12 Cited in Sasuga (2004).
13 See also Kotabe (1998) and Swamidass and Kotabe (1993).
14 See also Borrus, Ernst and Haggard (2000). For a description and analysis of the various terms used and how they correspond with each other, see Berger *et al* (2001).

5   Interpreting Chinese 'Power' in the Global Political Economy

1 On an interview on BBCs 'Newsnight' programme on 19 February 1997 commemorating Deng Xiaoping, former Prime Minister, Ted Heath said 'What happened was that for a month, there was a crisis in which the civil authority had been defied. They (the Chinese authorities) took action about it. We can criticise it in the same way people criticise Bloody Sunday in Northern Ireland, but that isn't by any means the whole story.'
2 PNTR is Permanent Normal Trade Relations – previously MFN – that China was granted by the US in 2000 to pave the way for WTO entry.
3 This quote is taken from Dorgan's web page, which includes a link to the text of the petition. See http://dorgan.senate.gov/issues/economy/chinatrade/ accessed on 21 August 2006.
4 These figures are a mixture of the data provided by Downs (2004: 23) and by the US Energy Information Administration's China brief (http://www.eia.doe.gov/emeu/cabs/china.html)
5 Unless otherwise cited, the data in this section is taken from the Ministry of Commerce web-pages, accessed on 21st August 2006.
6 By Lord Powell, Chair of the China-Britain Business Council. Oral Evidence to FAC (2000). It is notable that the visit of Jiang Zemin to the UK was considered as highly successful by the Chinese, not least because the UK visit was not marred by demonstrations and protests by Human Rights activists as a previous visit to Switzerland had been.
7 FAC (2000: Minutes of Evidence, Examination of Witnesses, Questions 140–159).

8 Unless otherwise cited, these statistics are taken from the Ministry of Commerce data sets on investment in China available at http://www.fdi.gov.cn – these statistics accessed on 3rd February 2006

9 Interview with Malaysian investor, Guangzhou Export Fair, April 2004.

10 I am grateful to Stephen Frost at City University in Hong Kong for this information.

11 Previously reported in the US in a Los Angeles Times article by Tempest (1996). The example was also repeated on Chinese television on a number of occasions during Zhu Rongji's visit to the USA in March 1999.

12 According to Hu Jintao 'at least 90 percent of US imports from China are goods that are no longer produced in the United States.... Even if not from China, the United States will still have to import these products from other suppliers' (CD 2006).

13 This information is taken from the American Federation of Labor and Congress of Industrial Organizations (AFLCIO) web pages devoted to the impact that Wal-mart has on jobs in the US and production processes overseas. It is fair to say that the AFLCIO is not Wal-mart's biggest fan, but very similar statistics can be found from a range of other less critical sources. See http://www.aflcio.org/corporatewatch/walmart/walmart_5.cfm

14 According to the official Chinese government webpage, http://english.gov.cn/ 2006-04/06/content_247295.htm accessed 23 August 2006. Morgan Stanley were also cited as Hu Jintao's source when he claimed that Chinese exports had created four million jobs in the US in 2004 (CD 2006).

15 Cited in Wu *et al* (2002: 96).

16 China had previously agreed in principle to only bilateral codes of conduct.

6 The Domestic Context: Stretching the Social Fabric?

1 Although the transition of the Indian economy comes close in population terms at least.

2 Indeed, I suspect that Gordon Chang's (2002) *The Coming Collapse of China* was in part intended as an antidote to such hyperbolic approaches – perhaps even deliberately exaggerating the potential for collapse. And it was Chang's book that in turn prompted Fan Gang's (2002) assessment of China's problems.

3 We should note that China already had large environmental problems before the start of the reform process – not least the deforestation and inappropriate land use that occurred in the rush to increase output in the Great Leap Forward. Mao's conviction that man could harness nature to support the socialist revolution has had environmental legacies that are still felt today. We should also note that China is far from unique in (ab)using resources and polluting during a phase of industrialisation. Nor is the Chinese leadership the only ruling elite in the world that is concerned that getting the balance wrong between prioritising the environment and promoting economic growth might have political (if not in this case electoral) consequences.

4 For example, increased and changing consumer demand (ie: car production increased by 80% in 2003 alone), increased production, increased waste,

demands for new types of housing, urbanisation and the creation of new mega-cities.

5 The source was cited as the UK Department for International Development by its Parliamentary Under-Secretary, Gareth Thomas, in a written answer to an MP on 8th March 2006 and recorded by Hansard http://www.publications.parliament.uk/pa/cm200506/cmhansrd/cm060308/text/60308w23.ht m#60308w23.html_dpthd0. However, a lower figure is used by the Department in their written materials and on their web pages. I have used it here as it provides an example of the difficulty in finding a definitive figure and not because it is the most reliable or 'best'.

6 https://www.cia.gov/cia/publications/factbook/geos/ch.html#Econ. Accessed 20 July 2006.

7 For the statistically and methodologically minded, Reddy and Minoiu (2005) outline not just the different figures, but also explain how the many different figures are calculated.

8 For example, in Gansu, over 21 per cent of registered peasants work elsewhere; 20.6 per cent in Ningxia; 18.4 per cent in Sichuan; 18 per cent in Anhui and so on.

9 The major difference here is that the unemployed are the younger generation, while the older generation dominate the 'laid-off' category.

10 See his various publications on http://www.msu.edu/~gilesj

11 Payment of premiums for five to ten years results in 18 months of benefits, and between one and five years of 12 months of benefits. The amount of the payment is set by local governments at a rate above the minimum living allowance, but less than the local minimum wage. Unemployment insurance provisions for ex farmers who have moved to employment in urban areas on a contract basis is limited to a lump sum dependent on the length of employment as long as their employers have paid premiums on their behalf for an unbroken one year period.

12 The report cited Callick (2001: 11) as the original in her 2001 chapter for Transparency International. But whilst Callick's paper does indeed point to the very high levels of corruption in China, she does not make this specific claim.

13 Other causes include the treatment of migrant workers, poor job prospects for college students, the lack of action over environmental disasters and so on.

14 See, for example, Li Peilin's (1995) early investigation into the impact of reform on China's social structure.

15 The reports cited here are based on interviews with Li after the publication of a chapter criticising mainstream Chinese research on the growth of the Chinese middle class. For an analysis of the original chapter (Li Chunling 2004), and other work on social stratification in China, see Fewsmith (2004).

16 Though we should note that those surveyed were given the list of 10 different strata that emerged from the original 2002 report and were constrained by the choices they were presented with. 56 per cent of those surveyed in the 2004 report thought that the classifications were about right.

17 Jiang Zemin's speech to the 16th Party Congress was officially translated by the party in English as 'Building a Well Off Society'. Whilst the term was

used by Deng Xiaoping, and is often associated with him in official state-ments, it has its origins in 'The Book of Songs' in traditional Chinese phi-losophy, being the stage before the creation of the perfect society of Great Harmony or *datong*.

18 For example, see People's Daily (2004a; 2004c; 2004e).
19 I am grateful to Kevin Hewison for this observation.
20 Private unpublished paper cited with author's permission.
21 This is sometimes referred to in English and Chinese as 'new socialist coun-tryside' (*xin shehuizhuyi nongcun*) – but the correct formal title is 'socialist new countryside'.
22 Officially the 'Office of the Leading Group for Adjustment and Renovation of the Old Industrial Base under the State Council'.
23 An argument refuted by the Ministry of Commerce. See http://dk2.mofcom.gov.cn/aarticle/chinanews/200412/20041200008390.html
24 In interviews with investors in Hong Kong, a local investor told me that he couldn't keep employees, as they left his factory (which stuck to legal limits for hours worked) to go to other factories where they could illegally work longer hours but make more money.

Conclusions

1 I particularly like Paul Foot's (2005) account of democratisation in the UK.

Bibliography

ADB (2003) *Private Sector Assessment in the People's Republic of China* (Manila: Asian Development Bank).

ADB (2004) *Poverty Profile of the People's Republic of China* (Manila: Asian Development Bank).

Ahn Byung-Joon (2004) 'The Rise of China and the Future of East Asian Integration', *Asia Pacific Review*, 11 (2): 18–35.

Akamatsu, K. (1962) 'A Historical Pattern of Economic Growth in Developing Countries', *The Developing Economies*, (March–August): 3–25.

Alden, E. and Harding, J. (2004) 'Bush's China Stance Hands Kerry a Big Stick', *Financial Times*, 30th April.

Amsden, A. (1989) *Asia's Next Giant: South Korea and Late Industrialization* (New York: Oxford University Press).

Babbin, J. and Timperlake, E. (2006) *Showdown: Why China Wants War with the United States* (Washington: Regnery).

Bacani, C. (2003) *The China Investor: Getting Rich with the Next Superpower* (Indianapolis: John Wiley).

Bachman, D. (1986) 'Differing Visions of China's Post-Mao Economy: The Ideas of Chen Yun, Deng Xiaoping, and Zhao Ziyang', *Asian Survey*, (March): 292–321.

Bachman, D. (1988) 'Varieties of Chinese Conservatism and the Fall of Hu Yaobang', *The Journal of Northeast Asian Studies*, (Spring): 22–46.

Bahl, R. (1999) *Fiscal Policy in China: Taxation and Intergovernmental Fiscal Relations* (Ann Arbor: University of Michigan Press).

Bai Shazhou (2004) 'The Three Types of Capitalists in China and Their Relations with the Government', *China Strategy*, 30th January: 21–5.

Balls, A. and Swann, C. (2006) 'US Attacks China Peg for Trade Deficit', *Financial Times*, 13th February.

Banister, J. (2005) *Manufacturing Employment and Compensation in China* (Washington: US Department of Labour).

Barboza, D. (2003) 'Textile Industry Seeks Trade Limits on Chinese', *New York Times*, 25th July.

Barshefsky, C. (1999) 'Statement of Ambassador Charlene Barshefsky Regarding Broad Market Access Gains from China WTO Negotiations' Office of the United States Trade Representative: Washington, 8 April.

Beeson, M. (2001) 'Globalization, Governance, and the Political-Economy of Public Policy Reform in East Asia', *Governance: an International Journal of Policy, Administration and Institutions*, 14(4): 481–502.

Berger, S. and Dore, R. (eds) (1996) *National Diversity and Global Capitalism* (Ithaca: Cornell University Press).

Berger, S., Kurz, C., Sturgeon, T., Voskamp, U. and Wittke, V. (2001) 'Globalization, Production Networks, and National Models of Capitalism – On the Possibilities of New Productive Systems and Institutional Diversity in an Enlarging Europe', University of Göttingen SOFI-Mitteilungen No. 29/2001.

Bergsten, C. (1997) 'The Asian Monetary Crisis: Proposed Remedies' prepared remarks to the U.S. House of Representatives Committee on Banking and Financial Services, November 13th, available at www.iie.com/publications/papers/paper.cfm?ResearchID=297

Bernard, M. (1991) 'The Post-Plaza Political Economy of Taiwanese-Japanese Relations', *Pacific Review*, 4 (4): 358–67.

Bernard, M. and Ravenhill, J. (1995) 'Beyond Product Cycles and Flying Geese: Regionalization, Hierarchy, and the Industrialization of East Asia', *World Politics*, 47 (2): 171–209.

Bernstein, R. and Dicker, R. (1994) 'Human Rights First', *Foreign Policy*, (Spring): 43–7.

Bernstein, R. and Munro, R. (1998) *The Coming Conflict with China* (New York: Vintage).

Bernstein, T. and Lu Xiaobo (2003) *Taxation Without Representation in Contemporary Rural China* (Cambridge: Cambridge University Press).

Bhaskaran, M. (2003) 'China as Potential Superpower: Regional Responses' (Berlin: Deutsche Bank Research Report, available at www.dbresearch.com/PROD/999/PROD0000000000050878.pdf

Bhatia, K. (2006) 'Remarks by Ambassador Karan K. Bhatia Deputy U.S. Trade Representative U.S.–China Business Council Forecast 2006 Conference', available at www.ustr.gov/assets/Document_Library/Transcripts/2006/January/asset_upload_file947_8798.pdf

Bhattasali, D. (2002) 'Accelerating Financial Market Restructuring in China', World Bank Trade Working Paper, available at siteresources.worldbank.org/INTRANETTRADE/Resources/bhattfinservices.pdf

Blecher, M. (2002) 'Hegemony and Workers' Politics in China', *China Quarterly*, (170): 283–303.

Bloomberg (2003) 'Evans Warns China to Comply with its WTO Commitments', *Bloombery*, 9 July: 12.

Bremner, B. with Carey, J. (2005) 'China's Wasteful Ways', *BusinessWeek*, 11th April.

Bonin, J. and Huang Yiping (2001) 'Dealing with the Bad Loans of the Chinese Banks', Columbia University APEC Studies Center Discussion Paper No. 13.

Borrus, M. and Zysman, J. (1997) 'Wintelism and the Changing Terms of Global Competition: Prototype of the Future?', Berkeley Roundtable on International Economy Working Paper No. 96b.

Borrus, M. and Zysman, J. (1998) 'Globalization with Borders: The Rise of 'Wintelism' as the Future of Industrial Competition', in John Zysman and Andrew Schwartz (eds) *Enlarging Europe: The Industrial Foundations of a New Political Reality* (Berkeley: University of California Press): 27–62.

Borrus, M., Ernst, D. and Haggard, S. (2000) 'Introduction: Cross Border Production Networks and the Industrial Integration of the Asia-Pacific Region', in Michael Borrus, Dieter Ernst and Stephan Haggard (eds) *International Production Networks in Asia: Rivalry or Riches?* (London: Routledge): 1–30.

Borrus, M. (1995) 'Left for Dead: Asian Production Networks and the Revival of US Electronics' Berkeley Roundtable on the International Economy Working Paper No. 100.

Bowles, P. and Dong Xiao-yuan (1994) 'Current Successes and Future Challenges in China's Economic Reforms', *New Left Review*, (208): 49–76.

Bratton, M. and van de Walle, N. (1994) 'Neopatrimonial Regimes and Political Transitions in Africa', *World Politics*, 46 (4): 453–89.

Braunstein, E. and Epstein, G. (2002) 'Bargaining Power and Foreign Direct Investment in China: Can 1.3 Billion Consumers Tame the Multinationals?', New School University Center for Economic Policy Analysis Working Paper No. 2002–13.

Brecher, J. and Costello, T. (2001) *Global Village or Global Pillage (Second Edition)*, (Cambridge, MA: South End Press).

Breslin, S. (1996a) *China in the 1980s: Centre-Province Relations in a Reforming Socialist State* (Basingstoke: Macmillan).

Breslin, S. (1996b) 'China: Developmental State or Dysfunctional Development', *The Third World Quarterly*, 17 (4): 689–706.

Breslin, S. (2003) 'Reforming China's Embedded Socialist Compromise: China and the WTO', *Global Change, Peace and Security*, 15 (3): 213–30.

Breslin, S. (2004) 'Greater China and the Political Economy of Regionalisation', *East Asia: An International Journal*, 21 (1): 7–23.

Breslin, S. (2005) 'China in the Asian Economy' in Barry Buzan and Rosemary Foot (eds) *Does China Matter? A Reassessment* (London: Routledge): 107–23.

Breslin, S. (2006) 'Foreign Direct Investment in the People's Republic of China: Preferences, Policies and Performance', *Policy and Society*, 25 (1): 9–38.

Breslin, S. and Hook, G. (eds) (2002) *Microregionalism and World Order* (Basingstoke: Palgrave Macmillan).

Brooke, J. (2004) 'Koreans Look to China, Seeing a Market and a Monster', *New York Times*, 10th February.

Brown, L. (1995) *Who Will Feed China? Wake-Up Call for a Small Planet* (Washington: WorldWatch Books).

Brown, O. (2004) 'Local Governments Rack Up Debt, Worrying Beijing', *Wall Street Journal*, 12th April: A18.

Byrd, W. (1990) 'Entrepreneurship, Capital, and Ownership' in William Byrd and Qingsong Lin (eds) *China's Rural Industry: Structure, Development, and Reform* (Oxford: Oxford University Press): 189–218.

Cai Yongshun (2002) 'Relaxing the Constraints from Above: Politics of Privatizing Public Enterprises in China', *Asian Journal of Political Science*, 10 (2): 94–121.

Calder, K. (1997) *Asia's Deadly Triangle: How Arms, Energy and Growth Threaten to Destabilize Asia-Pacific* (London: Nicholas Brealey Publishing).

Callick, R. (2001) 'East Asia and the Pacific' in Robin Hodess (ed.) *Global Corruption Report 2001* (Berlin: Transparency International): 10–22.

Camilleri, J. (2000) *States, Markets and Civil Society in Asia-Pacific* (Cheltenham: Edward Elgar).

Carter, C. and Li Xianghong (1999) 'Economic Reform and the Changing Pattern of China's Agricultural Trade', University of California Davis, Department of Agricultural and Resource Economics Working Paper No. 99–003.

Cao Yuanzheng, Qian Yingyi, and Weingast, B. (1999) 'From Federalism, Chinese Style, to Privatization, Chinese Style', *Economics of Transition*, 7 (1): 103–31.

CCP CC (1981) *Resolution on Certain Questions in the History of our Party Since the Founding of the People's Republic of China* (Beijing: Central Committee of the Communist Party of China).

CD (2002) 'China Enacts New Measures on Currency Control', *China Daily*, 28th May.

CD (2004) 'Four Reasons Why China Will Not Revalue RMB', *China Daily*, 6th April.

CD (2005) '26m Still in Poverty Despite Progress', *China Daily*, 5th April.

CD (2006) 'US Benefits from Trade with China: President Hu', *China Daily*, 20th April.

CECC (2005) *Congressional-Executive Commission on China Annual Report, 2005* (Washington: US Government Printing Office).

Chai Mi (2004) 'More Balanced Development', *Beijing Review* (13), available at www.bjreview.com.cn/200413/Cover-200413(B).htm

Chan, A. (1995) 'The Emerging Patterns of Industrial Relations in China and the Rise of Two New Labour Movements', *China Information*, 9 (4): 36–59.

Chan, A. (2001) *China's Workers Under Assault: the Exploitation of Labor in a Globalizing Economy* (Armonk: Sharpe).

Chan, A. and Zhu Xiaoyang (2003) 'Disciplinary Labor Regimes in Chinese Factories', *Critical Asian Studies*, 35 (4): 559–84.

Chan, G. (1999) *Chinese Perspectives on International Relations* (Basingstoke: Macmillan).

Chan, G. (2004) 'China and the WTO: the Theory and Practice of Compliance', *International Relations of the Asia-Pacific*, 4 (1): 47–72.

Chang Chun and Wang Yijiang (1994) 'The Nature of the Township Enterprise', *Journal of Comparative Economics*, 19 (3): 434–52.

Chang, G. (2002) *The Coming Collapse of China* (New York: Random House).

Che Jiahua and Qian Yingyi (1998a) 'Institutional Environment, Community Government, and Corporate Governance: Understanding China's Township-Village Enterprises', *Journal of Law, Economics, and Organization*, 14 (1): 1–23.

Che Jiahua and Qian Yingyi (1998b) 'Insecure Property Rights and Government Ownership of Firms', *Quarterly Journal of Economics*, 113 (2): 467–96.

Chen An (2002) 'Socio-Economic Polarization and Political Corruption in China: A Study of the Correlation', *Journal of Communist Studies & Transition Politics*, 18 (2): 53–74.

Chen An (2003) 'Rising Class Politics and its Impact on China's Path to Democracy', *Democratization*, 10 (2): 141–62.

Chen Chunlai (2002) 'Foreign Direct Investment in China: A Case Study' in *Austrian Foreign Trade Yearbook 2001–2002* (Federal Ministry for Economic Affairs and Labour, Vienna).

Chen Feng, Zhao Xingyuan, Huang Jiaoyu, Yang Mingjie, and Yuan Xixing (1996) *Zhongmei Jialian Caxiezheng (A History of Sino-American Rivalry)* (Beijing: Zhongguo Renshi).

Chen Shaohua and Ravallion, M. (2004a) 'How have the World's Poorest Fared since the Early 1980s?', *World Bank Research Observer*, 19 (2): 141–69.

Chen Shaohua and Ravallion, M. (2004b) 'China's (Uneven) Poverty Reduction' World Bank Policy Research Working Paper No. WPS 3408.

Chen Shin-Hong (2002) 'Global production networks and information technology: The case of Taiwan', *Industry and Innovation*, 9 (3): 249–65.

Chen Yixin (2000) 'Financial Services Liberalization in China: Conservative Gradualism', London: Royal Institute of International Affairs Briefing Paper No. 11.

Cheng, A. (2004) 'Beijing still baffled by soaring investments', *South China Morning Post*, 13th April.

Cheng, E. (2005) 'China: Sweeping Privatisations Spark Criticism', *Green Left Weekly*, (619) 16th March. Available at www.greenleft.org.au/back/2005/619/619p20.htm

Cheng, J. (2004) 'The ASEAN-China Free Trade Area: Genesis and Implications', *Australian Journal of International Affairs*, 58 (2): 257–77.

Cheng, L. and Kwan, Y. (2000) 'What are the Determinants of the Location of Foreign Direct Investment? The Chinese Experience', *Journal of International Economics*, 51 (2): 379–400.

Cheung Chiwai and Wong Kwan-Yiu (2000) 'Japanese Investment in China: A Glo-cal Perspective', in Si–Ming Li and Wing-Shing Tang (eds) *China's Regions, Polity, & Economy: A Study of Spatial Transformation in the Post-Reform Era* (Hong Kong: Hong Kong University Press): 97–132.

Cheung, Kui-Yin and Lin, Ping (2004) 'Spillover Effects of FDI on Innovation in China: Evidence From the Provincial Data', *China Economic Review*, 15 (1): 25–44.

Cheung, P., Chung, J. and Lin Zhimin (eds) (1997) *Provincial Strategies of Economic Reform in Post-Mao China: Leadership, Politics, and Implementation* (Armonk: Sharpe).

Chia Siow Yue and Lee Tsao Yuan (1993) 'Subregional Economic Zones: A New Motive Force in Asia-Pacific Development' in Fred Bergstein and Marcus Noland (eds) *Pacific Dynamism and the International Economic System* (Washington: Institute for International Economics): 225–69.

China Biz (2002) 'WTO-optimism on the Retreat – Analysis', *China Biz*, 3rd February.

China Currency Coalition (2004) *Petition for Relief Under Section 301(a) of the Trade Act of 1974, as Amended*, available at www.chinacurrencycoalition.org/pdfs/petition.pdf

Chinanews (2005a) 'China to Retain Not More Than 100 SOEs', 1st September, available at www.chinanews.cn/news/2005/2005-09-01/10265.html.

Chinanews (2005b) 'China to close unprofitable SOEs by 2008', 12th December, available at www.chinanews.cn/news/2005/2005-12-12/15671.html.

China News Digest (1996a) 'Chinese Researcher Urges Reforms in State Enterprises' available at http://museums.cnd.org/CND-Global/CND-Global.96.1st/CND-Global.96-03-13.html.

China News Digest (1996b) 'China's State-Owned Industry: Further Loss but Slow Reform' available at http://museums.cnd.org/CND-Global/CND-Global.96.4th/CND-Global.96-12-15.html.

China News Digest (1999) 'Debt-to-Equity Swaps Limited to Selected State Firms' available at http://museums.cnd.org/CND-Global/CND-Global.99.4th/CND-Global.99-11-07.html.

Chou, K.P. (2006) 'Downsizing Administrative Licensing System and Private Sector Development in China: A Preliminary Assessment', Asian Development Bank Institute (Tokyo) Discussion Paper No. 52.

Chowdhury, A. and Islam, I. (1993) *The Newly Industrialising Economies of East Asia* (London: Routledge).

Christensen, T. (2006) 'Fostering Stability or Creating a Monster? The Rise of China and U.S. Policy toward East Asia', *International Security*, 31 (1): 81–126.

Chua Chin Hon (2004) 'Chinese Middle Class? It's Just a Myth, Study Finds', *The Straits Times*, 27th January.

Chung, J. (1995) 'Studies of Central-Provincial Relations in the People's Republic of China: a Mid-Term Appraisal', *China Quarterly*, (142): 487–508.

Chung, J. (1999a) *Cities in China: Recipes for Economic Development in the Reform Era* (London: Routledge).

Chung, J. (1999b) 'A Sub-Provincial Recipe for Coastal Development in China: The Case of Qingdao', *China Quarterly*, (160): 487–508.

Chung, J., Hongyi Lai and Ming Xia (2006) 'Mounting Challenges to Governance in China: Surveying Collective Protesters, Religious Sects and Criminal Organizations', *The China Journal*, (56): 1–32.

Cotton, J. (1994) 'The State in the Asian NICs', *Asian Perspective*, 18 (Spring/ Summer): 39–56.

Coutts (2003) *Investment Perspective*, May/June 2003 (London: Coutts).

Cox, R. (1981) 'Social Forces, States and World Orders: Beyond International Relations Theory', *Millennium*, 10 (2): 126–55.

Cox, R. (1983) 'Gramsci, Hegemony and International Relations: An Essay in Method', *Millennium*, 12 (2): 162–75.

Cox, R. (1990) *Power, Production and World Order* (New York: Columbia University Press).

Crone, R. (1993) 'Does Hegemony Matter? The Reorganization of the Pacific Political Economy', *World Politics*, 45 (4): 501–25.

Crouch, C. and Streeck, W. (eds) (1997) *Political Economy of Modern Capitalism: Mapping Convergence and Diversity* (London: Sage).

Cumings, B. (1987) 'The Origins and Development of the Northeast Asian Political Economy: Industrial Sectors, Product Cycles, and Political Consequences', in Fred Deyo, (ed.) *The Political Economy of the New East Asian Industrialism* (New York: Cornell University Press): 44–83.

Cumings, B. (1997) 'Boundary Displacement: Area Studies and International Studies During and after the Cold War', *Bulletin of Concerned Asian Scholars*, 29 (1): 6–26.

Davidow, W. and Malone, M. (1992) *The Virtual Corporation – Structuring and Revitalizing the Corporation for the 21st Century* (New York: Harper Collins).

Davies, J. (1962) 'Towards a Theory of Revolution', *American Sociological Review*, 27 (1): 5–19.

de Bary, W. (1997) 'Constructive Engagement with Asian Values', *Columbia East Asia Review* (Fall), available at www.columbia.edu/cu/ccba/cear/issues/fall97/ graphics/special/debary/debary.htm

Deans, P. (1997) *Japan–Taiwan Relations, 1972–1992: Virtual Diplomacy And The Separation Of Politics And Economics* (University of Newcastle upon Tyne: PhD thesis).

Deans, P. (2000) 'The Capitalist Developmental State in East Asia', in Ronen Palan, and Jason Abbott with Phil Deans, *State Strategies in the Global Political Economy* (London: Pinter): 78–102.

Des Forges, R. and Luo Xu (2001) 'China as a Non-Hegemonic Superpower? The Use of History among the China Can Say No Writers and Their Critics', *Critical Asian Studies*, 33 (4): 483–507.

Desker, B. (2004) 'In Defence of FTAs: From Purity to Pragmatism in East Asia', *The Pacific Review*, 17 (1): 3–26.

Diamond, S. (1992) *Compromised Campus: The Collaboration of Universities with the Intelligence Community* (New York: Oxford University Press).

Dickson, B. (2002) 'Cooption and Corporatism in China: The Logic of Party Adaptation', *Political Science Quarterly*, 115 (4): 517–40.

Dickson, B. (2003) *Red Capitalists in China: The Party, Private Entrepreneurs, and Prospects for Political Change* (Cambridge: Cambridge University Press).

Ding Jianping (1998) 'China's Foreign Exchange Black Market and Exchange Flight: Analysis of Exchange-Rate Policy', *The Developing Economies*, 36 (1): 24–44.

Ding Kang (2004) 'Jiaru WTO Hou de Zhongguo Shehui Baozhang Zhidu: Tiaozhan yu Duice (WTO & China's Social Security System: Challenges and Countermeasures)', *Wuhan Daxue Xuebao: Zhexue Shehui Kexue Ban (Wuhan University Journal: Philosophy and Social Sciences Edition)*, 57 (2): 268–73.

Ding Xueliang (2000a) 'Informal Privatization Through Internationalization: The Rise of Nomenklatura Capitalism in China's Offshore Business', *British Journal of Political Science*, 30 (1): 121–46.

Ding Xueliang (2000b) 'The Illicit Asset Stripping of China's State Firms', *China Journal*, (43): 1–28.

Dittmer, L. (1990) 'Patterns of Elite Strife and Succession in Chinese Politics', *China Quarterly*, (123): 405–30.

Donnithorne, A. (1981) *Centre-Provincial Economic Relations in China*, Canberra: Australian National University Contemporary China Centre Working Paper 16.

Dornbusch, R. and Giavazzi, F. (1999) 'Heading off China's Financial Crisis', Bank of International Settlements Policy Paper No. 07b.

Dougherty, C. (2002) 'Chinese fall short on WTO promises', *The Washington Times*, 5th July.

Downer, A. (1997) 'Australia and China: Engagement and Cooperation', address to the 1997 Australia in Asia Series, Sydney, 10th September. Available at www.dfat.gov.au/media/speeches/foreign/1997/china10sept97.html

Downs, E. (2000) *China's Quest for Energy Security* (Santa Monica: Rand).

Downs, E. (2004) 'The Chinese Energy Security Debate', *China Quarterly*, (177): 21–41.

Duckett, J. (1998) *The Entrepreneurial State in China* (London: Routledge).

Duckett, J. (2003) 'China's Social Security Reform and the Comparative Politics of Market Transition', *Journal of Communist Studies and Transition Politics*, 19 (1): 80–101.

Duckett, J. (2004) 'State, Collectivism and Worker Privilege: A Study of Urban Health Insurance Reform', *China Quarterly*, (177): 155–73.

Ebel, R. (2005) China's Energy Future: The Middle Kingdom Seeks Its Place in the Sun (Washington: Center for Strategic and International Studies).

Economist (1995) 'China: World Trade Ordeal', *The Economist*, 4th November.

Economy, E. (2004) *The River Runs Black: The Environmental Challenge to China's Future* (Washington: Council on Foreign Relations).

Engels, F. (1970) 'Socialism: Utopian and Scientific' in Karl Marx and Fredrick Engels *Selected Works, Volume 3* (London: Progress): 95–151.

Ernst, D. (2001) 'The New Mobility of Knowledge: Digital Information Systems and Global Flagship Networks', Honolulu, East-West Center Working Papers, Economics Series No. 30.

FAC (2000) *Tenth Report, Session 1999–2000: Relations with the People's Republic of China* (Norwich: HMSO).

Fan Chengze and Grossman, H. (2001) 'Entrepreneurial Graft in China', *The Providence Journal*, 3rd May: B5.

Fan Gang (1999) 'Transition to Fiscal Federalism: Market – Oriented Reform and Redefinition of Central-Local Relations in China', in Kiichiro Fukusaku and Luiz de Mello (eds) *Fiscal Decentralization in Emerging Economies* (Paris: OECD): 223–38.

Fan Gang (2000), 'Lun Tizhi Guan de Dongtai Guocheng – Feiguoyou Bumen de Chengzhang yu Guoyou Bumen de Gaige (On Dynamic Process of Institutional Transition – The Growth of Non-State Sector and the Reform of the State Sector)', *Jingji Yanjiu (Economic Research)*, (January): 11–21.

Fan Gang (2002) 'How to View the Problems in China's Economy? – In Response to the Notion of "Coming Collapse of China"', *World Economy and China*, (5): 3–8.

Fan Gang and Zhang Xiaojing (2003) 'How Can Developing Countries Benefit from Globalization: The Case of China', *China & World Economy*, (6): 3–10.

Fang Li (2000) 'Yao Zhengshi Yanjiu Shijie Jingji Quanqiuhua Taojian Xia Guoji Zhengzhi Jingji Guanxi de Xin Tedian (Pay Attention to the New Characteristics of International Political Economy Relations in Researching World Economic Globalisation)', *Dangdai Shijie (Contemporary World)*, (2): 7–10.

Fang Ning, Wang Xiaodong and Song Qiang (1999) *Quanqiuhua Yinying xia de Zhongguo Zhilu' (China's Path Under the Shadow of Globalisation)* (Beijing: China Social Science Press).

Fedelino, A. and Singh, R. (2004) 'Fiscal Federalism' in Eswar Prasad (ed) *China's Growth and Integration into the World Economy* (Washington: IMF): 36–42.

Feenstra, R., Wen Hai, Woo, W. and Yao, S. (1998) 'The US–China Bilateral Trade Balance: Its Size and Determinants', University of California Davis Department of Economics Working Paper Number 98–09.

Felker, G. (2003) 'Southeast Asian Industrialisation and the Changing Global Production System', *Third World Quarterly*, 24 (2): 255–82.

Feng Guozhao and Liu Zunyi (1999) 'A New Estimation on the Trade Imbalance Between America and China', *International Economic Review*, (5–6): 4–12.

Ferguson, J. (2003) 'Renminbi Revaluation', NBR Briefing Paper No. 14, 22nd September.

Fernald, J., Edison, H. and Loungani, P. (1998) 'Was China the First Domino? Assessing Links between China and the Rest of Emerging Asia', Board of Governors of the Federal Reserve System International Finance Discussion Paper Number 604.

Fewsmith, J. (1999) 'China in 1998: Tacking to Stay the Course', *Asian Survey*, 39 (1): 99–113.

Fewsmith, J. (2001b) 'The Political and Social Implications of China's Accession to the WTO', *China Quarterly*, (167): 573–91.

Fewsmith, J. (2001a) *China Since Tiananmen: The Politics of Transition* (Cambridge: Cambridge University Press).

Fewsmith, J. (2004) 'Continuing Pressures on Social Order', *China Leadership Monitor*, No. 10.

Fewsmith, J. (2005) 'China under Hu Jintao', *China Leadership Monitor*, No. 14.

Financial Express (2002) 'Round Tripping – FDI: China, India May be on Par with Such Investments', *The Financial Express*, 5th June.

Fishman, T. (2005) China, *Inc.: How the Rise of the Next Superpower Challenges America and the World* (New York: Scribner).

Foot, P. (2005) *The Vote: How it Was Won and How it Was Undermined* (London: Viking).

Freeman, C. (2004) 'Witness Testimony: U.S.–China Trade' Preparations for the Joint Commission on Commerce and Trade Subcommittee on Commerce, Trade, and Consumer Protection, 31st March, available at energycommerce.house.gov/108/Hearings/03312004hearing1239/Freeman1914.htm

Fu Jing (2006) 'China's Oil Consumption, Imports Decreased', *China Daily*, 3rd February.

Fuller, T. (2006) 'Billions in Trade Gap, Pennies for Workers' *International Herald Tribune*, 4th August.

Funabashi, Y. (1988) *Managing the Dollar: From the Plaza to the Louvre* (Washington: Institute for International Economics).

Fung, K.C., Iizaka, H. and Tong, S. (2002) 'Foreign Direct Investment in China: Policy, Trend and Impact', Hong Kong Institute of Economic and Business Strategy Working Paper No. 1049.

Gamble, A., Payne, A., Hoogvelt, A., Dietrich, M. and Kenny, M. (1996) 'Editorial: New Political Economy', *New Political Economy*, 1 (1): 5–11.

Gao Peiyong (1999) 'Further Improving China's Financial and Taxation System', *World Economy and China*, (3–4): 41 and 45.

Gao Zhanjun and Liu Fei (1999) 'The Closure of GITIC: Latent Financial Risks and Government Approach', *World Economy and China*, (3–4): 51–66.

Geeraerts, G. and Men Jing (2001) 'International Relations Theory in China', *Global Society*, 15 (3): 251–76.

Geng Xiao (2005) 'Round-Tripping Foreign Direct Investment in the People's Republic of China: Scale, Causes and Implications', ADB Institute (Tokyo) Research Paper No. 58.

German Bundestag (2001) *Globalisation of the World Economy – Challengers and Responses* (Berlin: Study Commission (Select Committee) http://www.bundestag.de/gremien/welt/welt_zwischenbericht/zwb003_vorw_einl_engl.pdf

Gereffi, G., Korzeniewicz, M. and Korzeniewicz, R. (1994) 'Introduction: Global Commodity Chains' in Gary Gereffi, Miguel Korzeniewicz and Roberto Korzeniewicz (eds) Commodity Chains and Global Capitalism (Westport, CT: Praeger, 1993): 1–14.

Gertz, W. (2002) *The China Threat: How the People's Republic Targets America* (Washington: Regnery).

Giles, J., Park, A. and Fang Cai (2003) 'How has Economic Restructuring Affected China's Urban Workers?', Available at www.msu.edu/~gilesj/gilesparkcai.pdf

Gill, S. (1995) 'Globalisation, Market Civilisation, and Disciplinary Neoliberalism', *Millennium*, 24 (3): 399–423.

Gill, S. (2000) 'The constitution of global capitalism' Paper presented to a Panel: The Capitalist World, Past and Present at the International Studies Association Annual Convention, Los Angeles, 2000 available at www.theglobalsite.ac.uk/press/010gill.htm

Gills, B. and Philip, G. (1996a) – special issue of *The Third World Quarterly*, 17 (4).

Gills, B. and Philip, G. (1996b) 'Editorial: Towards convergence in development policy?: Challenging the 'Washington Consensus' and Restoring the Historicity of Divergent Development Trajectories', *The Third World Quarterly*, 17 (4): 585–91.

Gold, T., Guthrie, D. and Wank, D. (2002) 'An Introduction to the Study of Guanxi', in Thomas Gold, Doug Guthrie and David Wank (eds) *Social Connections in China: Institutions, Culture, and the Changing Nature of Guanxi* (Cambridge: Cambridge University Press): 3–20.

Goldstein, M. (2004) 'Adjusting China's Exchange Rate Policies', Institute for International Economics Working Paper Number 04–1.

Goodman, D. (1981) 'The 6th Plenum of the 11th Central Committee of the CCP: Look Back in Anger?', *China Quarterly*, (87): 518–27.

Goodman, D. (1985) 'The Chinese Political Order After Mao: "Socialist Democracy" and the Exercise of State Power', *Political Studies*, 33 (2): 218–35.

Goodman, D. (1986) *Centre and Province in the People's Republic of China: Sichuan and Guizhou 1955–1965* (Cambridge: Cambridge University Press).

Goodman, D. (ed.) (1997) *China's Provinces in Reform: Class, Commodity and Political Culture* (London: Routledge).

Goodman, D. (1998) 'In Search of China's New Middle Classes: the Creation of Wealth and Diversity in Shanxi During the 1990s', *Asian Studies Review*, 22 (1): 39–62.

Goodman, D. (2004a) 'The Campaign to "Open Up the West": National, Provincial-level and Local Perspectives', *China Quarterly*, (178): 317–34.

Goodman, D. (2004b) 'Localism and Entrepreneurship: History, Identity and Solidarity as Factors of Production' in Barbara Krug (ed) *The Rational Chinese Entrepreneur* (London: Routledge): 139–65.

Goodman, P. (2006) 'Foreign Currency Piles Up in China', *Washington Post*, 17th January: D01.

Green, S. (2003) *The Development of China's Stockmarket, 1984–2002: Equity Politics and Market Institutions* (London: Routledge/Curzon).

Groombridge, M. and Barfield, C. (1999) *Tiger by the Tail: China and the World Trade Organization* (Washington: the AEI Press).

Grugel, J. and Hout, W. (eds) (1998) *Regionalism Across the North South Divide* (London: Routledge).

Guang Zhang (2000) 'Governmental Policy Preferences and Foreign Capital Allocation: The Case of China', *Journal of Chinese Political Science*, 6 (2): 43–75.

Gunter, F. (1996) 'Capital Flight from the People's Republic of China', *China Economic Review*, 7 (1): 77–96.

Gunter, F. (2004) 'Capital flight from China: 1984–2001', *China Economic Review*, 15 (1): 63–85.

Guo Baogang (2003) 'Political Legitimacy and China's Transition', *Journal of Chinese Political Science*, 8 (1 & 2): 1–25.

Guo Shuyong (2004) 'Shilun Makesizhuyi Guoji Guanxi Sixiang ji qi Yanjiu Fangxiang (Discussion of the Research Method of Marxist International Relations Theory)', *Shijie Jingji yu Zhengzhi (World Economics and Politics)*, (4): 8–14.

Guo Sujian (1998) 'Enigma of All Enigmas: Capitalist Takeover? Assessment of the Post-Mao Economic Transformation', *Journal of Chinese Political Science*, 4 (1): 33–72.

Guo Sujian (2003) 'The Ownership Reform in China: What Direction and How Far?', *Journal of Contemporary China*, 12 (36): 553–73.

Guo Yong and Hu Angang (2004) 'The Administrative Monopoly in China's Economic Transition', *Communist and Post-Communist Studies*, 37 (2): 265–80.

Gurr, T. (1970) *Why Men Rebel* (Princeton: Princeton University Press).

Gutierrez, C. (2006) 'Remarks to Asia Society' available at hongkong.usconsulate.gov/uscn/trade/general/doc/2006/031401.htm

Haggard, S. (1990) *Pathways from the Periphery: The Politics of Growth in the Newly Industrializing Countries* (Ithaca: Cornell University Press).

Hale, D. and Hale, L. (2003) 'China Takes Off', *Foreign Affairs*, 82 (6): 36–53.

Haley, G., Tan, Chin Tiong and Haley, U. (1998) *The New Asian Emperors: The Overseas Chinese, Their Strategies and Competitive Advantages* (Burlington: Butterworth-Heinemann).

Hamilton, G. (1999) 'Asian Business Networks in Transition: or What Alan Greenspan Does Not Know About the Asian Business Crisis', in T.J. Pempel (ed.) *The Politics of the Asian Economic Crisis* (Ithaca: Cornell University Press): 45–61.

Hamilton, G. and Waters, T. (1995) 'Chinese Capitalism in Thailand: Embedded Networks and Industrial Structure', in Edward Chen and Peter Drysdale (eds) *Corporate Links and Foreign Direct Investment in Asia and the Pacific* (Pymble: Harper): 87–111.

Hamrin, C. (1990) *China and the Challenge of the Future, Changing Political Patterns* (Boulder, CO: Westview Press).

Han Deqiang (2000) *Pengzhuang: Quanqiuhua Xianjing yu Zhongguo Xianshi Xuanze (Collision: The Globalisation Trap and China's Real Choice)* (Beijing: Economic Management Press).

Hanson, G. and Feenstra, R. (2001) 'Intermediaries in Entrepôt Trade: Hong Kong Re-Exports of Chinese Goods', National Bureau of Economic Research Working Paper No. 8088.

Harding, H. (1987) *China's Second Revolution* (Washington: Brookings).

Harding, J. (1997) 'Jitters in Beijing', *Financial Times*, 10th November.

Harris, S. (2001) 'China and the Pursuit of State Interests in a Globalising World', *Pacifica Review*, 13 (1): 15–29.

Harrold, P. and Lall, R. (1993) 'China Reform and Development in 1992–93', World Bank Discussion Paper No. 215.

Hatch, W. (1998) 'Grounding Asia's Flying Geese: The Costs Of Depending Heavily On Japanese Capital And Technology', National Bureau of Asian Research Briefing Paper No. Hatch98.

Hatch, W. and Yamamura, K. (1996) *Asia in Japan's Embrace: Building a Regional Production Alliance* (Cambridge: Cambridge University Press).

Hay, C. and Marsh, D. (eds) (1999) *Putting the 'P' Back into IPE* a Special Edition of *New Political Economy*, 4 (1).

He Li (2003) 'Middle Class: Friends or Foes to Beijing's New Leadership', *Journal of Chinese Political Science*, 8 (1 & 2): 88–100.

He Qinglian (2000) 'China's Listing Social Structure', *New Left Review*, 5 (September/October): 68–99.

Head, K. and Ries, J. (1996) 'Inter-City Competition for foreign Direct Investment: Static and Dynamic Effects of China's Incentive Areas', *Journal of Urban Economics*, (40): 38–60.

Heartfield, J. (2005) 'China's Comprador Capitalism Is Coming Home', *Review of Radical Political Economics*, 37 (2): 196–214.

Heberer, T. (2003) 'Entrepreneurs in China and Vietnam as Strategic Players in Social and Political Change', *Journal of Communist Studies & Transition Politics*, 19 (1): 64–79.

Heilig, G. (1999) *ChinaFood. Can China Feed Itself?* (Laxenburg: IIASA).

Heilmann, S. (2005) 'Regulatory Innovation by Leninist Means: Communist Party Supervision in China's Financial Industry', *China Quarterly*, (181): 1–21.

Hendrischke, H. and Feng Chongyi (eds) (1999) *The Political Economy of China's Provinces: Comparative and Competitive Advantage* (London: Routledge).

Hennock, M. (2001) 'East Asian Pact Trades Up' *BBC News On-Line*, 7th November, news.bbc.co.uk/1/hi/business/1641613.stm

Heron, T. and Payne, A. (2002) 'Microregionalism across Caribbean America', in Shaun Breslin and Glenn Hook (eds), *Microregionalism and World Order* (Basingstoke: Palgrave): 42–65.

Hettne, B. (1999) 'Globalisation and the new Regionalism', in Björn Hettne, András Inotai, and Osvaldo Sunkel (eds), *Globalism and the New Regionalism* (London: Macmillan): 1–24.

Hettne, B. and Söderbaum, F. (2000) 'Theorising the Rise of Regionness', *New Political Economy*, 5 (3): 457–73.

Higgott, R. (1998) 'The Asian Economic Crisis: A Study in the Politics of Resentment', *New Political Economy*, 3 (3): 333–56.

Higgott, R. (2001) 'Taming Hegemony and Economics, Emboldening International Relations: The Theory and Practice of International Political Economy in an Era of Globalisation', in Stephanie Lawson (ed.) *International Relations Ten Years After the Fall of the Wall* (Cambridge: Polity Press): 91–108

Hiranuma I. (2002) 'Sugu soko ni aru kiki, shitsugyo maneku kudoka wa koshite kaihi suru (How to Avoid a Hollowed Out Industry That Will Lead to Unemployment)', *Toyo Keizai*, 5th January.

Hirst, P. and Thompson, G. (1999) *Globalization in Question* (Cambridge: Polity).

Ho, S. and Huenemann, R. (1984) *China's Open Door Policy: The Quest for Foreign Technology and Capital* (Vancouver: University of British Columbia Press).

Holm, H. and Sorensen, G. (eds) (1995) *Whose World Order? Uneven Globalization and the End of the Cold War* (Boulder: Westview).

Holst, D. and Weiss, J. (2004) 'ASEAN and China: Export Rivals or Partners in Regional Growth?', *The World Economy*, 27 (8): 1255–74.

Holz, C. (2003a) 'China's GDP Growth Numbers: Can We Believe Them?', *China Economic Quarterly*, (Q3): 30–40.

Holz, C. (2003b) 'Note on the definition of 'state-owned and state-controlled enterprises', available at ihome.ust.hk/~socholz/SOE-definition.htm, accessed 11/04/06.

Hong Kong SAR Census and Statistics Department (2005) *Annual Survey of Regional Offices Representing Overseas Companies in Hong Kong* (Hong Kong: Government Information Centre).

Hong Zhaohui (2004) 'Mapping the Evolution and Transformation of the New Private Entrepreneurs in China', *Journal of Chinese Political Science*, 9 (1): 23–42.

Hornik, R. (2002) 'Who Needs Hong Kong?', *Fortune*, 2nd May.

Hou Yu (2004) 'Local Protectionism: The Bottleneck of China's Economic Development', *IIAS Newsletter*, (33): 24.

Hou, J. (2002) 'China's FDI Policy and Taiwanese Direct Investment (TDI) in China' Hong Kong University of Science and Technology, Centre for Economic Development Working Paper No. 0206.

Houde, M.F. and Lee, H. (2000) 'Main Determinants and Impacts of Foreign Direct Investment on China's Economy', OECD Working Paper on International Investment No. 2000/4.

Hout, T. and Lebreton, J. (2003) 'The Real Contest Between America and China', *Asian Wall Street Journal*, 16th September.

Howell, J. (1993) *China Opens Its Doors – The Politics Of Economic Transition* (Boulder: Harvester Wheatsheaf).

Howell, J. (1998) 'An Unholy Trinity? Civil Society, Economic Liberalisation and Democratisation in Post-Mao China', *Government and Opposition*, 33 (1): 56–80.

Hsu Chih-Chia (2002) 'The Increasingly Uneven Distribution of Wealth in Mainland China', Division of Strategic and International Studies Peace Forum (China Studies) Essay No. 08/21/2002.

Hu Angang (2000) *Corruption and Anti-Corruption in China* (Beijing: Chinese Academy of Social Sciences) mimeo.

Hu Angang (2002) 'Public Exposure of Economic Losses Resulting from Corruption', *World Economy and China*, (4): 44–9.

Hu Yong (2005) 'Measuring Our Greenness', *China Business International*, 1st January.

Huang Jikun and Rozelle, S. (2003) 'The Impact of Trade Liberalization on China's Agriculture and Rural Economy', *SAIS Review*, 23 (1): 115–31.

Huang Yasheng (1998) *Foreign Direct Investment in China: An Asian Perspective* (Singapore: Institute of Southeast Asian Studies).

Huang Yasheng (2003) *Selling China: Foreign Direct Investment During the Reform Era* (Cambridge: Cambridge University Press).

Huang Yasheng (1996) *Inflation and Investment Controls in China: The Political Economy of Central-Local Relations During the Reform Era* (New York: Cambridge University Press).

Huchet, J.F. and Richet, C. (2002) 'Between Bureaucracy and Market: Chinese Industrial Groups in Search of New Forms of Corporate Governance', *Post-Communist Economies*, 14 (2): 169–201.

Hughes, C. (1997) 'Globalization and Nationalism: Squaring the Circle in Chinese IR Theory', *Millennium*, 26 (1): 103–24.

Hughes, C. (1999) 'Japanese Policy and the East Asian Currency Crisis: Abject Defeat or Quiet Victory?', University of Warwick, Centre for the Study of Globalisation and Regionalisation Working Paper No. 24.

Hughes, C. (2006) *Chinese Nationalism in the Global Era* (London: Routledge).

Hund, M. (2003) 'ASEAN Plus Three: Towards a New Age of Pan-East Asian Regionalism? A Skeptic's Appraisal', *The Pacific Review*, 16 (3): 383–417.

Huntington, S. (1996) *The Clash of Civilizations and the Remaking of World Order* (New York: Simon and Schuster).

Hurrell, A. (1995) 'Explaining the Resurgence of Regionalism in World Politics', *Review of International Studies*, 21 (4): 331–58.

Hurrell, A. and Woods, N. (eds) (1999) *Inequality, Globalization, and World Politics* (Oxford: Oxford University Press).

Hutzler, C. (2003) 'China's New Leadership Indicates Change of Focus', *Wall Street Journal*, 25th February.

Ianchovichina, E., Sethaput, S.N., and Min Zhao (2004) 'Regional Impact of China's WTO Accession', in Kathie Krumm and Homi Kharas (eds) *East Asia Integrates: A Trade Policy Agenda for Shared Growth* (Washington: World Bank): 57–78.

Isogai, T. Morishita, H. and Rüffer, R. (2002) 'Analysis of Intra- and Inter-Regional Trade in East Asia: Comparative Advantage Structures and Dynamic Interdependency in Trade Flows', Bank of Japan International Department Working Paper No. 02-E-1.

Israel, C. (2006) 'Testimony of Chris Israel U.S. Coordinator for International Intellectual Property Enforcement Before the US–China Economic and Security Review Commission 'Piracy and Counterfeiting in China'', available at www.uscc.gov/hearings/2006hearings/written_testimonies/06_06_07wrts/Chris_Israel.pdf

Ito, J. (2002) 'Why TVEs have Contributed to Inequality in China', Washington: International Food Policy Research Institute Environment and Production Technology Division Discussion Paper Number 91.

Jackson, J. (1989) *The World Trading System: Law and Policy of International Relations* (Cambridge, Mass: MIT Press).

Jackson, S. and Mosco, V. (1999) 'The Political Economy of New Technological Spaces: Malaysia's Multimedia Super Corridor', *Journal of International Communication*, 6 (1): 23–40.

Jia Kang (2002) 'Study on Local Government Public Debt Financing in the People's Republic of China' Paper presented at ADB Conference on Local Government Finance and Bond Market Financing, available at www.adb.org/Documents/Events/2002/LG_Finance_Bond_Market/PRC_report.pdf

Jia Kang (2003) 'Contingent Debt in China's Public Sector', *World Economy and China*, (3): 14–18.

Jiang Xiaoyuan (2003) 'Geographical Distribution of Foreign Investment in China: Industrial Clusters and Their Significance', *World Economy and China*, (1): 16–24.

Jiang, C. Y. (2000), 'Xiangzhenqiye Zijinlaiyuan yu Rongzijiegoude Dongtaibianhua: Fenxi yu Sikao (Fund Resources of Township Enterprises And The Dynamic Change in Their Financing Structure: Analysis and Considerations)', *Jingji Yanjiu (Economic Research)*, (February): 34–9.

Jiang Wenran (2006) 'China's Energy Engagement with Latin America', *Jamestown Foundation China Brief*, 6 (16): 3–6.

Jin Bei (1997) 'The International Competition Facing Domestically Produced Goods and the Nation's Industry', *Social Sciences in China*, 18 (1): 65–71.

Johnson, C. (1966) *Revolutionary Change* (Boston: Little, Brown).

Johnson, C. (1981) *MITI and the Japanese Miracle: Industrial Policy 1925–1975* (Stanford: Stanford University Press).

Johnson, C. (1987) 'Political Institutions and Economic Performance: The Government–Business Relationship in Japan, South Korea, and Taiwan' in Fred Deyo (ed.) *The Political Economy of the New East Asian Industrialism* (Ithaca: Cornell University Press): 136–64.

Johnson, C. (1997) 'Preconception vs. Observation, or the Contribution of Rational Choice Theory and Area Studies to Contemporary Political Science', *PS: Political Science and Politics*, 30 (2): 170–4.

Johnson, D. (1999) 'China's Reforms – Some Unfinished Business', University of Chicago Office of Agricultural Economics Research Working Paper No. 99–08.

Johnston, A. (2003) 'Is China a Status Quo Power?', *International Security*, 27 (4): 5–56.

Kagan, R. (2005) 'The Illusion of 'Managing' China', *Washington Post*, 15th May.

Kang Xiaoguang (2002), 'Weilai 3–5 Nian Zhongguo Dalu Zhengzhi Wendingxing Fenxi (On Mainland China's Political Stability over the Next 3–5 Years)', *Zhanlue yu guanli (Strategy and Management*, 23 (2): 1–15.

Kasaba, R. (1998) 'Towards a New International Studies', available at jsis.artsci.Washington.edu/programs/is/toanewis.html

Kawai, M. and Bhattasali, D. (2001) 'The Implications of China's Accession to the World Trade Organisation' paper presented at Japan and China: Economic Relations in Transition Jan 2001 Tokyo. Cited with authors' permission.

Khan, A. and Riskin, C. (2001) *Inequality and Poverty in China in the Age of Globalization* (New York: Oxford University Press).

Khanna, J. (ed.) (1995) *Southern China, Hong Kong, and Taiwan: Evolution of a Subregional Economy* (Washington: The Center for Strategic and International Studies).

Kotabe, M. (1998) 'Global sourcing strategy in the Pacific: American and Japanese multinational companies', in M. Czinkota and M. Kotabe (eds), *Trends in International Business: Critical Perspectives* (Oxford: Blackwell): 238–56.

Krasner, S. (1994) 'International Political Economy: Abiding Discord', *Review of International Political Economy*, 1 (1): 13–19.

Kristof, N. (2003) 'The China Threat?', *New York Times*, 20th December.

Krug, B. (1997) 'Privatisation in China: Something to learn from?', in Herbert Giersch (ed.) *Privatisation at the Turn of the Century* (Berlin: Springer): 269–93.

Kurlantzick, J. (2006) 'China's Charm: Implications of Chinese Soft Power', Carnegie Endowment Policy Brief No. 47, June.

Kwan, C. (1994) *Economic Interdependence in the Asia Pacific Region: Towards a Yen Bloc* (London and New York: Routledge).

Kwan Chi Hung (2002) 'Primary Stage of Socialism or Primitive Capitalism?', *China in Transition*, 25th October, available at www.rieti.go.jp/en/china/02102501.html

Kwong, J. (1997) *The Political Economy of Corruption in China* (Armonk: Sharpe).

Kynge, J. (1998) 'Zhu Assails Padded Growth Figures', *The Financial Times*, 17th December.

Kynge, J. (2002) 'Survey – China & The World Trade Organisation', *Financial Times*, 15th March.

Kynge, J. (2006) *China Shakes the World: The Rise of a Hungry Nation* (London: Weidenfeld & Nicolson).

Lai Hongyi (2001) 'Behind China's World Trade Organization Agreement with the USA', *Third World Quarterly*, 22 (2): 237–55.

Lam, W. (1999) *The Era of Jiang Zemin* (New Jersey: Prentice Hall).

Lardy, N. (1995) 'The Role of Foreign Trade and Investment in China's Economic Transformation', *China Quarterly*, (144): 1065–82.

Lardy, N. (1998) *China's Unfinished Economic Revolution* (Washington: Brookings).

Lardy, N. (2000) 'Is China a "Closed" Economy?', Prepared Statement for a Public Hearing of the United States Trade Deficit Review Commission, 24th February, available at www.brook.edu/dybdocroot/views/testimony/lardy/20000224.htm

Lardy, N. (2002) *Integrating China into the Global Economy* (Washington: Brookings).

Lasswell, H. (1936) *Politics: Who Gets What, When, How* (New York: McGraw-Hill).

Lau, L., Qian Yingyi and Roland, G. (2000) 'Reform Without Losers: An Interpretation of China's Dual Track Approach to Transition', *Journal of Political Economy*, 108 (1): 120–63.

Lau, R. (1997) 'China: Labour Reform and the Challenge Facing the Working Class', *Capital and Class*, (61): 45–80.

Lautard, S. (1999) 'State, Party, and Market: Chinese Politics and the Asian Crisis', *International Political Science Review*, 20 (3): 285–306.

Leftwich, A. (1995) 'Bringing Politics Back In: Towards a Model of the Developmental State', *Journal of Development Studies*, 31 (3): 400–27.

Lemoine, F. and Unal-Kesenci, D. (2004) 'Assembly Trade and Technology Transfer: The Case of China', *World Development*, 32 (5): 829–50.

Lewis, J. and Xue Litai (2003) 'Social Change and Political Reform in China: Meeting the Challenge of Success', *China Quarterly*, (176): 926–42.

Li Chunling (2004) 'Zhongchanjieceng: Zhongguo Shehui Zhide Guanzhu de Renqun' (The Middle Stratum: A group in Chinese Society Worth Paying Attention To), in Ru Xin, Lu Xueyi, and Li Peilin (eds) *2004 Nian: Zhongguo Shehui Xingshi Fenxi yu Yuce (Analysis and Prognosis of the Features of Chinese Society: 2004)* (Beijing: Shehui Kexue Wenxian Press).

Li Hongbin and Rozelle, S. (2003) 'Privatizing Rural China: Insider Privatization, Innovative Contracts and the Performance of Township Enterprises', *China Quarterly*, (176): 981–1005.

Li Jie, Qiu, L. and Sun Qunyan (2003) 'Interregional Protection: Implications of Fiscal Decentralization and Trade Liberalization', *China Economic Review*, 14 (3): 227–45.

Li Lianjiang (2002) 'The Politics of Introducing Direct Township Elections in China', *China Quarterly*, (171): 704–23.

Li Qiang (2002) 'Nike, Adidas, Reebok and New Balance Made in China', *China Labor Watch*, 25th October.

Li Fangchao (2006) 'NGOs in Difficulty, Survey Shows', *China Daily*, 24th April.

Li Zhaoxing (2003) 'Speech at US–China Business Council', *People's Daily* (online edition), 23rd September.

Li, D. (1996) 'Ambiguous Property Rights in Transition Economies', *Journal of Comparative Economics*, 23 (1): 1–19.

Li, L. (1998) *Centre and Province: China 1978–1993: Power as Non-Zero-Sum* (Oxford: Oxford University Press).

Li Peilin (ed.) (1995) *Zhongguo Xinshiqi Jieji Jieceng Baogao (Report on Class and Social Stratification in China's Market Transition)* (Shenyang: Liaoning People's Press).

Lian Yue and Xue Yong (2004) 'Bieba 'Zhongchanjieji' Yangsuhua (Don't Debase 'Middle Class)', *Nanfang Dushi Bao*, 19th March.

Lin, J. and Liu Zhiqiang (2000) Fiscal Decentralization and Economic Growth in China', *Economic Development and Cultural Change*, 49 (1): 1–21.

Liu Yuanli, Rao Keqin and Hsiao, W. (2003) 'Medical Expenditure and Rural Impoverishment in China', *Journal of Health, Population and Nutrition*, 21 (3): 216–22.

Liu, A. (1992) 'The Wenzhou Model of Development and China's Modernization', *Asian Survey*, 32 (8): 696–711.

Liu Yingqiu (2002) 'Development of Private Entrepreneurship in China: Process, Problem and Countermeasures' in *Entrepreneurship in Asia: Playbook for Prosperity* (online publication by the Maureen and Mike Mansfield Foundation Program available at www.mansfieldfdn.org/programs/program_pdfs/ent_china.pdf).

Liu Weisheng (ed.) (2002) *Wenhua Baquan Gailun (An Outline of Cultural Hegemony)* (Shijiazhuang: Hebei People's Press).

Liu Xiguang and Liu Kang (1997) *Yaomohua Zhongguo de Beihou (Behind the Demonisation of China)* (Beijing: China Social Sciences).

Lu Di (2002) 'Yapian Zhanzheng Jiaopian Zhanzheng he Guojihua (The Opium War, Film War and Internationalisation)' in Yin Hong (ed.) *Quanqiuhua he Meiti (Globalisation and Media)* (Beijing: Qinghua University Press): 217–28.

Lu Xiaobo (2000) 'Booty Socialism, Bureau-preneurs and the State in Transition: Organizational Corruption in China', *Comparative Politics*, 32 (3): 273–94.

Lu Xueyi (2002) *Dangdai Zhongguo Shehui Jieceng Yanjiu Baogao (Research Report on Contemporary China's Social Strata)* (Beijing: Chinese Academy of Social Sciences).

Lu Xueyi (ed.) (2004) *Dangdai Zhongguo Shehui Liudong (Mobility in Contemporary Chinese Society)* (Beijing: Social Sciences Academic Press).

Luthje, B. (2002) 'Electronics Contract Manufacturing: Global Production and the International Division of Labor in the Age of the Internet', *Industry and Innovation*, 9 (3): 227–47.

McGregor, R. (2006) 'Data Show Social Unrest on the Rise in China', *Financial Times*, 16th January.

Macfarquhar, R. (1996) 'The Party's Armageddon', *Time International*, 13th May.

Makin, J. (1997) 'Two New Paradigms', *Economic Outlook*, 1st October.

Marsh, D. and Savigny, H. (2004) 'Political Science as a Broad Church: The Search for a Pluralistic Discipline', *Politics*, 24 (3): 155–68.

Masaharu, H. (2002) 'China and the WTO: The Effect on China's Sociopolitical Stability', *Japan Review of International Affairs*, (Summer): 1–18.

Matsuzaki, Y. (1997) 'Hon Kon: tai Chu kyoten to shite no genjo, in K. Ishihara (ed.), *Chugoku Keizai no Kolusaika to Higashi Ajia* (Tokyo: Ajia Keizai Kenkyusho): 139–68.

Menges, C. (2005) *China: The Gathering Threat* (Nashville: Thomas Nelson).

Min Zhao (2006) 'External Liberalization and the Evolution of China's Exchange System: an Empirical Approach' World Bank China Research Paper No. 4 available at www.worldbank.org.cn/english/content/Working_Paper4.pdf

Mittleman, J. (1999) 'Rethinking the "New Regionalism" in the Context of Globalisation', in Björn Hettne, András Inotai and Osvaldo Sunkel (eds), *Globalism and the New Regionalism* (Basingstoke: Macmillan): 25–53.

Montinola, G., Qian Yingyi, and Weingast, B. (1996) 'Federalism, Chinese Style: The Political Basis for Economic Success', *World Politics*, 41 (1): 50–81.

Morgan, J. (2004) 'Contemporary China, Anachronistic Marxism? The Continued Explanatory Power of Marxism', *Critical Asian Studies*, 36: 1 (2004): 65–90.

Morrison, W. (2002) 'Issue Brief for Congress Received through the CRS Web' Order Code IB91121 China–U.S. Trade Issues 2002.

Mosher, S. (2000) *Hegemon: China's Plan to Dominate Asia and the World* (New York: Encounter).

Murphy, D. (2003) 'Can Makers Worry China is Planning a U-turn', *Wall Street Journal*, 31 July.

Murray, G. (1998) *China: The Next Superpower: Dilemmas in Change and Continuity* (Basingstoke: Palgrave Macmillan).

Naím, M. (2003) 'Only a Miracle Can Save China', *Financial Times*, 15th September.

Naughton, B. (1995) *Growing out of the Plan: Chinese Economic Reform, 1978–1993* (Cambridge: Cambridge University Press).

Naughton, B. (1997) 'Introduction: The Emergence of the China Circle', in Barry Naughton (ed.), *The China Circle: Economics and Electronics in the PRC, Taiwan, and Hong Kong* (Washington: Brookings): 3–37.

Naughton, B. (2000) 'China's Trade Regime at the end of the 1990s,' in Ted Carpenter, and James Dorn (eds) *China's Future: Constructive Partner or Emerging Threat?* (Washington: Cato Institute): 235–60.

Naughton, B. (2003) 'How Much Can Regional Integration Do to Unify China's Markets?', in Nicholas Hope, Dennis Yang, and Mu Yang Li (eds) *How Far Across the River? Chinese Policy Reform at the Millennium* (Stanford: Stanford University Press): 204–32.

Naughton, B. (2005) 'SASAC Rising', *China Leadership Monitor*, (14): 1–11.

New York Times (2002) 'Economic Juggernaut: China is Passing US as Asian Power', *New York Times*, 29th June.

Nolan, P. (2003) *China at the Crossroads* (Oxford: Polity Press).

Nye, J. (2005) 'The Rise of China's Soft Power', *The Wall Street Journal Asia*, 29th December.

O'Quinn, R. (2005) *Overview Of The Chinese Economy* (Washington: US Congress Joint Economic Committee Publication).

O'Brien, K. (2001) 'Villagers, Elections and Citizenship in Contemporary China', *Modern China*, 27 (4): 407–35.

Ohmae, K. (1995) *The End of the Nation State* (London: HarperCollins).

Oi, J. (1992) 'Fiscal Reform and the Economic Foundations of Local State Corporatism in China', *World Politics*, 45 (1): 99–126.

Oi, J. (1995) 'The Role of the Local State in China's Transitional Economy', *China Quarterly*, (144): 1132–50.

Oi, J. (1999) *Rural China Takes Off: Institutional Foundations of Economic Reform* (Berkeley: University of California Press).

Olson, M. (1963) 'Rapid Growth as a Destabilizing Force', *Journal of Economic History*, 23 (4): 529–52.

Oman, C. (1999) 'Globalization, Regionalization, and Inequality', in Andrew Hurrell and Ngaire Woods (eds) *Inequality, Globalisation and World Politics* (Oxford: Oxford University Press): 36–65.

Overholt, W. (1994) *The Rise of China: How Economic Reform is Creating a New Superpower* (London: Norton).

Parris, K. (1993) 'Local Initiative and National Reform: The Wenzhou Model of Development', *China Quarterly*, (134): 242–63.

Payne, A. (1998) 'The New Political Economy of Area Studies', *Millennium*, 27 (2): 253–73.

Payne, A. and Gamble, A. (1996) 'Introduction: The Political Economy of Regionalism and World Order' in Andrew Gamble and Anthony Payne (eds) *Regionalism and World Order* (Basingstoke: Macmillan): 1–20.

Pearson, M. (1997) *China Business Elites: the Political Consequence s of Economic Reform* (Berkeley: University of California Press).

Pei Minxin (2002) 'China's Governance Crisis', *Foreign Affairs*, (September–October): 96–109.

Pei Minxin (2006) *China's Trapped Transition: The Limits of Developmental Autocracy* (Cambridge, MA: Harvard University Press).

People's Daily (2000) 'Market Decides Commodity, Service Prices in China', *People's Daily* (online edition), 30th September.

People's Daily (2001a) 'Details of Xiamen Smuggling Case Exposed', *People's Daily* (online edition), 26th July.

People's Daily (2001b) 'Interview: Long Yongtu on China's WTO Entry', *People's Daily* (online edition), 12th November.

People's Daily (2004a) 'China Making Efforts to Cultivate Middle Income Class', *People's Daily* (online edition), 26th March.

People's Daily (2004b) 'China's 'Green GDP' Index Facing Technology Problem, Local Protectionism', *People's Daily* (online edition), 3rd April.

People's Daily (2004c) 'Middle Class Grows in China as More Farmers Move to Cities', *People's Daily* (online edition), 2nd August.

People's Daily (2004d) 'China's Development at a Critical Point – Common Prosperity or Half in Poverty?', *People's Daily* (online edition), 12th August.

People's Daily (2004e) 'How to Optimize Social Structure in China?', *People's Daily* (online edition), 16th August.

People's Daily (2005a) 'China's Trust Investment Companies Report Growing Busines, *People's Daily* (online edition), 19th January 2005.

People's Daily (2005b) 'China has Socialist Market Economy in Place', *People's Daily* (online edition), 13th July.

People's Daily (2005c) 'Who Takes the Lion's Share in Sino-US Textile Trade?', *People's Daily* (overseas edition), 31st August.

People's Daily (2005d) 'Party School Journal Warns Against China's Widening Income Gap', *People's Daily* (online edition), 20th September.

People's Daily (2005e) 'China Becomes Major Victim of Trade Protectionism', *People's Daily* (online edition), 30th October.

People's Daily (2005f) 'China revises 2004 GDP up by 16.8 percent', *People's Daily* (online edition), 20th December.

People's Daily (2006a) 'Improve Welfare of 200 Million Rural Workers: Experts', *People's Daily* (online edition), 1st May.

People's Daily (2006b) 'Facts and Figures: China's Drive to Build Socialist New Countryside', *People's Daily* (online edition), 5th March.

People's Daily (2006c) 'RMB has Appreciated by 3.8% Relative to U.S. Dollar', *People's Daily* (online edition), 13th August.

Pomfret, J. (2001) 'Seeds of Revolt in Rural China: Farmers' Heroes Give a Voice to Besieged Taxpayers', *The Washington Post*, 8th May.

Poncet, S. (2005) 'A Fragmented China: Measure and Determinants of Chinese Domestic Market Disintegration', *Review of International Economics*, 13 (3): 409–30.

Potter, D., Goldblatt, D., Kiloh, M. and Lewis, P. (eds) (1997) *Democratization* (Cambridge: Polity).

Price, A., Weld, C., Nance, S., and Zucker, P. (2006) *The China Syndrome: How Subsidies and Government Intervention Created the World's Largest Steel Industry* (Washington: Wiley Rein and Fielding LLP for the American Iron and Steel Institute, The Steel Manufacturers Association, The Specialty Steel Industry of North America and the Committee of Pipe and Tube Imports).

Qin Chuan (2005) 'Government Turns up NGO Volume', *China Daily*, 26th April.

Ramo, J. (2004) *The Beijing Consensus: Notes on the New Physics of Chinese Power* (London: Foreign Policy Centre).

Rauch, J. and Trindade, V. (2002), 'Ethnic Chinese Networks in International Trade', *Review of Economics and Statistics*, 84 (1): 116–30.

Rawski, T. (2002a) 'Beijing's Fuzzy Math', *The Wall Street Journal*, 22nd April.

Rawski, T. (2002b) 'Where's the Growth?', *Asian Wall Street Journal*, 19th April.

Reddy, S. and Minoiu, C. (2005) *Chinese Poverty: Assessing the Impact of Alternative Assumptions*. Mimeo, available at ssrn.com/abstract=799844

Rigby, T. (1982) 'Introduction: Political Legitimacy, Weber and Communist Mono-Organisational Systems', in T.H. Rigby and Ference Fehér (eds), *Political Legitimation in Communist States* (Basingstoke: Macmillan): 1–26.

Roach, S. (2002) 'Global: China's Heavy Lifting', *Morgan Stanley Global Economic Forum*, 6th March.

Roberts, D. (2005) 'China: Go West, Westerners', *BusinessWeek*, 3rd November.

Roberts, D. and Einhorn, B. with Webb, A. (2001) 'While Taipei's Politicians Defend Independence, Business Leaders Want to fully Unite The Economies', *Business Week*, 11th June.

Roberts, D. and Kynge, J. (2003) 'How Cheap Labour, Foreign Investment and Rapid Industrialisation are Creating a New Workshop for the World', *Financial Times*, 4th February.

Roden, M. (2000) *The International Political Economy of Contemporary US–China Relations* (University of Sheffield: PhD Thesis).

Rodrik, D. (1997) *Has Globalization Gone too Far?* (Washington: Institute for International Economics).

Rosen, Daniel (2003) 'Low-Tech Bed, High-Tech Dreams', *China Economic Quarterly*, (Q4): 20–7.

Ross, R. (1997) 'Why Our Hardliners are Wrong', *The National Interest*, (49): 42–51.

Ruggie, J. (1982) 'International Regimes, Transactions and Change: Embedded Liberalism in the Post World War Economic Order', *International Organization*, 36 (2): 379–415.

Sassen, S. (1999) 'Embedding the Global in the National: Implications for the Role of the State', in David Smith, Dorothy Solinger and Steven Topik (eds), *States and Sovereignty in the Global Economy* (London: Routledge): 158–70.

Sasuga, K. (2004) *Microregionalism and Governance in East Asia* (London: Routledge).

Schultz, M., Söderbaum, F. and Öjendal, J. (2001) 'Introduction: A Framework for Understanding Regionalization' in Michael Schultz, Frederik Söderbaum, and Joakim Öjendal (eds) *Regionalization in a Globalizing World: A Comparative Perspective on Forms, Actors and Processes* (London: Zed): 1–24.

Segal, G. (1999) 'Does China Matter?', *Foreign Affairs*, 78 (5): 24–36.

Segal, P. (2003) 'How Washington Can be a Hyper-Power and a Hyper-Borrower: Foreign Buyers of US Bonds are Banking on a Stable US Consumer Market', *YaleGlobal*, 2nd September.

Seligson, M. and Passe-Smith, J. (eds) (1998) *Development and Underdevelopment: the Political Economy of Global Inequality* (Boulder: Lynne Rienner).

Shambaugh, D. (2004/5) 'China Engages Asia: Reshaping the Regional Order', *International Security*, 29 (3): 64–99.

Shen Liren and Dai Yuanchen (1990) 'Woguo "Zhuhou Jingji" De Xingcheng Ji Chi Biduan He Genyuan (The Creation, Origins and Failings of Feudal Economies in China)', *Jingji Yanjiu (Economic Research)*, (3): 12–20.

Shen, S. (2007) *Nationalism and the Changing Politics of Diverse Publics: The Interpretation of Chinese Public Reaction to Sino-American Relations, 1999–2003* (University of Oxford: PhD Thesis).

Shenkar, O. (2004) *The Chinese Century: The Rising Chinese Economy and Its Impact on the Global Economy, the Balance of Power, and Your Job* (Philadelphia: Wharton School).

Shi Bin (2004) 'Guoji Guanxi Lilun "Zhongguo Shi Tansuo" de Jige Jiben Wenti (Some Fundamental Questions of "Chinese Type Explorations" of International Relations Theory)', *Shijie Jingji yu Zhengzhi (World Economics and Politics)*, (5): 8–13.

Shi Tianjian (1999) 'Village Committee Elections in China: Institutionalist Tactics for Democracy', *World Politics*, 51 (3): 385–412.

Shih, V. (2004) *Not Quite a Miracle: Factional Politics, Inflationary Cycles, and Non-Performing Loans in China* (Harvard University: PhD Thesis).

Shirai, S. (2002) 'Banking Sector Reforms in the People's Republic of China – Progress and Constraints', in UNESCAP-ADB, *Rejuvenating Bank Finance for Development in Asia and the Pacific* (New York: United Nations): 49–98.

Shu Wei (2004a) 'Transfer Pricing in China: New Transfer Pricing Developments in China', *Deloitte Tax*, July, available at www.deloitte.com/dtt/cda/doc/content/Bulletin_TP0304E(1).pdf

Shu Wei (2004b) 'Transfer Pricing in China: China Issues Formal Advance Pricing Agreement Rules', *Deloitte Tax*, September, available at www.deloitte.com/dtt/cda/doc/content/TP0504(1).pdf

Shu Wei (2004c) 'Transfer Pricing in China: China Amends Transfer Pricing Rules', *Deloitte Tax*, November, available at www.deloitte.com/dtt/cda/doc/content/tp0604E.pdf

Sicular, T. (1998) 'Capital Flight and Foreign Investment: Two Tales From China and Russia', *The World Economy*, 21 (5): 589–602.

Sklair, L. (1995) *Sociology of the Global System* (Baltimore: John Hopkins University Press).

Smart, A. (2000) 'The emergence of Local Capitalisms in China: Overseas Chinese Investment and Pattern of Development', in Si–Ming Li and Wing-Shing Tang (eds) *China's Regions, Polity, & Economy: A Study of Spatial Transformation in the Post-Reform Era* (Hong Kong: University of Hong Kong Press): 65–95.

Smil, V. (1993) *China's Environmental Crisis: An Enquiry into the Limits of National Development* (Armonk: Sharpe).

Smil, V. (2004) *China's Past, China's Future: Energy, Food, Environment* (London: Routledge/Curzon).

Smith, M. (2002) 'Taiwan: Post-Congress push for China links', *Asia Times*, 3rd December.

Snitwongse, K. (2003) 'A New World Order in East Area?', *Asia-Pacific Review*, 10 (2): 36–51.

Solinger, D. (1982) 'The Fifth National People's Congress and the Process of Policymaking: Reform, Readjustment and the Opposition', *Issues and Studies*, 18 (8): 63–106.

Solinger, D. (2001) 'Why we Cannot Count the "Unemployed"', *China Quarterly*, (167): 671–88.

Solinger, D. (2003) 'State and Society in Urban China in the Wake of the 16th Party Congress', *China Quarterly*, (176): 943–59.

Solinger, D. (2005) 'The Creation of a New Underclass in China and its Implications', University of California, Irvine Center for the Study of Democracy Working Paper No. 05'10.

Song Jung-a (2003) 'Samsung to Move Most PC Production to China', *Financial Times*, 19th September.

Song Qiang, Zhang Zangzang and Qiao Bian (1996) *Zhongguo Keyi Shuo Bu (China Can Say No)* (Beijing: Zhonghua Gongshang Lianhe Press).

Song Xinning (2001) 'Building International Relations Theory with Chinese Characteristics', *Journal of Contemporary China*, 10 (26): 61–74.

Song Xinning and Chan, G. (2000) 'International Relations Theory In China', in Weixing Hu, Gerald Chan and Daojiong Zha (2000) *China's International Relations in the 21st Century: Dynamics of Paradigm Shift* (Lanham: University Press of America): 15–40.

State Council (1997) *On Sino-US Trade Balance* (Beijing: Information Office of the State Council of the People's Republic of China).

State Council (2004) *China's Social Security and Its Policy* (Beijing: Information Office of the State Council of the People's Republic of China).

Steinfeld, E. (2004) 'China's Shallow Integration: Networked Production and the New Challenges for Late Industrialization', *World Development*, 32 (11): 1971–87.

Strange, S. (1990) 'The Name of The Game' in: Nicholas X. Rizopoulos (ed.) *Sea Changes: American Foreign Policy in a World Transformed* (New York: Council on Foreign Relation Press): 238–73.

Strange, S. (1994) 'Wake up Krasner! The World *Has* Changed', *Review of International Political Economy*, 1 (2): 209–19.

Strange, S. (1996) *The Retreat of the State* (Cambridge: Cambridge University Press).

Stratford, T. (2002) 'Testimony to The Office of the United States Trade Representative Regarding China's Implementation of its WTO Commitments', 18th September.

Stubbs, R. (2002) 'ASEAN Plus Three: Emerging East Asian Regionalism?', *Asian Survey*, 42 (3): 440–55.

Studwell, J. (2003) *The China Dream: The Quest for the Last Great Untapped Market on Earth* (New York: Grove Press).

Sturgeon, T. (1997) 'Does Manufacturing Still Matter? The Organizational Delinking of Production from Innovation', Berkeley Roundtable on International Economy Working Paper No. 92B.

Subramanian, K. (2002) 'FDI: Any lessons from China?', *The Hindu*, 18th November.

Swamidass, P. and Kotabe, M. (1993) 'Component Sourcing Strategies of Multinationals: An Empirical Study of European and Japanese Multinationals', *Journal of International Business Studies*, 24 (1): 81–100.

Taipei Times (2001) 'China Investigates Multi-Billion Dollar Tax Rebates Fraud', *Taipei Times*, 3rd March.

Tangri, R. (1999) *The Politics of Patronage in Africa: Parastatals, Privatisation and Private Enterprise* (Trenton: Africa World Press).

Tanner, M. (2004) 'Protests Now Flourish in China', *International Herald and Tribune*, 3rd June.

Tempest, R. (1996) 'Barbie and the World Economy', *Los Angeles Times*, 22nd September.

Thomas, G. (2001) *Seeds of Fire: China and the Story Behind the Attack on America* (Tempe: Dandelion).

Tian Ye (2000) 'Guanyu Guoji Zhengzhi Jingji Zhong Buqueding Xing de Lilun Tantao (A Discussion about the Uncertain Nature of International Political Economy Theory)', *Guoji Luntan (International Forum)*, 2 (4): 62–7.

Timperlake, E. (1999) *Red Dragon Rising: Communist China's Military Threat to America* (Washington: Regnery).

Ting Gong (1997) 'Forms and Characteristics of China's Corruption in the 1990s', *Communist and Post-Communist Studies*, 30 (3): 277–88.

Tong, J. (1989) 'Fiscal Reform, Elite Turnover and Central Provincial Relations in Post Mao China', *The Australian Journal of Chinese Affairs*, (22): 1–28.

Tongzon, J. (2005) 'ASEAN-China Free Trade Area: A Bane or Boon for ASEAN Countries?', *The World Economy*, 28 (2): 191–210.

Trebilcock, M. and Howe, R. (1999) *The Regulation of International Trade* (London: Routledge).

Tsai, K. (2004) 'Off Balance: The Unintended Consequences of Fiscal Federalism in China', *Journal of Chinese Political Science*, 9 (1): 7–26.

Tseng, W. and Zebregs, H. (2002) 'Foreign Direct Investment in China: Some Lessons for Other Countries', IMF Policy Discussion Paper No. PDP/02/03.

Tsui, K. and Wang Youqiang (2004) 'Between Separate Stoves and a Single Menu: Fiscal Decentralization in China', *China Quarterly*, (177): 71–90.

UNCTAD (2001) *World Investment Report 2001* (New York: United Nations).

Underhill, G. (2000) 'Conceptualising the Changing Global Order', in Richard Stubbs and Geoffrey Underhill (eds) *Political Economy and the Changing Global Order*, (Oxford: Oxford University Press): 3–24.

Unger, J. and Chan, A. (1995) 'Corporatism in China: A Developmental State in an East Asian Context', in Barrett L. McCormick and Jonathan Unger (eds) *China after Socialism: In the Footsteps of Eastern Europe or East Asia?* (Armonk: Sharpe): 95–129.

USCBC (2002) 'China's WTO Implementation Efforts: An Assessment of the First Nine Months of China's WTO Membership', Written Testimony by the United States–China Business Council, Prepared on 3rd September, available at www.uschina.org/public/testimony/testimony13.pdf

US–China Security Review Commission (2002) 'The National Security Implications of the Economic Relationship Between the United States and China', available at www.uscc.gov/researchpapers/2000_2003/reports/ch4_02.htm

US Department of State (2005) *China: Country Reports on Human Rights Practices, 2005* (Washington: Department of State) available at www.state.gov/g/drl/rls/hrrpt/2005/61605.htm

USGAO (2002) 'World Trade Organization: Selected U.S. Company Views about China's Membership' United States General Accounting Office Report to Congressional Committees, September, available at www.gao.gov/cgi-bin/getrpt?GAO-02-1056

Van Wolferen, K. (1990) *The Enigma of Japanese Power* (New York: Vintage).

Various (2004) 'Abstracts from the Seminar on International Relations Research Methods', *World Economics and Politics*, (1): 14–29.

Voon, J. (1998) 'Export Competitiveness of China and ASEAN in the US Market', *ASEAN Economic Bulletin*, 14 (3): 273–91.

Wade, R. (1990) *Governing the Market: Economic Theory and the Role of Government in East Asian Industrialization* (Princeton: Princeton University Press).

Wœver, O. (1998) 'The Sociology of a Not So International Discipline: American and European Developments in International Relations', *International Organization*, 52 (4): 687–727.

Walder, A. (2002) 'Privatization and Elite Mobility: Rural China, 1979–1996', Stanford Institute for International Studies APARC Working Paper.

Walder, A. (2004) 'The Party Elite and China's Trajectory of Change', *China: An International Journal*, 2 (2): 189–209.

Waldron, A. (2002) 'China's Economic Façade', *Washington Post*, 21st March.

Wang Dan (2001) 'China Trying to Redefine the Party', *Taipei Times*, 5th July.

Wang Hui (2004) 'The Year 1989 and the Historical Roots of Neoliberalism in China', *Positions: East Asia Cultures Critique*, 12 (1): 7–70.

Wang Huning (1988a) 'An Economic Analysis of the Reform of China's Political-Administrative System', *Shehui Kexue Zhanxian (Social Sciences Frontline)*, (2): 107–115 translated in JPRS 27th October.

Wang Huning (1988b) *'Zhongguo Bianhuazhong De Zhongyang He Difang Zhengfu De Guanxi: Zhengzhi De Hanyi* (Ramifications of Changing Relationship Between Central and Local Government in China)', *Fudan Xuebao (Fudan University Journal)*, (5): 1–8 and 30.

Wang Jinchang (2004) 'Cong "Yangcong" Dao "Ganlan" Zhongguo Shehui Jiegou Jiang Ruhe Youhua (How to Modernise China's Social Structure From "Onion" to "Olive" Shaped)' Beijing Television News Report Transcript available at www.cpirc.org.cn/yjwx/yjwx_detail.asp?id=2793

Wang Jincun (1999) '"Global Democratization" – Camouflage of the US Hegemony', *World Economy and China*, (4): 28–31.

Wang Jun (2004) 'Zhongguo de Guoji Guanxi Lilun: Zhong Zhutixing Shijiao (Chinese International Relations Theory: A Subjective Viewpoint)', *Shijie Jingji yu Zhengzhi (World Economics and Politics)*, (2): 26–30.

Wang Luolin, Liu Shucheng and Liu Rongcang (1999) 'An Opportunity to Raise the Ultimate Consumption Rate While Restarting the Economy', *World Economy and China*, (5–6): 4–8.

Wang Shaoguang (2003) 'Jiegui Haishi Nalai: Zhengzhixue Bentuhua de Sikao (Catching Up or Borrowing: Reflections on the Localisation of Political Science' in Gong Yang (ed.) *Sichao – Zhongguo Xinzuopai ju qi Yingxiang (Ideological Trends – China's New Left and Their Influence)* (Beijing: Zhongguo Shehui Kexue Chubanshe).

Wang Shaoguang and Hu Angang (1993) *Zhongguo Guojia Nengli Baogu (Report on China's State Capacity)* (Shenyang: Liaoning People's Press).

Wang Shaoguang and Hu Angang (2001) *The Chinese Economy in Crisis: State Capacity and Tax Reform* (Armonk: East Gate).

Wang Yiwei (2004) 'Weishenme Meiyou Zhongguo de Guoji Guanxi Lilun? (Why is there No Chinese International Relations Theory?)', *Shijie Jingji yu Zhengzhi (World Economics and Politics)*, 1: 21.

Wang Yizhou (1995) *Dangdai Guoji Zhengzhi Xilun (Analysis of Contemporary International Politics)* (Shanghai: Shanghai People's Press).

Wang Yizhou (1998) *Xifang Guoji Zhengzhi Xue: Lishi yu Lilun (Western International Political Study: History and Theory* (Shanghai: Shanghai People's Press).

Wang Yizhou (2000) 'Political Stability and International Relations in the Process of Economic Globalisation – Another Perspective on Asia's Financial Crisis', available at http://www.iwep.org.cn/chinese/gerenzhuye/wangyizhou/wenzhang/political%20stability%20and%20international%20relation.pdf

Wang Yizhou (2003) *Quanqiu Zhengzhi he Zhongguo Waijiao: Tanxun Xinde Shijiao yu Jieshi (Global Politics and Chinese Diplomacy: Exploring New Viewpoints and Explanations)* (Beijing: World Knowledge Press).

Wang Yong (1998) 'Momentum vital for GDP Exports Require Stimulus', *China Daily*, 21st May.

Wang Zhengyi (2004) 'Conceptualizing Economic Security and Governance: China Confronts Globalization', *The Pacific Review*, 17 (4): 523–4.

Wank, D. (1998) *Commodifying Chinese Communism: Business, Trust, and Politics in a South Coast City* (Cambridge: Cambridge University Press).

Watts, J. (2004) 'China Admits First Rise in Poverty Since 1978', *The Guardian*, 20th July.

Watts, J. (2006) 'Be Here Now', *The Guardian*, 26th August.

Wedeman, A. (1997) 'Stealing from the Farmers: Institutional Corruption and the 1992 IOU Crisis', *China Quarterly*, (152): 81–107.

Wedeman, A. (2003) *From Mao to Market: Rent Seeking, Local Protectionism, and Marketization in China* (New York: Cambridge University Press).

Weidenbaum, M. and Hughes, S. (1996) *The Bamboo Network: How Expatriate Chinese Entrepreneurs Are Creating a New Economic Superpower in Asia* (New York: Simon and Schuster).

Weitzman, M. and Xu, C. (1994), 'Chinese Township Village Enterprises as Vaguely Defined Cooperatives', *Journal of Comparative Economics*, 18 (2): 121–45.

White, G. (1984) 'Changing Relations Between State and Enterprise in Contemporary China: Expanding Enterprise Autonomy', in Neville Maxwell and Brian McFarlane (eds) *China's Changed Road to Development* (Oxford: Pergamon): 43–60.

White, L. (1998) *Unstately Power: Volume 1, Local Causes of China's Economic Reforms* (Armonk: Sharpe).

White, L. (1999) *Unstately Power: Volume 2, Local Causes of China's Intellectual, Legal, and Governmental Reforms* (Armonk: Sharpe).

Whiting, A. (1995) 'Chinese Nationalism and Foreign Policy after Deng', *China Quarterly*, (142): 297–315.

Whitley, R. (1999) *Divergent Capitalisms – The Social Structuring and Change of Business Systems* (Oxford: Oxford University Press).

WTO (2001) *Accession of the People's Republic Of China, WTO Document No. WT/L/432* (Cambridge: Cambridge University Press for the World Trade Organization).

Wolf, C. (2002) *Straddling Economics and Politics: Cross-Cutting Issues in Asia, the United States, and the Global Economy* (Santa Monica: Rand).

Wolf, C., Yeh, K., Zycher, B., Eberstadt, N. and Lee, S. (2003) *Fault Lines in China's Economic Terrain* (Santa Monica: Rand).

Wolf, F. (2003) 'Excerpts: Rep. Wolf Says China Won't Let U.S. Monitor Rights', Office of International Information Programs, U.S. Department of State, available at canberra.usembassy.gov/hyper/2000/0719/epf318.htm

Wolfowitz, P. (1997) 'Bridging Centuries: Fin de Siecle all Over Again', *National Interest*, 76 (47): 3–8.

Womack, B. (1982) 'The 1980 County-Level Elections in China: Experiment in Democratic Modernization', *Asian Survey*, 22 (3): 261–77.

Wong, C. (1988) 'Interpreting Rural Industrial Growth in the Post-Mao Period', *Modern China*, 14 (1): 3–30.

Wong, C. (1991) 'Central-Local Relations in an Era of Fiscal Decline: The Paradox of Fiscal Decentralization in Post-Mao China', *China Quarterly*, (128): 691–715.

Wong, C. (1992) 'Fiscal Reform and Local Industrialization: The Problematic Sequencing of Reform in Post-Mao China', *Modern China*, 18 (2): 197–227.

Wong, C. (1997) 'Rural Public Finance', in Christine Wong (ed.) *Financing Local Government in the People's Republic of China* (Oxford: Oxford University Press): 213–82.

Wong, C., Heady, C. and Wing Thye Woo (1995) *Fiscal Management and Economic Reform in the People's Republic of China* (Hong Kong: Oxford University Press).

Woo, Wing Thye (1999) 'The Economics And Politics Of Transition To An Open Market Economy: China', OECD Development Centre Technical Paper No. 153.

Wood, E. (1981) 'The Separation of the Economic and the Political in Capitalism', *New Left Review*, (127): 66–95.

World Bank (1998) *China 2020: Development Challenges in The New Century* (New York: World Bank).

World Bank (2002) *Global Development Finance 2002* (New York: World Bank).

World Bank (2003) 'Thailand Economic Monitor, May 2003', available at www.worldbank.or.th/monitor/economic/2003may.shtml

Wu Churen (1998) 'Leaders Water the Statistical Data, the Only Beneficiaries are Official Careers – False Reporting and Report Manipulation Smooth Official Career Paths', *Caifang Bao*, 1st June, available at www.usembassy-china.org.cn/sandt/STATFAKE.html

Wu, F., Poa Tiong Siaw, Yeo Han Sia and Puah Kok Keong (2002) 'Foreign Direct Investments to China and Southeast Asia: Has Asean Been Losing Out?' in *Economic Survey of Singapore*, (Third Quarter): 96–115.

Wu, F. and Tang, L. (2000) 'China's Capital Flight, 1990 –1999: Estimates and Implications', *Review of Pacific Basin Financial Markets and Policies*, 3 (1): 59–75.

Xie Ping (1999) 'Financial Reform in China: Review and Future Challenges', *World Economy and China*, (9–10): 5–13.

Xinhua (2002) 'All About Xiaokang', *Xinhuanet*, 10th November.

Xu Chenggang and Zhuang Juzhong (1998) 'Why China Grew: The Role of Decentralization', in Peter Boone, Stanislaw Gomulka, and Richard Layard (eds) *Emerging from Communism: Lessons from Russia, China, and Eastern Europe* (Cambridge, MA: MIT Press): 183–212.

Yahuda, M. (2004) 'Gerald Segal's Contribution' in Barry Buzan and Rosemary Foot (eds) *Does China Matter? A Reassessment* (London: Routledge): 1–10.

Yang Guohua and Cheng Jin (2001) 'The Process of China's Accession to the WTO', *Journal of International Economic Law*, 4 (2): 297–328.

Yang Yao (2004) 'Government Commitment and the Outcome of Privatization', in Takatoshi Ito and Anne O. Krueger (eds) *Governance, Regulation, and Privatization in the Asia-Pacific Region* (Chicago: University of Chicago Press): 251–78.

Yang Yongzheng and Tyers, R. (2000) 'Weathering the Asian Crisis: The Role of China', Australian National University Asia Pacific School of Economics and Management Working Paper No 00–1.

Yang Yunhua (1999) 'Dangdai Zhanzheng Qishi Lu (Revelations on Contemporary Warfare)' *Xinhua Bulletin* 28 June 1999, available at zz-www.sd.cninfo.net/news/990628/25.htm accessed 23 March 2001.

Yardley, J. (2004) 'China Faces Stiff Challenge to Create Work', *International Herald Tribune*, 29th May.

Yep, R. (2000) 'The Limitations of Corporatism for Understanding Reforming China: An Empirical Analysis in a Rural County', *Journal of Contemporary China*, 9 (25): 547–66.

Yep, R. (2002) 'Maintaining Stability in Rural China: Challenges and Responses', Brookings Institution Center for Northeast Asian Policy Studies Working Paper, available at www.brook.edu/views/papers/fellows/2002_yep.htm

Yep, R. (2004) 'Can 'Tax-for Fee' Reform Reduce Rural Tension in China? The Process, Progress and Limitations', *China Quarterly*, (177): 42–70.

Yeung, G. (2001) *Foreign Investment and Socio-economic Development in China: The Case of Dongguan* (Basingstoke: Palgrave).

Yong Deng and Wang Fei-ling (eds) (1999) *In the Eyes of the Dragon: China Views the World* (Lanham: Rowman and Littlefield).

Young, A. (2000) 'The Razor's Edge: Distortions and Incremental Reform in the People's Republic of China', *The Quarterly Journal of Economics*, 115 (4): 1091–135.

Yu Yongding (1999) 'China's Macroeconomic Situation and Future Prospect', *World Economy and China*, (2): 4–13.

Yu Yongding (2006) 'A Look at China's Readjustment of Mode of Economic Growth', *People's Daily* (online edition), 22nd August.

Yu Yongding, Zheng Bingwen, and Song Hong (eds) (2000) *Zhongguo 'RuShi' Yanjiu Baogu: Jinru WTO de Zhongguo Chanye (Research Report on China's Entry into WTO: The Analysis of China's Industries)*, (Beijing: Social Sciences Documentation Press).

Zeng Huaguo (2006) *Globalization and Media Governance in the People's Republic of China (1992–2004)* (University of Warwick, PhD Thesis).

Zha Daojiong (1999) 'Chinese Considerations of "Economic Security"', *Journal of Chinese Political Science*, 5 (1): 69–87.

Zha Daojiong (2005) 'Comment: Can China Rise?', *Review of International Studies*, 31 (4): 775–85.

Zhang Honglin (2002) 'Why Does China Receive So Much Foreign Direct Investment?', *World Economy and China*, 10 (3): 44–58.

Zhang Xudong (2001) 'Challenging the Eurocentric, Cold War View of China and the making of a Post-Tiananmen Intellectual Field', *East Asia*, (Spring/Summer): 3–57.

Zhang Ye (2003) 'China's Emerging Civil Society', Brookings Institution Center for Northeast Asian Policy Studies Working Paper, available at www.brook.edu/fp/cnaps/papers/ye2003.pdf

Zhang Yongjin (1998) *China in International Society Since 1949: Alienation And Beyond* (Basingstoke: Macmillan).

Zhang Yongjin (2000) 'The "English School"' in China: A Story Of How Ideas Travel And Are Transplanted', Canberra: Australian National University Department of International Relations Working Paper No. 2000/4.

Zhang Zhongli (1988) *'Shanghai He Shanghai Jingjiqu Zai Zhongguo Jingji Xiandaihua Zhong De Diwei He Zuoyong* (The Position and Role of Shanghai and its Economic Zones in the Modernisation of China's Economy)', *Shehui Kexue (Social Sciences)*, (1): 18–22.

Zhao Linghua (1999) 'An Analysis of the Forms of Irregular Capital Flows in China', *International Economic Review*, (3–4): 7–13.

Zhao Suisheng (2000) 'Chinese Nationalism and Its International Orientations', *Political Science Quarterly*, 115 (1): 1–33.

Zhao Xiao (1999) 'Jingzheng, Gonggong Xuanze yu Zhidu Bianqiang (Competition, Public Choice and System Change)', Beijing University China Centre for Economic Research Working Paper No. C1999025.

Zheng Bijian (2005) 'China's 'Peaceful Rise' to Great Power Status', *Foreign Affairs*, 84 (5): 18–24.

Zheng Shiping (1997) *Party Vs State in Post-1949 China – The Institutional Dilemma* (Cambridge: Cambridge University Press).

Zheng Shiping (2003) 'Leadership Change, Legitimacy, and Party Transition in China', *Journal of Chinese Political Science*, 8 (1 & 2): 47–63.

Zheng Yongnian (1999) 'Political Incrementalism: Political Lessons from China's 20 Years of Reform', *Third World Quarterly*, 20 (6): 1157–77.

Zheng Yongnian (2004) *Globalization and State Transformation in China* (Cambridge: Cambridge University Press).

Zhou Pailin (ed.) (2002) *Meiguo Xin Baquan Zhuyi (The New American Hegemonism)* (Tianjin: Tianjin People's Press).

Zhou Shaohua (1987) 'Establishing a National Tax Reform System is Urgently Necessary for Continued Reform', *Shijie Jingji Daobao (World Economic Herald)* 24th August. Translated and reported in Joint Publications Research Service, 3rd November.

Zhu Li (1987) *'Zijin Fengpei de Zhuyao Gaibian* (Major Changes in the Distribution of Funds in China)', *Jingji Guanli (Economic Review)*, (9): 4–9.

Zhu Wenli (2001) 'International Political Economy from a Chinese Angle', *Journal of Contemporary China*, 10 (26): 45–54.

Zweig, D. (2002) *Internationalizing China: Domestic Interests and Global Linkages* (Ithaca: Cornell University Press).

Zweig, D. and Bi Jianhai (2005) 'China's Global Hunt for Energy', *Foreign Affairs*, 85 (5): 25–38.

Index

Printed and bound by CPI Group (UK) Ltd, Croydon, CR0 4YY

CPI Antony Rowe
Chippenham, UK
2016-12-23 21:54